India and New Zealand in a Rising Asia

Issues and Perspectives

India and New Zealand in a Rising Asia

Issues and Perspectives

Editors

Man Mohini Kaul

Vibhanshu Shekhar

PENTAGON PRESS

First Published in 2012

Published by

PENTAGON PRESS
206, Peacock Lane, Shahpur Jat,
New Delhi-110049
Phones: 011-64706243, 26491568
Telefax: 011-26490600
email: rajan@pentagonpress.in
website: www.pentagonpress.in

Cataloging in Publication Data—DK
Courtesy: D.K. Agencies (P) Ltd. <docinfo@dkagencies.com>

India and New Zealand in a rising Asia : issues and perspectives / editors, Man Mohini Kaul, Vibhanshu Shekhar.
p. cm.
Includes bibliographical references and index.
ISBN 9788182746527

1. India—Foreign relations—New Zealand. 2. New Zealand—Foreign relations—India. 3. New Zealand—Foreign relations—Asia. 4. Asia—Foreign relations—New Zealand. I. Kaul, Man Mohini. II. Shekhar, Vibhanshu.

DDC 327.54093 23

Printed at Aegean Offset Printers, Greater Noida (U.P.)

Contents

About the Contributors

Amit Singh is Associate Fellow, National Maritime Foundation, New Delhi.

Amrita Dey is Research Associate, Department of South and Southeast Asian Studies, Kolkata University, Kolkata.

Anushree Chakraborty is Research Associate, National Maritime Foundation, New Delhi.

G.Vijay Kumar Reddy is Assistant Professor, Centre for Southeast Asian & Pacific Studies, Sri Venkateshwara University, Tirupati.

Ganganath Jha is Professor, School of International Studies, JNU, New Delhi.

Man Mohini Kaul is Professor, School of International Studies, JNU, New Delhi.

Mohor Chakraborty is Assistant Professor, South Calcutta Girls' College, Kolkata.

Nabeel A Mancheri is affiliated with the National Institute of Advanced Studies, Bangalore.

P. Krishna Mohan Reddy is Assistant Professor, Department of History, Sri Venkateshwara University, Tirupati.

Renu Sharma is a journalist associated with the Network 18.

Rupakjyoti Borah is Assistant Professor, Petroleum University, Gujarat.

Ruth Rhea Khan is Ph.D. Scholar, School of International Studies, JNU.

Tridib Chakraborty is Professor, Department of International Relations, Jadavpur University, Kolkata.

Vibhanshu Shekhar is Research Fellow, Indian Council of World Affairs, New Delhi.

Introduction

Man Mohini Kaul and Vibhanshu Shekhar

As India emerges a rising power in the Asia-Pacific and gets more and more integrated, it finds comprehensive expansion in its engagement with the countries of the region. It has witnessed greater economic integration and multi-faceted strategic engagement with every country in the region. The wide-ranging nature of engagement is both at country-to-country level and in the multilateral cooperative forums.

A somewhat similar level of enhanced strategic engagement can be perceived in India's engagement with New Zealand, one of the most important players in the South Pacific and an ardent advocate of regional concerns. The bilateral trade between the two countries has gone up by 100 per cent during the last five years. Both India and New Zealand are dialogue partners of the Association of Southeast Asian Nations (ASEAN) and members of several regional cooperative forums such as ASEAN Regional Forum (ARF), East Asia Summit (EAS) and ASEAN+ Defence Ministerial Meetings (ADMM+). These interactions at the institutional level have poised the two countries towards greater strategic engagement on the issues, vital for constructive and comprehensive engagement in the Asia-Pacific. New Zealand has also facilitated India's engagement with the Pacific Island countries via media Pacific Islands Forum (PIF), of which India is a dialogue partner since 2002.

Any bilateral cooperation and partnership requires an appropriate understanding of the strategic priorities, foreign policy choices and normative concerns of the partner. Ironically, New Zealand, for long, remained mainly an area of darkness, due to lack of interest on the part of analysts and academics in India. Moreover, much of India's foreign policy focus on South Pacific centred around its relations with Australia and its troubled diaspora in Fiji.

There are two principal worldviews that India has offered on New Zealand, located in the distant maritime terrain of South Pacific. One perspective reflects a somewhat bureaucratic, issue-driven, ignorance-reflective and cooperation-seeking approach of the Indian government, engaging irregularly at bilateral level, and periodically and more regularly in several regional multilateral forums. The two sides, until the end of the 20th century, did not exhibit any sense of shared understanding or urgency in expanding the bilateral relations either horizontally or vertically. In fact, the relationship between the two multicultural and democratic nation-states can, at best, be described as 'indifferent and business as usual' relationship. Both India and New Zealand have looked at the world as well as at each other from different lenses and the dynamics of engagement has revolved primarily around the issue of diaspora, commonwealth, and normative positioning over discussions in the UN General Assembly. The second perspective is based on popular imagination of New Zealand driven primarily by common bonds of cricket, and scenic beauty of the country promoted extravagantly by the Indian film industry.

The dynamics of this relationship became more substantial during the first decade of the 21st century. The process of globalisation, the changing geopolitical realities in the form of growing emergence of Asia as the new gravity of global power politics has hastened its process of engagement with Asia. In the new emerging scenario the two nation-states have sought better interaction, more avenues for strategic and normative engagement and the pressing need for developing a shared understanding over the changing geopolitical realities of the Asia-Pacific. The two countries are now major stakeholders in several important cooperative forums and are vigorously pursuing bilateral relations which are inclusive and not exclusive in nature.

This book is an effort to develop an Indian perspective on hitherto a somewhat neglected and overlooked but important relationship of the Asia-Pacific.

A Small Power Dreams Big

New Zealand represents one of the few cases of 'small power advocating big change in the international order.' While describing America's relations with New Zealand as an important relationship, the US Secretary of State, Hillary Clinton characterised New Zealand as a country that punches way above its weight.

The desire for playing a prominent role in the global bodypolitik has come primarily from the long-standing belief of the ruling political elite in the creation of a 'just and safer' international order and looming challenges to the global security. Two areas especially highlight it—nuclear non-proliferation and climate change. While multilateralism remains the main vehicle of New Zealand's much-advocated normative recipe to manage the global problems, economic diplomacy continues to guide practical aspects of the country's strategic behaviour. New Zealand's growing focus on the eastern Asian hemisphere is essentially an outcome of growing economic linkages with the region.

In the first decade of the 21st century, New Zealand, as part of its Asia policy, has been keen to enlarge its relations with the rising Asian countries like India and China. Notwithstanding the apprehensions that abound in scholarly circles regarding the simultaneous rise of India and China, New Zealand views both as essential partners in its engagement with the region. No longer is New Zealand's Foreign Policy just South Pacific centric, it has enlarged its scope and is vigorously engaging with ASEAN countries, with East Asia and with India. It is apparent that the well thought out Asia policy of New Zealand is being implemented through effective initiatives, which has paid dividends in it being accepted as an important part of the emerging regional order.

Structure and Outline of the Book

The first chapter of the book **India in New Zealand's Asia Policy** by **Man Mohini Kaul** evaluates the evolution of India-New Zealand relations through the prism of New Zealand's Asia policy. India is emerging as an important focus of this policy that seeks to further strengthen its relations with Asian countries. She also examines the geo-political and geo-strategic considerations that are shaping this relationship. Both India and New Zealand are witnessing tumultuous changes in the regional order, which have a significant bearing on this relationship dictated, to a large extent by the economic integration taking place in the region and by the rising complexity of security threats.

In the fast-changing geopolitical strategic environment, India and New Zealand have shown remarkable dynamism in adjusting their security policies to the changing environment. A good deal of their diplomacy is directed at promoting their economic and strategic well being through forging cooperative ties. This has resulted in their participation in institutionalised meetings, both at bilateral and multilateral level; and these regular interactions have lead to better understanding of each other's security needs and aspirations.

The second chapter **New Zealand's Foreign Policy in the 21st Century** by **Vibhanshu Shekhar** offers an insight into the emerging contours of New Zealand's foreign policy in the 21st century. The key drivers of the change have come from both domestic as well as systemic sources, augmenting new sets of relationships and giving new thrusts to New Zealand's foreign policy. Its foreign policy has seen constant improvisations at regular intervals reflecting changing domestic priorities, and the regional and global structures of power. He argues that New Zealand's foreign policy during the 21st century is essentially a product of its reassessment of (a) emerging prospects of cooperation and integration in the Asia-Pacific, and (b) strategic constraints posed by the prevailing uncertainty surrounding the rise of China as the dominant player in the region. Moreover, while integrative processes have interconnected the economic interests of the regional stakeholders and governmental actors, inter-linkages among people and the non-governmental spaces across the region have grown, facilitated by the process of globalisation, the revolution in information technology, and shrinkage of business space.

The third chapter **Does the FTA Really Matter? Trends in India-New Zealand Economic Relations** by **Nabeel A Mancheri** delves into economic aspects of India-New Zealand bilateral relations. The two countries, consequent upon India's growing demands and New Zealand's increase in the exports, have begun to strengthen bilateral economic relations. The finalisation of India-New Zealand Comprehensive Economic Partnership Agreement (CEPA) would increase the bilateral trade value by three hundred per cent by 2015. A Free Trade Agreement will lead to greater economic cooperation, and would increase trade and investment opportunities for both sides.

The fourth chapter **India's Engagement with New Zealand: What Ails the Relationship?** by **Rupakjyoti Borah** attempts to highlight important dimensions of India-New Zealand engagement and key challenges facing the bilateral relationship. Two major drivers of greater engagement have come in the form of India's economic liberalisation and the onset of Look East policy. New Zealand's strong condemnation of India's nuclear tests in May 1998 and the former's ambivalence over the process of granting a NSG (Nuclear Suppliers Group)-waiver to the latter have acted as spoilers in the bilateral relations. The under-utilisation of the Indian diaspora in New Zealand has proved to be an important road-block in promoting the bilateral engagement.

The fifth chapter **Role of Diaspora in India's Relations with New Zealand** by **Ganganath Jha** brings forth growing significance of diaspora in India-New Zealand relations. The two countries are important players in their respective regions and they can effectively use soft power to attract each other for mutual benefits. The Indian diaspora offers a huge source of soft power and a strategic bridge in bringing the two countries together. The appointment of Anand Satyanand as the Governor General has shown New Zealand's determination to pursue the principle of multiculturalism and offer equal rights to all ethnic groups in the matters of governance.

The sixth chapter **Multiculturalism in New Zealand: Reality or Rhetoric?** by **G. Vijay Kumar Reddy and P. Krishna Mohan Reddy** examines the existing debate about the utility and applicability of the principle of multiculturalism to govern New Zealand's domestic political and social life. In spite of the writings or statements by the government officials, there is fear and concern among the immigrants from Asia regarding economic discrimination. The problem of multiculturalism in New Zealand is a manifestation of the Treaty of Waitangi which simply looks through the eyes of White New Zealanders and indigenous Maoris ignoring other minority groups and immigrants from Asia. It is becoming increasingly clear that in future, the immigrants are going to play a significant role not only in the economy but also in other fields in New Zealand.

The seventh chapter **Tackling Terrorism: the New Zealand Way** by **Renu Sharma** highlights New Zealand's approach towards terrorism and its methods and strategies for managing it. It is clearly evident that stringent measures have been taken both at the domestic as well as at the bilateral and multilateral level. The two disasters of 9/11 and the Bali bombing of October 2002, prompted New Zealand government to strengthen its homeland security that includes the ability to deter, prevent and handle any acts of terrorism on its shore. It has significantly increased its intelligence, law enforcement, and border and transport capabilities. New Zealand has offered military assistance to the US-led 'War on Terror' by sending SAS troops to Afghanistan and by sending frigates to be part of the Maritime Interdiction Force in the Persian Gulf. In line with the UN Security Council resolution 1373 on counter-terrorism, New Zealand government enacted Terrorism Suppression Act (2001) which also highlighted the causes and targets of terrorism.

The eighth chapter **New Zealand-China Relations in the 21st Century: NZ Perspective on Rising China** by **Anushree Chakraborty** aims to examine the evolving relations of New Zealand with China over the years. The primary aim of her chapter is to understand New Zealand's perspective of the Asian superpower —China, considering the fact that Wellington is currently an active participant of the Asia Pacific regional architecture. She highlights that in addition to the traditional western allies including the US, Britain and Australia, over the last three decades, China has become the primary focus of New Zealand's foreign policy.

The ninth chapter **India and New Zealand: The Evolving Domain in East Asian Community Building** by **Tridib Chakraborty and Mohor Chakraborty** has discussed in detail the interests and strategic priorities of India and New Zealand in East Asia, evolving patterns of their engagement in the East Asian forums, and their contribution towards the process of East Asian community building. They argue that New Zealand perceived its evolving tempo in the sphere of regionalism and community building as a two-way process, not only seeking to build greater understanding of Asia in New Zealand, but also underlining the relevance of New Zealand to its key partners in the region through a long-term and sustained commitment to contributing to the development of the region as a whole. The EAS has offered India and New Zealand a much-needed platform for the two countries to discuss and develop a common understanding over the issue of East Asian community building. The space that was developed between India and New Zealand was further expanded when the two countries met for the second consecutive time in Cebu, the Philippines to participate in the second EAS, held on 15-19 January 2007. The leaders of the two countries voiced their concerted opinion on issues of politico-economic importance like poverty eradication, energy, education, mitigation of natural disaster, economic development and regional integration.

The tenth chapter **New Zealand's Re-engagement with the United States** by **Ruth Rhea Khan** offers an insight into New Zealand's relations with perhaps one of the most controversial alliance partners—the USA. There has been growing desire among New Zealand policy makers to consolidate its relations with the most powerful global player and also the ultimate security guarantor in the Asia-Pacific. She has characterised New Zealand-US relations as a time-tested partnership experiencing normal ebbs and flows with a brief tumultuous interlude. She argues that the nuances of re-engagement are undergoing a fundamental transformation as newer concerns are mushrooming in the form of common concerns of regional stability and security in the Southwest Pacific and archipelagic Southeast Asia.

The New Zealand-United States re-engagement was strengthened significantly with the singing of the Wellington Declaration on 4 November 2010. The declaration is termed as a 'new strategic partnership' with the United States with the desire to work together in the Asia-Pacific in the field of strategic, economic, inter-governmental as well as non-governmental and regional cooperation.

The eleventh chapter **Towards Closer Partnership: New Zealand-Southeast Asia Relations** by **Man Mohini Kaul and Amrita Dey** offers an Indian perspective on the evolution and trajectory of New Zealand's relations with the countries of Southeast Asia and the region as a whole. They argue that both New Zealand and ASEAN share common concerns in the 21st century over global issues—terrorism, Weapons of Mass Destruction (WMDs), climate change and other non-traditional security issues. Besides, New Zealand has an important role within Southeast Asia through its membership of the Five Power Defence Arrangement (FPDA) and as a new member of East Asia Summit (EAS), ASEAN Plus Defence Ministerial Meeting (ADMM+), Asia-Pacific Economic Cooperation (APEC) and ASEAN-Australia-New Zealand Summit level engagement. Similar growth is seen in the economic relations of New Zealand with Southeast Asia.

The last chapter **South China Sea Dispute: Policy Options for India and New Zealand** by **Amit Singh** explores the policy options for both New Delhi and Wellington while facing the escalation of hostility in the South China Sea (SCS) dispute, one of the most destabilising developments in the recent years in the Asia-Pacific. The SCS is not only a strategic maritime link between the Pacific and the Indian Ocean, but also a vital gateway for shipping in East Asia and is, thus, economically and strategically important to the emerging economies of the Asia-Pacific. The dispute has the potential to adversely affect the strategic and economic stakes of the regional maritime nations like India and New Zealand. Therefore, it is high time for New Delhi and Wellington to address the issue substantially rather than symbolically.

This book, we hope, will bring forth a holistic picture of New Zealand collating the existing worldviews and new trends emerging out of changing politico-strategic landscape of the Asia-Pacific in the 21st century. It is an attempt on the part of Indian scholars (both experts and young research scholars) to develop an Indian perspective on New Zealand as an actor and a stakeholder in the global and regional politics of the Asia-Pacific.

1

India in New Zealand's Asia Policy

ManMohini Kaul

In the 1980's New Zealand's Labour Prime Minister David Lange, asserted that his country's foreign policy was being "increasingly shaped by the reality of our location. We now not only accept but celebrate what the map tells us... that we are a South Pacific nation."[1] Since then, New Zealand's foreign policy and strategic thinking has undergone a major transformation. Its foreign policy is now focused on furthering its economic, political and strategic interests through greater engagement with Asia. This strengthening of relations with Asian countries was greatly influenced by the important transition taking place in the international order. As noted by a well known scholar, this transition has been attributed to the "wealth and power moving from the North and the West to the East and the South, and the old order dominated by the United States and Europe giving way to one increasingly shared with non-Western rising states."[2]

The Asian orientation in New Zealand's foreign policy has led to convergence of strategic and security interests with regional countries and mutual desire for greater economic engagement. However, it needs to be clarified that although, New Zealand's focus is no longer confined to its periphery, South Pacific does continue to remains a critical area which impacts "significantly on New Zealand's security and defence policy thinking."[3]

The basic thrust of this paper is to holistically evaluate the evolution of India-New Zealand relations through the prism of New Zealand's Asia policy. India is an important focus of this policy through which New Zealand aims to strengthen its relations with Asian countries.[4] The paper will also examine the geo-political and geo-strategic considerations that are shaping this relationship. Both India and New Zealand are witnessing tumultuous changes in the regional order, which have a significant bearing on this relationship which to a large extent is dictated by the economic integration taking place in the region and by the rising complexity of security threats. In other words, this relationship is now no longer just dependent on the Commonwealth connections and common interest in cricket etc. Much of the bilateral relationship is being shaped by the process of globalisation which is integrating economies "and the resultant deepening of interdependence."[5]

New Zealand's Asia Policy

Orientation towards Asia

With Britain joining the European Common Market in 1973, New Zealand lost the trade benefits it was having from its major trading partner. In order to find alternative markets it found new markets in economically booming East Asia and Southeast Asia. Although, the change in New Zealand's policy perspective had been slow in taking shape, it pursued bilateral relations with Japan and the core countries of the Association of Southeast Asian Nations (ASEAN). The response from the ASEAN countries was warm, which got translated by the inclusion of New Zealand into ASEAN, as a Dialogue Partner in 1975.[6] New Zealand was among the first Dialogue Partners along with Australia and Japan, "to hold Summits with ASEAN in 1977."[7] This can be appreciated better if it is pointed out that India became a Sectoral Dialogue Partner of ASEAN only in January 1992, and a full Dialogue Partner in December 1995. Inclusion of India in ASEAN process became possible only after its foreign and economic policy underwent a change in the early 90's.The end of the Cold War, saw India adopting a vividly pragmatic policy in keeping with the globalised world and the positive developments taking place in the economic environment of its extended neighbourhood.

As stated earlier, New Zealand's quest for economic partners in Asia had made it first turn to Japan, which emerged as a major economic power in the region. The relationship between the two has evolved into one of partnership where both are keen to help resolve common regional security issues like maritime security and nuclear proliferation in Asia. Both, New Zealand and Japan are also cooperating in multilateral institutions like Asia Pacific Economic Cooperation (APEC) and in the still evolving East Asia Summit (EAS). Similarly, New Zealand's engagement with Southeast Asian countries, which grew through economic needs, has over the years grown into multifaceted relationship. Thus, New Zealand has emerged as an important participant in the economic integration taking place in Southeast Asia and East Asia, thanks to its quest for economic cooperation.[8] Importantly, the increase in trade with East Asia and the ASEAN countries brought about a major change in its restrictive migration policy towards Asians. Like Australia, its reorientation from Europe to Asia would not have been acceptable, unless it opened its borders to Asians.[9] Today the face of New Zealand is fast changing from a white settler country to that of a multicultural state.

In Southeast Asia, New Zealand has security links with traditional partners Malaysia and Singapore, who are its partners in the Five Power Defence Agreement (FPDA) of 1977. According to the Defence White Paper 2010, "FPDA will remain for New Zealand a crucial security link with Southeast Asia."[10] As for trade relations with ASEAN countries, New Zealand exports have grown immensely when compared to previous years especially with Indonesia and Vietnam.[11] Economic linkages with ASEAN were further strengthened when New Zealand and Australia jointly signed FTA with ASEAN in Cha-am, Phetchaburi, Thailand on 27 February 2009, which established the ASEAN-Australia-New Zealand Free Trade Area (AANZFTA Agreement).[12] Through the AANZFTA Agreement, ASEAN, Australia and New Zealand are able to create a Free Trade Area of over 600 million people with a combined GDP of US$ 2.3 trillion.[13] According to data issued by ASEAN, the total trade in 2010 between ASEAN and New Zealand was $6.75 billion having progressively gone up from US$ 5.3 billion in 2009.[14] The signing of the FTA was held by New Zealand to be important as it would "help to ensure that New Zealand remains an integral part of this unfolding regionalisation and that the process remains open and outward looking."[15]

These positive initiatives in the economic sector have helped New Zealand in deepening its relations not only with ASEAN, but with other Asian countries as well. In the rising Asia of the twenty first century, New Zealand is successfully pursuing the first dictum of economic cooperation which is based on building "a network of free trade agreements."[16] Thus, both at the bilateral and multilateral level New Zealand is vigorously pursuing economic cooperation with Asian countries. Of the top 10 trading partners of New Zealand, six are from Asia.

In the first decade of this century, as part of its Asia policy, New Zealand has paid special attention to its policy of closer engagement with India. The immediate gains for New Zealand from this active socialising of India, has resulted in greater economic engagement and closer cooperation in strategic sphere. There is a growing convergence between the two countries in the new geopolitics of the region, which is also being shaped by India's emergence "as an economic, political and strategic power with influence that extends beyond South Asia..."[17] However, there are some apprehensions within New Zealand policy makers that "the rise in power of both China and India...could put some strain on neighbouring countries especially Burma, but also Pakistan."[18]

Even so, India and New Zealand have shown remarkable dynamism in adjusting their security policies to the changing environment. A good deal of their diplomacy is directed at promoting economic and strategic wellbeing through forging cooperative ties. This has resulted in their participation in institutionalised meetings, both at bilateral and multilateral level; and these regular interactions have led to better understanding of each other's security needs and aspirations.[19]

Rise of China and India

With China, New Zealand's economic cooperation is growing extensively. China has emerged after Australia as the second largest trading partner of New Zealand, the US is in the third place while Japan, which was previously ahead is now much behind. It is obvious that New Zealand policy makers have not hesitated in engaging with China, in spite of China's authoritarian regime and its deplorable human rights record. In fact it has the distinction of being the first OECD country to sign the FTA with China.[20] In the 21st century, both realism and pragmatism are dictating international politics of all countries including India and New Zealand, as they interact with China to forge robust ties and more dynamic relationship.

However, many analysts and prominent public figures in New Zealand have expressed their dissent with some of the decisions taken by the Key administration in its engagement with China. They have been particularly critical of the policy of appeasement of China as seen in Prime Minister Key's refusal to meet the visiting Dalai Lama in December 2009. In the past, former Prime Ministers David Lange and Helen Clark had met Dalai Lama very warmly when he had come to New Zealand. In order to dispel the criticism and clarify the China policy of the current government, New Zealand Foreign Minister gave a statement explaining the significance of China to New Zealand. He stated rather candidly: "I do not believe that the vast majority of New Zealanders have any real sense of just how important our relationship with China has been in cushioning our economy through the global economic storm, and sparing this country some of the dramatic fallout experienced by small, vulnerable exporter nations elsewhere."[21] Evidently, New Zealand's relations with China have evolved faster than they have with India. The economic benefits accruing to New Zealand and its close partner Australia from their growing links with China far outweigh the shared commonalities with India.

China and India are the two major Asian countries, vying to maximise their influence in the emerging economic architecture that is acquiring institutional shape and form in the region. However, perceptions about them differ in the region. India's economic rise and its integration with Southeast Asia are welcomed by the ASEAN countries, which see in India the capability to balance China's presence as an 'economic centre and competitor'.[22] Though, compared to China's high economic growth, India has 'miles to go'. With the signing of the ASEAN-China Free Trade Area (ACFTA), the largest free trade area in terms of population and the third largest in terms of nominal GDP were created.[23] Yet, inspite of its effort to be acceptable to ASEAN countries through its show of generosity and fairness in signing economic treaties, the ASEAN countries continue to be apprehensive of China's military might and economic rise and its long term plans. The apprehensions have been further aggravated with China's recent assertive behaviour, which seems to have proved those analysts right, who had have all along doubted China's assertion of a "peaceful rise." They held that "China had long term hegemonic ambitions in the region."[24] There is no doubt that the unresolved issues of South China Sea, Taiwan and North Korea continue to remain potential flashpoints.

India too, is concerned about its own security from China's militarisation and its presence and influence in the neighbouring countries like Myanmar. According to some analysts there is a perceptible strategy of China to contain India by engaging and arming India's neighbours.[25] China, finds India's growing linkage and interest in Southeast Asia and East Asia intrusive, as was obvious when it opposed India's membership of EAS. It was due to ASEAN's effort that India along with Australia and New Zealand was included as members. By laying the criteria for membership, ASEAN put itself effectively in the driver's seat and is central to EAS process.[26] China supports ASEAN's centrality in the EAS.

In spite of competing interests, trade between India and China is increasing at an incredible pace. The number of Indian tourists visiting China is a result of an admiration in India for China's economic success. China is now India's second largest trading partner after the United States, and the Indian and Chinese business communities are pleased about the enhanced economic and trade relations between the two countries. However, the strengthening of economic integration has not resolved the border issue. Nevertheless, both the countries are keen to continue with the dialogue process so that the "phenomenal growth" seen in trade does not suffer.[27] Also, it is held that there is a convergence of views on many issues where both the countries have taken common positions.[28] According to the Indian side, "the relationship could easily be described as a very complex engagement in the world".[29] For this very reason, India is carefully watching the US moves in Asia-Pacific. It does not want to openly antagonise China, even though the US does see India as a balancing force to China's rising power in East Asia.

Security Dimensions

From the outset, China's assertiveness and military posturing in the region has irked many countries including ASEAN states, the United States, Japan, and South Korea. As enumerated by Professor Christensen in his article in Foreign Affairs, the following cases are illustrative of China's assertive diplomacy. In the first case, China warned US and South Korea to desist from conducting joint naval exercises in international waters near China. In the second incident, it asserted in May 2010 that South China Sea was China's area of "core interest", while in the third case China's military posturing in East China Sea, created tension between China and Japan.[30] Some of the concerns felt in the region were mentioned officially by New Zealand although in somewhat muted language. It was stated: "The pace of China's military modernisation and force projection programme, and the response this could prompt from neighbouring states, may test the relationships of the major regional powers."[31]

Developments in the South China Sea

India and New Zealand are committed to support efforts to safeguard freedom of commerce and navigation. Both are concerned about the maritime environment in Asia-Pacific and are keen to safeguard SLOCs from inimical powers. New Zealand's "ninety-nine percent exports of its merchandise goods (by volume) travel by sea,"[32] while, "almost, 55% of India's trade with the Asia Pacific transits" through the sea lanes in the South China Sea.[33] Any obstruction to free passage of ships through these waters would have major consequence for India's maritime interests, both here and in the Indian Ocean. The major dispute in recent times has been the Chinese assertion of sovereignty over the South China Sea which has resulted in a very complex situation which could lead to serious discord in this area. South China Sea is rich in oil and gas reserves and has crucial sea lanes which are important to those whose trade depends on these routes. Strategically it is important for the US to continue to maintain its prominence in Asia-Pacific.[34] China's rising power and its assertive behaviour has led to much scholarly debate and analyses on China's intentions and its consequences on the regional order. Some of the critics like John Hemmings, hold the view that what is being witnessed is the emergence of China's grand strategy and the developments in the South China Sea could lead to serious discord between the US and China.[35] Dr Kerry Brown of the Asia Programme at Chatham House, London, is equally critical of China. In his view: "China is becoming much more confident in the region and there are signs it is becoming giddy with success. It has become much more influential much more quickly than it expected."[36]

In such a complex situation the regional stakeholders, have to contend with the new power projections and new equations such as between the United States and Vietnam. In this unfolding security dynamics, India is the new entrant in the South China Sea imbroglio. This is due to the Oil and Natural Gas Corporation (ONGC) Videsh Limited engaging in oil and gas exploration projects in the blocks that are claimed by Vietnam. In July 2011, China had warned India to "leave Chinese waters," after the Indian naval ship INS Airavat had made a goodwill visit to Vietnam.[37] India called this a violation of the "freedom of navigation in international waters" including in the South China Sea.[38] At the EAS meet in Bali on 18 November 2011, Prime Minister Manmohan Singh firmly rejected China's objections to its presence in the South China Sea. He was quoted to have told the Chinese Prime Minister Wen Jiabao, "that Indian interests were 'purely commercial' and sovereignty claims must be settled according to international law."[39]

Indian interest in the South Pacific

Connected with the above mentioned strategic dimension, there are crucial developments in the South Pacific which could put at risk the stability and security of this region. In fact, the South Pacific is now part of the new term in vogue—"Indo-Pacific", which as India's former foreign secretary Shyam Saran, writes "is a logical corollary to India's Look East Policy having graduated to an Engage East policy."[40] Till recently the South Pacific had received little attention from the Indian decision makers, with interaction mostly limited to the major South Pacific powers Australia and New Zealand and very little contact with the island states of the South Pacific. There are three major explanations for India's attitude. One, the colonial status of the South Pacific countries with decolonisation process starting as late as 1962, restricted India's interaction. Two, the major metropolitan countries of the region, Australia and New Zealand, had chosen the policy of alignment in the 1940s and 1950s, and this was heightened during the Cold War. Three, the island states were tied to the metropolitan powers through their aid dependence, thus limiting scope for trade and commerce with India.[41] In addition, India's closed economy, domestic problems, hostile geo-strategic setting and its faith in non-alignment were other reasons for its disinterest in a region which it felt was under the US influence.

In the changing strategic atmosphere, New Zealand realises that India should play a significant and constructive role in the economic development of the South Pacific Island countries. Perhaps, India is also seen as a balancer to China, whose presence in the micro nations of South Pacific has grown in the last ten years. Many see these aid dependent island states lured by what is called the "cheque book diplomacy" of China. India on the other hand was indifferent towards a region which till recently did not feature on its security agenda. It is the growing convergence with Australia and New Zealand on issues of security and trade that India's interest in the South Pacific was reinforced. In an address at the second India-ASEAN Summit in September 2003, the then Foreign Minister Yashwant Sinha stated that India's Look East Policy which had focused primarily on ASEAN countries earlier in Phase 1 had expanded in Phase II, the "definition of East extending from Australia to China and East Asia with ASEAN as its core".[42] India's relationship with the island states became more proactive, only after its inclusion in 2002 as a dialogue partner in the Pacific Islands Forum (PIF). Getting India involved in PIF was obviously initiated by the two antipodean nations.

However, among the island states, Fiji has been the focus of India's attention due to the presence of Indian Diaspora here. Unlike New Zealand, India has not shunned relations with the current government of Commodore Bainimarama who had carried a coup against a democratic government in 2006. Indian policy makers are of the opinion that Bainimarama's government is less racist than the regimes which followed the coups of 1987 and 2000.[43] India's ties with Fiji, in a way, prevent China from gaining leverage in Fiji especially when the two regional powers Australialia and New Zealand, have no equation with the present administration in Fiji.

There is a need for greater linkages with the South Pacific, and it is heartening to note that of late there is a noticeable rising interest in the South Pacific littoral states, as evident from the current writings of Indian strategic analysts and former diplomats. Also, with the growing interaction with New Zealand on the increase, India's interaction with the remote island states of the South Pacific will also increase.

Strategic Partnerships

The US

In any discourse on New Zealand's policy towards Asia in general and India in particular, Australia and the US perspectives have played a critical role in New Zealand's security policies and in its strategic posture. Both Australia and the US have embarked on a policy of engaging India, and this has had a definitive impact on New Zealand's foreign policy approach towards India.

The security ramifications of the emerging new challenges in international politics of Asia Pacific, has led to the forging of strategic partnerships with like minded countries which may not have been allies during the Cold War period. It has been seen that today even those countries that were "once far from American orbit, like Vietnam and India, are being driven closer to it by China's aggressive assertion of territorial claims."[44] The US which had earlier a strong presence and interest in Southeast Asia and South Pacific, had almost disengaged itself for some time due to its preoccupation in the Middle East.

The US is responding to the concerns being expressed by its allies and strategic partners in the changing strategic dimensions in the region, and is reengaging with both the South Pacific and Southeast Asia. Also, "... for all the fear of China's rise, the United States remains the predominant military power in the Pacific."[45] On 23 October 2011, the US Defence Secretary Leon E. Panetta in a statement clearly assured of the US involvement in the region at the ASEAN Defence Ministers Meeting (ADMM) in Bali, Indonesia.[46] President Barrack Obama, too reiterated the US commitment to the security of the region and supported India's emergence as a major Asian power which according to him would play a crucial role in the shaping of Asia-Pacific.[47]

Interestingly, the US ties with New Zealand had suffered a setback during David Lange's administration from 1984 to1989. Relations improved in 2001, when New Zealand participated in the US-led war against terrorism in

Afghanistan.[48] Relations were further energised when New Zealand and the United States signed the Wellington Declaration on 4November 2010. Both sides heralded it as a declaration which would further strengthen their partnership through "a new focus on practical cooperation in the Pacific region; and enhanced political and subject-matter dialogue—including regular Foreign Ministers' meetings and political-military discussions."[49]

Australia

New Zealand's most crucial partner is Australia, both in economic and strategic terms.[50] Nevertheless, inspite of such close connections, New Zealand has differed with Australia on many issues like the Kyoto Protocol, and in signing of the Treaty of Amity and Cooperation (TAC). New Zealand's commitment to climate change and its sensitivity towards the concerns of the South Pacific states, led it to ratify the Kyoto Protocol on 19 December2002.[51] Australia ratified it on 3 December 2007, only when the new Prime Minister Kevin Rudd came to power and took immediate steps to ratify the treaty, which his predecessor Johan Howard had refused to sign.[52] India and even China "the world's second biggest emitter of greenhouse gases"[53] ratified the Kyoto Protocol, the former in August 2002 and the latter in September 2002.

In the signing of the TAC as well, New Zealand took an independent stand when it signed the TAC on 25 July 2005. The signing of the TAC with ASEAN countries was a prerequisite for membership of the EAS. Australia signed the TAC with great reluctance only after its leaders were explicitly told by the ASEAN, that there was no way their country could be included without first signing it. Ultimately, just before the first EAS meeting to be held in Kuala Lumpur on 14 December 2005, Australia signed the TAC on 10 December 2005. India had signed the TAC much earlier on 8 October 2003. These two instances mentioned above, in a way reflect that at times the close partners do differ in their perceptions even when they do share strategic space and ideas.

India-New Zealand Bilateral Relationship

Cold War Years

After India became independent it decided to pursue an independent and active non-aligned foreign policy attuned with India's national interests. It placed itself outside the power blocs, and refused to be drawn into any military pact sponsored by any of the superpowers. India began to play an increasingly important role in Asian-African affairs. The exigencies of the Cold War and political and economic considerations at home had a hand in the shaping of India's foreign policy. Though India and New Zealand shared membership of the Commonwealth and interacted in other forums as well, they had no shared history or direct geographical proximity to bring them together. India identified the South Pacific as the "American lake." This perception was based on Australia and New Zealand's alignment with the US and by their restrictive immigration policy, which aimed at protecting their Anglo Celtic identity.

After the Second World War, New Zealand like Australia opted for an alliance with the "big and powerful friend" the United States and its economy continued to be tied to the western markets. Though the Immigration Amendment Act of 1961 removed certain restrictions, it was still very difficult for an Asian to "gain entry" into New Zealand.[54] By 1990, its economic and security perceptions changed and bilateral relations with Asia including India were being sought .The economic transformation taking place in its immediate neighbourhood and beyond made New Zealand adopt a more outward looking policy. After all, "...the economic concern for New Zealand is far from theoretical. Among the fears is that regional economic groupings could be formed which exclude NZ and that might result in this country facing a future in which it withers in its region."[55] New Zealand's commercial interests benefited with the economic liberalization in Asia, trade with Asia increased and so did its positive stance towards Asian migration.

New Era in India's Foreign Policy

In India the end of the Cold War, brought about some soul searching. This resulted in Prime Minister Narsimha Rao initiating economic reforms and announcing the "Look East Policy" in 1992. Closed economy and set attitudes of Indian policy makers had not done much for Indian image either globally or regionally.[56] By the end of 1980's, it was clear that India was being marginalised from every other regional or sub regional forum whether it was ASEAN or APEC. On the one hand, there was a peaceful country like India, with no hegemonic designs, on the other hand, there was China gaining a strong foothold in the region, irrespective of its dubious past record. With one masterly stroke Narsimha Rao's "Look East Policy," wiped away the earlier constricted thinking and approach that had been a handicap in its acceptance by ASEAN nations and established India as a country of consequence in the region. The new strategy to promote India's links with the ASEAN had immediate positive fallout with the ASEAN responding immediately by making India a Sectoral Dialogue Partner of the ASEAN in January 1992 and a full Dialogue Partner in December 1995. In July 1996, India was made a member of the ARF. India's elevation to a Summit partner of ASEAN during the Phnom Penh Summit of November 2002 was an acknowledgement of India's emergence as a key player in the Asia Pacific region. Australia and more slowly New Zealand too responded positively to this "new era" in India's foreign and economic policy.

The Look East Policy resulted in increased bilateral and multilateral interaction with countries to its east. It also led Indian policy makers to look beyond the immediate east and take note of Australia and New Zealand and the South Pacific island states. Since both these countries were already actively involved in meetings at institutional and at bilateral levels in Southeast Asia, India's dialogue partnership of ASEAN, helped in forging closer relations with them. Membership of ARF, created a common security platform through which they could cooperate in building a security community based on the objectives set by ARF. The objectives of the ARF were outlined in the First Chairman's Statement of 1994"to foster constructive dialogue and consultation on political and security issues of common interest and concern; and to make significant contributions to efforts towards confidence-building and preventive diplomacy in the Asia-Pacific region."[57] Although critics have called ARF a talking shop, the ARF meetings held on the recent developments in the South China Sea, of which India and New Zealand are two of the 27 members, had according to some security experts ended with positive results.[58]

While, geographically apart and culturally different, India and New Zealand do share certain commonalities which span from shared belief in democracy to multiculturalism. In addition, they are part of growing regional architecture and are members of various regional and international forums. Both are keen to strengthen this partnership as has been apparent from various reciprocal high level visits in recent years. The highlight of these high level visits was the one made by the then Governor-General of New Zealand, Anand Satyanand, who is of Indian descent. All efforts are being geared to make up for the lost time during which New Zealand had lagged behind other countries, in enhancing relations with rising India. Evidently, the political elite is doing its utmost best to make the right gestures and the right statements to signify India's growing significance to New Zealand. In a statement on 11 May 2011, the New Zealand Trade Minister Tim Grosner stated: "India is fast emerging as a super power. It will be in the top three during the next decade along with the U.S. and China. It has become a top priority of our foreign policy agenda aimed at enhancing the economic engagement."[59] These were no empty words, the bilateral trade figures for 2010, amounted to US$750 million showing a steady rise in trade when compared to previous years.[60] Deepening of relations between them, has led New Zealand to support India's bid for permanent seat in the UN Security Council.[61]

Challenges

Although, there are challenges in the form of nuclear issues over which the two have differences, the real challenge for both the countries is to ensure that the inevitable minor irritants which affect relationships do not impact on overall bilateral ties. The relationship with New Zealand suffered a setback when it criticised India's nuclear tests of May 1998. New Zealand's stand can be better understood if briefly its anti-nuclear policy is reviewed. New Zealand has been at the vanguard of international movement against nuclear proliferation and is a vocal supporter of NPT and CTBT. On 4 June 1987, New Zealand Parliament passed the Nuclear Free Zone, Disarmament and Arms Control Bill and thus "became the only country in the world which has attempted to legislate disengagement from nuclear deterrence."[62] Prime Minister Helen Clark in her talk at Oxford on 1 October 2007 emphasised the importance of anti nuclear policy to New Zealanders, which resulted in the legislation of 1987 Act—declaring the country nuclear free. According to her, this Act "enjoyed strong public support then, and does to this day—to the extent that it has become an accepted part of New Zealand's identity. Politicians tamper with it at their peril. It is a cornerstone of our independent foreign policy."[63]

Pursuit of close relations with India seems to have softened New Zealand's stand vis a vis India's civil nuclear programme. Like Australia and the US, which have strategic partnership with India, it too has in the present century common strategic interests that it shares with India. Australian Prime Minister Julia Gillard's decision to sell uranium to India was supported by the American President Obama on his visit to Australia on the 16 November 2011.He stated, "India is a big player and the Australia-India relationship is one that should be cultivated..."[64] The US-India nuclear deal and the US support for India's peaceful use of nuclear energy has had a positive effect on New Zealand's policy towards India's civil nuclear programme. This was evident during New Zealand's Prime Minister John Key's visit to India in June-July 2011. The Joint Statement of 28 June 2011 stated, "Both sides share the vision of a nuclear weapon free world. New Zealand welcomes increased engagement between India and the multilateral export control regimes."[65] It is hoped that the single issue of New Zealand's position towards India in the Nuclear Suppliers Group (NSG) will not dictate the positive course of existing bilateral relations.

Strategic Relations

Though there is a growing economic integration in Asia, it is becoming extremely difficult to predict the future contours of politico-strategic dynamics of the region. The internal challenges in some of the countries of South and Southeast Asia have serious security implications, as these could jeopardise prospects for peace and stability in the region. In so many ways India and New Zealand are natural allies. Both have vested interest in stability and peace in Asia and for that very reason the defence cooperation between the two countries has increased in the past few years. There is a need towards strategic convergence which would lead to better coordination in facing non-traditional security challenges. Needless to say, defence cooperation is essential for the safety of sea lanes and the choke points like the Malacca straits. Combined security effort is needed to combat threat from terrorist activities especially maritime terrorism.

Since, it is not possible to fight these "asymmetrical wars" alone, India is seen as a natural partner by most of those in the region. Its navy has the capability to respond immediately to threats in the neighbouring seas. With the proliferation of non-traditional threats, there is a need for a multi dimensional and cooperative approach. Many of these cooperative efforts especially those related to intelligence sharing and enhanced military contacts will help in assuaging anxieties about India's emerging dominant role. Such cooperation is now the basic component of India's foreign and defence policy in the region. This multilateral cooperation has taken the form of 13-nation Milan exercise hosted by the Indian Navy which includes ships from New Zealand as well.[66] It is based on common threat perceptions "with India having a leading role in combating maritime terror, poaching, gun and drug-running."[67] As an Indian Ocean nation, India has an important role in ensuring maritime security in the Indian Ocean Region (IOR). Besides, there is a need to put together combined efforts at disaster management which due to climate change have become a common occurrence in the region.

Since 2001, there have been enhanced contacts between New Zealand and India at the defence level. It is important to enumerate some of these contacts as these reflect the new warmth in this relationship. On 9 October 2001, Indian naval war ships visited Wellington. On 2 July 2006, another Indian naval ship 'Tabar' visited Auckland. In addition, there have been a number of bilateral high level visits of senior officials from the Army, Air Force, and Navy.[68] These interactions have led to exchange of views which help in understanding each other's security perceptions essential for building security cooperation. In an effort at upgrading its defence relations with India, New Zealand took the initiative in June 2011, to appoint a Defence Adviser to India who would be able to facilitate better defence linkages between them.[69] At the regional level their defence linkages have increased through their participation in the ADMM+ process.

Economic Linkages

India has emerged a key promoter of economic cooperation in the region. The recent trade figures are reflective of a more open and less discriminatory regime coming into play in India. The bilateral economic engagement between India and New Zealand has been progressively increasing. The two-way goods trade between New Zealand and India is valued at over NZ$1.25 billion (up from NZ$950 million two years ago). Exports were worth NZ$917 million for the year ending March 2011, and had doubled in the past two years.[70] India is now New Zealand's 7th largest market. Imports from India were valued at NZ$370 million for the year ending March 2011.[71]

New Zealand exports to India are limited to coking coal, wool, logs, sheep skin leather, raw hides and skins, Indian exports too are limited to diamond jewellery, bed linen, table linen, garments and footwear.[72] However, going by

New Zealand official source, there are excellent investment opportunities for India in sectors as varied as forestry, energy resources especially coal, and the IT. The bilateral trade and business relations have substantial potential to grow. [73] Already there is a presence of various Indian companies and banks who have invested in New Zealand. Some of these are : Mahindra-Satyam, HCL Technologies, CMC, WIPRO, Infosys, TCS, Tata Steel, New India Assurance Co. Ltd and Bank of Baroda and Bank of India.[74] In India, New Zealand's ANZ Bank has a branch in Mumbai and ANZ Bank's global IT and processing hub is based in Bangalore.[75]

In order to further develop investment and trade links, several areas of co-operation were identified during the visit of Minister of Commerce & Industry Anand Sharma, to New Zealand on May 8-10, 2011.[76] These were, post-harvest technologies/logistic management for the agriculture sector, renewable energy sector, including wind and geo-thermal energy, tourism, films (including animation films); pharmaceuticals, education, IT enabled services and financial services.[77] Once Free Trade Agreement (FTA) is signed by the two countries, it will tremendously boost the bilateral economic and trade relations. A number of initiatives have been taken to facilitate and accelerate the process and it is expected that India would be signing FTA sooner than latter.

People-to-People Links

Although, majority of New Zealand population is of Anglo Celtic ethnicity, of late there has been a steady increase in immigration from Asia. Of these according to 2006 census, Indians are about 100,000. Many of them are Indo-Fijians, who came in the wake of Fijian crisis which began with the March and September 1987 coups. According to New Zealand government source, Indian Minister of Overseas Indian Affairs regularly visits New Zealand and keeps in touch with the Indian community there.

There has been an increase in the number of Indian tourists and students going to New Zealand. Not only has it helped to build people to people contact, it is generating economic benefits as well through tourism, which is an important industry for New Zealand. In 2004, the number of Indian tourists was estimated to be 16,000; in March 2011 their number had increased to over 30,000. India is New Zealand's 10th largest source of visitors.[78] The number of fee paying Indian students to New Zealand has also grown and is growing significantly, in 2008, there were 4,600 Indian students and today their number has increased to 12,000, which is contributing more than $1 billion a year to New Zealand exchequer. Indian students number fourth after those coming from China, South Korea and Japan. These fee paying students are crucial to New Zealand's economy and education industry.[79]

This new Indian Diaspora is an "important point of contact" for the growth of bilateral relations. New Zealand has profited from the presence of Indian Diaspora who have maintained their links with India, and their presence has helped the growing proximity between New Zealand and India. This growth in bilateral relations is clearly a product of globalization and the changed economic scenario in India. With the growing relationship, people to people contact is helping to build mutual understanding to a large extent. Also, the increase in the number of Asians in New Zealand is somewhat changing its insular character. According to a New Zealand diplomat, "We are of course now a much more multicultural society than ever before. Large waves of immigrants from the South Pacific, and particularly Asia, have transformed the cultural landscape—some would say not before time. That is a reality and it's a stimulating one. Multiculturalism is alive and well."[80]

Conclusion

It is reasonable to assume from the broad contours of New Zealand foreign policy delineated above that New Zealand is diligently pursuing its Asia policy; and in keeping with this policy, it has enhanced close economic, political and strategic relations with the "rising India". In the new millennium, the international environment is becoming more complex, giving shape to new patterns of relationship along with new centres of power. New Zealand, like others, wants to engage economically with both the rising powers in Asia. In 2007, the then Labour Prime Minister Helen Clark had explicitly explained the rationale behind the Asia Policy of New Zealand. She said, "The countries of Asia today are undergoing rapid and fundamental changes. We have much to learn from these changes. If we can keep pace, many new opportunities will open to us."[81]

Although, economic relations with China continue to be strong, simultaneously, New Zealand's economic engagement with India too is growing. India has an advantage over China as it is perceived to be a peace loving democratic country, having the capability to contribute towards economic, political and strategic well-being of the region, this perception is shared by New Zealand with the US, Australia, Japan, South Korea and ASEAN. To sum up, India-New Zealand relations have evolved in the backdrop of India's Look East Policy and New Zealand's Asia Policy. With a growing multicultural identity and having important strategic interests in Asia, New Zealand's partnership with India would be vital for both the countries, in dealing with future challenges emanating from the region. Unlikely partners of the past are today natural partners in the emerging regional order of the twenty first century.

End Notes

1. Quoted in Stephen Henningham, *France and the South Pacific: A Contemporary History*, University of Hawaii Press, Honolulu (1992), p. 224.

2. G. John Ikenberry, "The Future of the Liberal World Order: Internationalism after America", *Foreign Affairs*, New York (May/June 2011), vol.90, no.3, p. 56.
3. Graham Fortune, "New Zealand's Approach to Pacific Security" in Jenny Bryant-Tokalau and Ian Frazer, ed., *Redefining the Pacific? Regionalism Past, Present and Future*, Ashgate Publishing Ltd, Hampshire, England (2006) p. 58.
4. New Zealand MFAT: *Our Future with Asia,* http://www.mfat.govt.nz/Media-and-publications/Publications/Asia-White-Paper/0-asia-strategy.php
5. Michael Yahuda, The International Politics of the Asia-Pacific 2nd ed., Routledge Curzon, London, (2003) p. 13.
6. ASEAN-New Zealand Relations http://www.asean.org/5826.htm
7. Ibid.
8. New Zealand Ministry of Defence: *Defence White Paper 2010,* http://www.defence.govt.nz/reports-publications/defence-white-paper-2010/chapter3-nz-strategic-outlook-to-2035.html
9. Hal Hill, *East Asia: Australia's Asia-Pacific Connections*, Economics Division Working Papers, Research School of Pacific Studies, Australian National University (1994) p. 7.
10. New Zealand Ministry of Defence: *Defence White Paper 2010,* http://www.defence.govt.nz/reports-publications/defence-white-paper-2010/chapter3-nz-strategic-outlook-to-2035.html
11. Murray McCully, " New Zealand And China In The 21st Century", 26 June 2010, http://www.scoop.co.nz/stories/PA1006/S00423.htm
12. ASEAN http://www.aseansec.org/index.html
13. Agreement on Australia-New Zealand FTA Enters into Force,12 January 2010, http://www.asean.org/24194.htm
14. ASEAN-New Zealand Relations, http://www.asean.org/5826.htm
15. New Zealand Ministry Of Foreign Affairs andTrade: Agreement establishing the ASEAN-Australia-New Zealand Free Trade Area, http://www.asean.fta.govt.nz/assets/Downloads/asean-factsheet.pdf
16. Toyoo Gyohten," The Future of Asia"in Indermit Gill, Yukon Huang, and Homi Kharas ed., East Asian Visions:Perspectives on Economic Development,World Bank Washington (2007), p. 74.
17. See Michael Yahuda, *The International Politics of the Asia-Pacific* (RoutledgeCurzon,2004, London) 2nd ed. p. 341.
18. New Zealand Ministry of Defence: *Defence White Paper 2010,*http://www.defence.govt.nz/reports-publications/defence-white-paper-2010/chapter3-nz-strategic-outlook-to-203
19. For details see the recent Joint Statement issued during the visit of New Zealand Prime Minister John Key to India in June 2011, http://mealib.nic.in/?2010201117789
20. New Zealand Ministry Of Foreign Affairs and Trade: Agreement On Free Trade Agreement between New Zealand and China, http://www.chinafta.govt.nz/1-The-agreement/index.php
21. Murray McCully, "New Zealand and China In The 21st Century", (26 June 2010, http://www.scoop.co.nz/stories/PA1006/S00423.htm
22. C. Raja Mohan, "India and the Balance of Power" *Foreign Affairs,* (July 2006), http://www.realclearpolitics.com/articles/2006/2007/india and the balance of power.html
23. Backgrounder: ASEAN-China Free Trade Area, 18 November 2011, *Xinhua net,* http://news.xinhuanet.com/english2010/china/2011-11/18/c_131254269.htm
24. Mark Beeson, "Southeast Asia and the Major Powers: The United States, Japan and China", in Mark Beeson ed., *Contemporary Southeast Asia: Regional Dynamics, National Differences* (2004), Palgrave Macmillan, Hampshire, p. 209.

25. Mohan Malik, "*China's Strategy of Containing India*", http//www.pinr.com/report.phb?ac+view_printable&report_id=434&language_id=1
26. The criteria are: Full Dialogue Partner of ASEAN; Member has acceded to or agrees to accede to the Treaty of Amity and Cooperation in Southeast Asia. (TAC); and has substantive relations with ASEAN.
27. *The Hindu*, 18 November 2011.
28. Ibid.
29. Ibid.
30. Thomas J. Christensen, "The Advantage of an assertive China: Responding to Beijng's Abrasive Diplomocy", *Foreign Affairs,* vol, 90, no. 2 (March/April 2011), p. 55.
31. New Zealand Ministry of Defence: *Defence White Paper 2010,* http://www.beehive.govt.nz/sites/all/files/White_Paper_Final.pdf
32. New Zealand Ministry of Defence: *Defence White Paper 2010,* http://www.defence.govt.nz/reports-publications/defence-white-paper-2010/chapter2-national-security-defence.html
33. Amit Singh, "South China Sea Dispute and India,National Maritime Foundation," New Delhi (25 September 2011), http://saeagroup.com/articles/2011/sept/south-china-sea-dispute-and-india.html
34. Charles Scanlon, "South China Sea tensions rattle China's neighbours", http://www.bbc.co.uk/news/world-asia-pacific-15578083
35. Ibid.
36. Ibid.
37. Liu Sheng, "India makes waves with South China Sea oil and gas exploration", *Global Times,* (17 September 2011), http://www.globaltimes.cn/NEWS/tabid/99/ID/675647/India-makes-waves-with-South-China-Sea-oil-and-gas-exploration.aspx
38. Ibid.
39. Indrani Bagchi, "PM Manmohan Singh to China's Wen Jiabao: Back off on South China Sea", *TNN* (19 November 2011), http://timesofindia.indiatimes.com/india/PM-Manmohan-Singh-to-Chinas-Wen-Jiabao-Back-off-on-South-China-Sea/articleshow/10786454.cms
40. Shyam Saran," Mapping the Indo-Pacific: India and the strategic inter-linkage between Indian and Pacific Oceans",*The Indian Express,* (29 October 2011).
41. Man Mohini Kaul, "Imagining the South Pacific: An Indian Construct of the Region" in N.N. Vohra ed., India and Australasia: History, Culture and Society, New Delhi, Shipra Publications, 2004, p. 132.
42. C. Raja Mohan, "Is India an East Asian Power? Explaining New Delhi's Security Politics in the Western Pacific, ISAS Working Paper, No. 81, (11 August 2009), p. 6.
43. For New Zealand view see David McCraw, "New Zealand, Fiji and Democracy," *Commonwealth and Comparative Politics,* vol.47, no.3, (July 2009), pp. 267-86.
44. *The Economist,* (24-30 September 2011), p. 46.
45. Ibid.
46. U.S. Department of Defense: Statement to ASEAN Defense Ministers, As Prepared for Delivery by Secretary of Defense Leon E. Panetta, Bali, Indonesia, Sunday,(23 October 2011), http://www.defense.gov/speeches/speech.aspx?speechid=1624
47. Barack Obama's speech to Parliament, *Herald Sun,* (17 November 2011).
48. Country Profile 2006: New Zealand, *The Economist Intelligence Unit* (2006), p.12
49. Ibid.
50. New Zealand Ministry of Defence: *Defence White Paper 2010,* http://www.nzdf.mil.nz/downloads/pdf/public-docs/2010/defence_white_paper_2010.pdf

51. New Zealand Emission Unit Register, http://www.eur.govt.nz/about-us/about-the-kyoto-protocol
52. Australia ratifies Kyoto Protocol, *The Sydney Morning Herald*, 3 December 2007, http://www.smh.com.au/news/environment/rudd-signs-kyoto-deal/2007/12/03/1196530553203.html
53. China ratifies global warming treaty, 4 September, 2002, *CNN*, http://archives.cnn.com/2002/WORLD/africa/09/03/kyoto.china.glb/index.html
54. Donald Denoon and Philippa Mein Smith with Marivie Wyndham, *A History of Australia, New Zealand, and the Pacific*, Oxford (2000), p. 212.
55. *The National Business Review*, 12 December 2003.
56. See ManMohini Kaul, "ASEAN-India Relations During the Cold War" in Fredric Grare and Amitabh Mattoo ed., *India and ASEAN; The politics of India's Look East Policy*,New Delhi: Manohar Publishers (2001), pp. 41-66 and "Indian Perspectives on Security Dimensions of India and Southeast Asia", inV.R. Raghavan and Karl Fischer ed., *Security Dimensions of India and Southeast Asia*, (New Delhi: Tata McGraw-Hill, 2005) pp. 3-21.
57. ARF http://aseanregionalforum.asean.org/about.html
58. Daljit Singh "South China Sea developments at the ASEAN Regional Forum", http://www.eastasiaforum.org/2011/08/03/south-china-sea-developments-at-the-asean-regional-forum/
59. *The Hindu*, 12 May 2011
60. Mukul G. Asher and Rahul Sen "India-New Zealand PTA: Broaden it for Balanced Gains", http://www.eastasiaforum.org/2011/04/01/india-new-zealand-pta-broaden-it-for-balanced-gains/
61. New Zealand announces new initiatives for India, *Indian Newslink*, 29 June 2011, http://www.indiannewslink.co.nz/index.php/archives_2011/july_1_2011/new-zealand-announces-new-initiatives-for-india.html
62. Alan Burnett, The A-NZ-US Triangle, Canberra (1988), p. 93.
63. Helen Clark, "New Zealand Foreign Policy, Nuclear Age Peace Foundation," Oxford, England (1 October 2007), http://www.wagingpeace.org/articles/2007/10/05_clark_nz_disarmament.php
64. Obama backs Australia's u-turn on uranium sale to India, *Daily News and Analysis*, Melbourne (16 November 2011), http://www.dnaindia.com/world/report_obama-backs-australia-s-u-turn-on-uranium-sale-to-india_1613362
65. Joint Statement on the State Visit of PM of NZ, 29 June 2011, http://www.scoop.co.nz/stories/PA1106/S00480/joint-statement-on-the-state-visit-of-pm-of-nz.htm
66. Navy's Milan exercise to become Asia-Pacific taskforce, Rediff News, (9 February 2010), http://news.rediff.com/report/2010/feb/09/milan-exercise-to-become-asia-pacific-taskforce.htm
67. Ibid.
68. High Commission of India: India NewZealand Bilateral Relations, Wellington, (15 November 2011), http://www.hicomind.org.nz/index.php/india-and-new-zealand/
69. John Hartevelt, "Closer defence ties with India signalled" (29 June 2011), http://www.stuff.co.nz/national/politics/5205114/Closer-defence-ties-with-India-signalled
70. New Zealand Ministry Of Foreign Affairs and Trade : *Republic of New Zealand*, http://www.mfat.govt.nz/Countries/Asia-South-and-Southeast/India.php
71. Ibid.
72. Ibid.
73. Ibid.

74. Ibid.
75. Ibid.
76. Ibid.
77. Ibid.
78. New Zealand Ministry of Foreign Affairs and Trade : *Republic of New Zealand* http://www.mfat.govt.nz/Countries/Asia-South-and-Southeast/India.php
79. Ibid.
80. Talk by Christopher Laidlaw at the International Centre, New Delhi (12 April 2004).
81. Helen Clarke, *op. cit.*, n. 63.

2

New Zealand's Foreign Policy in the 21st Century

Vibhanshu Shekhar

Introduction

No matter how insulated and isolated a country is, it can not remain unaffected from the fundamental transformation taking place in the global *bodypolitik* of the 21st century. The impact is all the more pervasive for a globally connected country whose half of the economy depends on foreign trade and that advocates greater activism in international relations, trade policies and issues of global concern. New Zealand is one such integrated and inter-connected nation-state driven by a unique blend of pragmatism and normativism on several issues of international significance. As a result, substantial transformation is manifest in New Zealand's strategic world view and foreign policy priorities as it traverses in the changed politico-strategic and economic environment of 21st century.

New Zealand no longer remains either psychologically or economically dependent on the Western world. Its foreign policy has developed an independent character and a view of its own, tuned with the changing realities of the 21st century. New Zealand's foreign policy has undergone a major change during the last twenty years in the form of greater Asianisation of its strategic priorities and its economic engagements. Moreover, Wellington's policy stances over several issues of global and regional significance, such as nuclear non-proliferation, climate change, or its alliance partnerships, have demonstrated its conscious pursuit of its foreign policy priorities and, sometimes, in defiance of its regional and strategic partners.

Drivers of New Zealand's Foreign Policy

The nature and trajectories of New Zealand's foreign policy during the last six decades have been shaped by three important catalysts—normative dynamics and divergence of bipartisan politics, changing regional and international structures of power, and the pattern of New Zealand's global economic engagement. These catalysts have exhibited two distinct characteristics. First, these drivers have been prominent in influencing the evolution of the fundamental tenets of New Zealand's foreign policy. As a result, their contributions have also been obvious and self-explanatory. For example, while New Zealand's entry into ANZUS (Australia, New Zealand, United States Security Treaty) was a result of its recognition of growing importance of the United States for New Zealand's security, its exit from the treaty was driven by growing regionalisation of New Zealand's foreign policy, a trend driven primarily by domestic normative considerations of the Labour party. Second, even though they can be understood as operating separately, often in divergent directions, they should not be understood as watertight categories. They have, on occasions, mutually reinforced as well as opposed each other.

The domestic catalysts have factored primarily in the form of ideologies and priorities of New Zealand's two ruling political parties—National and Labour parties. Their differences, according to David McCraw, have been much more pronounced in the context of (a) scope and normative exposition of the foreign policies, and (b) importance assigned to cooperation with allies and to the role of economic interests in the country's strategic behaviour.[1] The influence of domestic drivers over New Zealand's foreign policy over the decades has been manifested in the dynamic of economic engagement with the outside world, issues of human rights, Asian immigration and multiculturalism, and nuclear non-proliferation.

International catalysts can be divided into two categories—regional and global strategic discourses. Until the end of the Cold War era, the regional worldview remained confined to South Pacific but the regional today seems to incorporate the entire Asia-Pacific. Therefore, the attendant changes taking place in the region are impacting upon the foreign policy decisions in a much more obvious manner. In other words, both New Zealand and Asia are becoming closer to each other. Asia figures more prominently today in New Zealand articulation of its foreign policy priorities.

Alliances have come to significantly influence New Zealand's foreign policy priorities. Wellington has relied for the security on its principal alliance partners—Britain and the USA—for the most part of 20th century, whether it is Britain during the first half of 20th century or the United States of America during the second half of the 20th century. Therefore, New Zealand's foreign policy has been influenced by the strategic priorities of these two principal alliance partners. New Zealand participated in the World War II as a part of British alliance system. Similarly, it participated in the Korean and Vietnam Wars as an alliance partner of the USA. The two types of government, national and Labour have not differed much, howsoever, in their propensity to become involved in others' conflicts.

Perhaps, one of the most important catalysts for shaping New Zealand's foreign policy is the dynamic of its international economic relations. Foreign trade constitutes more than 50 per cent of New Zealand's Gross National Product (GNP). In fact, New Zealand's foreign policy seems to closely follow the pattern of its economic engagement. New Zealand's trading partners are also seen as important strategic partners. Britain remained the principal trading as well as strategic partner during the Colonial times. Australia and USA have remained principal strategic and trading partners during the Cold War and Post-Cold War eras. The eastern Asian hemisphere has emerged as the most important strategic focus of New Zealand's foreign policy in the 21st century and China, the second largest trading partner, has become a focus area of New Zealand's foreign policy in the 21st century.

Evolution of New Zealand's Foreign Policy

New Zealand's Foreign Policy has seen constant improvisations at regular intervals reflecting changing domestic priorities, and the regional and global structures of power. Though fundamentals of New Zealand's foreign policy have evolved gradually, two distinctive eras could be identified, which have had overwhelming impact on the agendas and strategies of New Zealand's foreign policy in the 21st century.

Era of Floating between the Alliances

An important element of New Zealand's Foreign Policy has been its security alliances formed with three players—Australia, United Kingdom and the USA. These three countries have, for several reasons, been capable of effecting substantial influence in New Zealand's foreign relations. Britain remained New Zealand's principal alliance partner until the end of the World War II. The World War II developments—Japan's attack on Pearl Harbour, Britain's loss of Singapore base, the Japanese bombardment over Australia's Northeastern port of Darwin, and the emergence of the United States of America—prompted New Zealand to look towards regional consolidation and the USA as the new alliance partner. The Japanese incursions to the South Pacific and Australia during the World War II had brought home the point that New Zealand remained vulnerable as an Anglo-Saxon island in the Asian continent.

One of the first major steps that New Zealand took towards consolidating its position in the immediate neighbourhood was to sign the Canberra Pact in 1944 with Australia. The pact was not a security treaty, rather provided a platform for the two countries to develop common understanding on issues of mutual interest. Perhaps, the most definitive step towards alliance formation was taken by New Zealand in 1951 when it along with Australia and USA signed a security treaty in 1951, known as ANZUS treaty. The treaty entered into force in 1952 and it provided for collective security and defence measures in the case of armed attack against any of the signatories in the Pacific Ocean. The article V of the treaty declared that "an armed attack on any of the Parties is deemed to include an armed attack on the metropolitan territory of any of the Parties, or on the island territories under its jurisdiction in the Pacific or on its armed forces, public vessels or aircraft in the Pacific."[2] The treaty also allowed the transit and harbouring of the American warships carrying nuclear vessels along the Australia and New Zealand ports. The New Zealand security forces, as a part of its obligations under the ANZUS treaty, participated both in the Korean and Vietnam Wars.

The National government of New Zealand consolidated its alliance relationship with Australia, United Kingdom and the USA when it along with other countries formed in 1954 an offense-defence security treaty known as Southeast Asia Treaty Organisation (SEATO). The members of SEATO were Australia, France, New Zealand, Pakistan, the Philippines, Thailand, the United Kingdom, and the United States. Moreover, the alliance reflected primarily an anti-communist outlook and was dissolved in 1977 after many members had lost interest in the grouping. New Zealand became a part of another alliance with Britain, France, Malaysia and Singapore in 1971, known as Five Powers Defence Agreement (FPDA). The basic objective of the FPDA was to provide security and military assistance in case of any threat to Malaya and Singapore.

These alliances, which came to characterise New Zealand's security and defence posturing during the Cold War era, according to Jim Rolfe, were essentially a part of New Zealand's strategy of balancing against a potential threat either in the form of re-militarised Japan or a communist China.[3] Moreover, these alliances not only shaped New Zealand's foreign relations with these principal partners but also with other countries and other regions. The ANZUS treaty gave a definitive shape to New Zealand's foreign relations not only in the South Pacific rather also in other theatres of America's global containment of communism. Similarly, the alliances of SEATO and FPDA came to characterise New Zealand's strategic engagement with Southeast Asia and Europe. New Zealand maintained its military presence in Southeast Asia first as a part of British contingent and later as a part of ANZUS for the larger part of Cold War years.

Labour Interregnum and Beyond: towards Normative Posturing

New Zealand's alliance-driven, West-oriented, and economic and military-centric foreign policy underwent a tectonic shift during the 1980s under the Labour leadership of David Lange. The ascendancy of the Labour party brought its normative posturing, regional focus and independent approach to the centre-stage of foreign policy debates.[4] David McCraw argues that this normative posturing was essentially an extrapolation of the Labour party's domestic considerations onto its international behaviour with the objective of creating a just and humane world.[5]

> "On the basis of this more active and self-reliant regional role, we will seek to consolidate, reorder where necessary and expand our important and substantial bilateral relationships with the United States and Australia. Over time, it seems to me likely that the underlying ties and interests which bind together the ANZUS partners will reassert themselves, leading to a resumption in due course of trilateral defense cooperation. If and when this occurs, however, such cooperation may well take a different form. Certainly, in any future trilateral defense cooperation, New Zealand will be a more independent, self reliant and valuable partner."[6]

New Zealand government began to shed its dependence on its Western alliance system and assert greater independence in their foreign policy making processes. In addition to the Labour's normative focus, another important factor effecting the change came in the form of New Zealand's reduced economic and trade transactions from the West and growing share of the Asia-Pacific including Australia and the rest of South Pacific in New Zealand's foreign trade. The West, led by Western Europe began to lose its position as the preeminent market of New Zealand's goods. The growing domestic opposition to New Zealand's participation in the wars of Britain and the United States of America further triggered the former's dissociation from the latter. In fact, the alliance-centric foreign policy came under severe criticism.

Nuclear non-proliferation stands out as the most conspicuous example of normative positioning in the Labour party's foreign policy under the leadership of David Lange and the impact of domestic variables on Wellington's international relations. The Labour party of New Zealand had aggressively opposed and launched international campaign against the French nuclear testing in the region. Emphasising on New Zealand's no nuclear policy, David Lange, the then Prime Minister of New Zealand wrote, "there is simply no need for nuclear weapons to be brought into New Zealand. The strategic environment does not call for nuclear weaponry... Successive New Zealand governments have affirmed that ANZUS is not a nuclear alliance.[7] New Zealand banned the transit of the American nuclear vessels in its territorial waters that led to the former's suspension from the ANZUS in 1985. This move threatened New Zealand's break from its most powerful and the most dependable alliance system. New Zealand signed the Rarotonga Treaty in 1985 that declared South West Pacific as a nuclear weapon free zone and passed the New Zealand Nuclear Free Zone Act (NZNFZA) in 1987.

South Pacific emerged as a priority area of New Zealand's foreign policy as discourses of regionalism and regional identity began to draw greater attention. It is argued that New Zealand's turn towards Southwest Pacific is an appreciation of the local 'Maori tradition of belonging to the region.'[8] New Zealand shares constitutional and other politico-administrative relations with the Cook Island, Niue and Tokelau and their citizens are also citizens of New Zealand.[9] New Zealand is a member and an active participant in the Pacific Island Forum.

New Zealand's involvement in the South Pacific comprised of three key elements—participation and cooperation under the South Pacific Forum, economic assistance for the development to the countries of the region, and maintenance of peace and security in the region. Conflict and peace-building, and according to John Henderson, constituted important considerations for New Zealand's policies towards the Pacific Island Countries (PICs).[10] New Zealand intervened in the Bougainville crisis and mediated dialogue between the parties in the conflict. New Zealand severely criticised the coup in Fiji in 2000 and overthrow of the democratically elected government led by the Prime Minister of Indian origin, Mahendra Choudhary.[11] While these conflicts were taking place primarily in the Melanesian region, Polynesia, which formed the focus of New Zealand's policy towards South Pacific, drew attention for the French nuclear testing in the region.[12] A large part of these aids went to sectors of health, education, local capacity building, and other sectors of governance. In addition to the advocacy of peace-building and developmental assistance, New Zealand regional focus revolved around its normative posturing over issues of global concern, such as nuclear non-proliferation, climate change, human rights, and governance.

East Asia began emerging as a priority area in New Zealand's foreign policy during the 1990s as economic relations and diasporic linkages began to bring the two sides closer. These processes were also supported by the political leadership of New Zealand, which began to develop inter-governmental and strategic relationships with the countries of Asia that essentially meant East Asia. Moreover, the overall relationship followed economic trajectories.

Nevertheless, these changes were not sudden, rather had evolved over the years, reflecting intense debate and discussion within the country. One can safely argue that many of the initiatives adopted and implemented by the Labour government of David Lange were actually conceived and initiated under the Labour government of Norman Kirk. For example, New Zealand's declaration of NZNFZA, according to Kevin Clements, was a culmination of 'eleven years of campaigning by the New Zealand Peace Movement in collaboration with the New Zealand Labour Party, the Social Credit League and the Values Party.'[13]

New Zealand's Foreign Policy in the 21st Century: New Realities, New Strategies

The geo-political realities of the Asia-Pacific have undergone fundamental changes during the last twelve years. The politico-strategic landscape of the region is characterised today by its emergence as a global economic hub and an arena of great power rivalries, a shift in the gravity of power from the trans-Atlantic to the Asia-Pacific, the emergence of China and India as new power centres, the re-construction of regional boundaries, growing emphasis on multi-polarity, regional economic integration, and the primacy of ASEAN (Association of Southeast Asian Nations)-driven multilateralism. New Zealand's foreign policy during the 21st century is essentially a product of its reassessment of (a) emerging prospects of cooperation and integration in the Asia-Pacific, and (b) strategic constraints posed by the prevailing uncertainty surrounding the rise of China as a dominant player in the region. While integrative processes have interconnected the economic interests of the regional stakeholders and governmental actors, inter-linkages among people and the non-governmental spaces across the region have grown, facilitated by the process of globalisation, the revolution in information technology, and shrinkage of business space.

The rise of China has been entwined with a sense of fear and an uncertainty as to whether it is a peaceful or conflict-prone process.[14] China's rise has coincided with the rise of India as an important strategic player in the Asia-Pacific. With its sustained economic growth, enhanced strategic presence in East Asia, long-standing 'China-threat' theory and a great power posturing, the perception of countries about India has changed from one of an insular South Asian hegemon to an important strategic player with the material capability of altering the balance of power in the region, what C Raja Mohan characterises as 'a swing state'.[15]

As China and India have emerged as Asian powerhouses, the Asia-Pacific has become a theatre, where each of them is vying for greater strategic influence, setting in motion big-power rivalry in the region. There is a greater degree of Chinese assertion in Asia coupled with efforts to prevent the emergence of any alternative power centre in the continent. China first opposed the idea of forming the East Asia Summit, then tried to scuttle the entry of Australia, India and New Zealand into the grouping, and in the face of failure, decided to take over the agenda of the EAS by proposing to hold the summit in the Beijing. The Chinese diplomatic offensive has invited varied responses from different countries in the region. The formation of the EAS is, in fact, the manifestation of ASEAN's policy of engaging with major players in the region and the entry of three new players including New Zealand into the EAS is an outcome of the balancing efforts of Japan and the ASEAN countries. ASEAN's unequivocal declaration of holding the annual summit of EAS within the region was a response to the Chinese offer of holding the second summit in Beijing.[16]

These changes have impacted upon New Zealand's foreign policy in two definitive ways—introducing new elements and consolidating processes initiated during the 1990s. Moreover, the changing geopolitical realities of the 21st century have added new sense of pragmatism into New Zealand's normative posturing.

Eastern Asian Hemisphere Gains Prominence

The eastern Asian hemisphere has emerged as the new focal point of NZ's foreign policy priorities. To quote Robert Ayson, "New Zealand's engagement with a changing Asia would be the country's most important foreign policy issue over the next 50 years."[17] While the Statement of Intent on Asia, released by New Zealand's Ministry of Foreign Affairs and Trade in 2008 considers Asia as 'the near neighbourhood,' the White Paper on Asia of 2007 identified Asia 'as a region that will carry greater weight in the future.'[18] To quote Helen Clark, New Zealand's former Prime Minister,

> "It is important that New Zealand casts its interest in Asia and it must be a high priority interest, firmly in the context of that continuity of having developed substantive relationships since the Second World War. New Zealand must not invite the accusation that it is only a fair weather friend there for the good times and for the business."[19]

Though the shift in New Zealand's foreign policy towards Asia had begun taking place during the Post-Cold War era, the emergence of Asia as the new driver of global economic growth has hastened the process in the 21st century. In other words, New Zealand's Asia focus is no longer merely a normative posturing, rather a practical necessity. Asia today for New Zealand is not merely East Asia rather refers to the entire Eastern Asian Hemisphere covering the geographical space between India, China Japan and Indonesia. The Asia focus today reflects changing economic relations of New Zealand, a willful acceptance of its geographical reality, and growing emphasis on developing shared values within the continental socio-cultural fabric.

The West, which has traditionally been New Zealand's important foreign policy focus, has shown economic stagnation and signs of deep-seated economic crisis, and, therefore, reduced economic exchanges. On the other hand, New Zealand's economic exchange with the eastern Asian hemisphere has increased manifold, facilitating deeper engagement at political, institutional, inter-governmental, as well as people-to-people levels.

With the trade volume of more than US$33 billion, the Eastern Asian hemisphere (excluding Australia and South Pacific) constitutes more than 40 per cent of New Zealand's total trade. Six of New Zealand's current top 10 trading partners are located in Asia.[20] Moreover, New Zealand has signed bilateral FTAs with China, Malaysia, Singapore, South Korea, Thailand, and multilateral FTA with the entire ASEAN grouping. As a member of East Asia Summit, New Zealand is also a part of deliberations over Comprehensive Economic Partnership in East Asia (CEPEA). Moreover, New Zealand is negotiating an FTA with India, Japan, and Vietnam.[21]

New Zealand has responded to the growing significance of Asia by adopting a two-pronged strategy of engaging with Asia, as identified by the White Paper of 2007 on Asia. First, "no matter what the area of interest—business, politics, education, culture—building strong relationships is vital."[22] Second, "New Zealand needs to look at ways in which it can build a greater shared future in the region, making a bigger contribution to Asia as well as focusing on what we can gain for New Zealand."[23] The first strategy reflects on identifying newer areas of engagement with Asia and the second strategy aims at consolidating the existing relationship.

China takes the Centre Stage, India Follows Suit

New Zealand's region-centric policy towards Asia seems to have received additional stimulus from the actor-driven changes in the region. In this context, both China and India have emerged as the winners of this transformation. China has emerged as an important focus area of New Zealand's Asia policy and increasingly viewed as a panacea for New Zealand's economic situation.[24] Highlighting the dynamic of its relationship with China, the New Zealand Prime Minister, John Key declared that the relationship with China is 'unquestionably and unashamedly an economic relationship.'[25] The total bilateral trade between the two sides crossed NZ$10 billion in 2010 that saw the emergence of China as the second largest trading partner of New Zealand after Australia. The bilateral trade picked up after the signing of FTA in 2008. The two countries have agreed to double the volume of bilateral trade to NZ$20 billion by 2015.

The bilateral relationship received a major breakthrough in 1999 when the then Chinese President, Jiang Zemin visited New Zealand followed by the reciprocal visit of the then New Zealand Governor General of New Zealand, Michael Hardie Boys' to China to 'set a seal on high-level contact.' Since then, the bilateral relationship has grown in many directions including the military relationships. The Chinese PLAN (People's Liberation Army Navy) ships have made visits to the New Zealand ports and the New Zealand naval ships have made similar visits to the Chinese ports.[26] Moreover, New Zealand has engaged with China in the several cooperatives forums of ASEAN and South Pacific.

India did not figure earlier in any major way in New Zealand's foreign policy, an awakening that has dawned upon the policy makers from both the sides only recently. India was not economically very attractive nor were there enough avenues for the two countries to engage except the commonwealth and the UN bodies. Three developments seem to have triggered New Zealand's favourable disposition towards New Delhi—India's sustained growth story, new platforms for politico-strategic and economic cooperation in the form of ASEAN cooperative processes, and increasing diasporic relations. As a result, the two countries have begun waking up to the need of stronger political, strategic and economic linkages. The bilateral trade, which is merely US$1 billion, has shown potential for growth. The two sides are also discussing the feasibility study of India-New Zealand Free Trade Agreement.

Towards pan-Asia-Pacific Cooperation and Institution-building

An important focus of New Zealand's foreign policy during the 21st century has been towards greater participation in the ASEAN-driven cooperative processes. New Zealand was one of the first three countries (along with Australia and Japan) to sign the dialogue partnership with ASEAN in 1977. New Zealand, since then, has engaged with ASEAN as a dialogue partner, a member of ASEAN Regional Forum (ARF), summit partnership along with Australia, a member of East Asia Summit since 2005, and a member of ASEAN Plus Defence Ministerial Meetings (ADMM+) since October 2010. Besides, New Zealand has participated in several track-II level ASEAN cooperative processes. The primary objectives of New Zealand's participation in these forums are to become a part of ASEAN-led processes of economic integration, develop engagement with the ASEAN countries and its dialogue partners, and utilise these forums to advocate its own foreign policy agendas, especially over issues on Non-Traditional Security (NTS). Nevertheless, New Zealand's advocacy of its own visions and priorities has been limited. New Zealand has shown greater enthusiasm in participating in the regional deliberations over creating an all-encompassing and inclusive East Asian Security architecture.

New Zealand's participation in the ASEAN cooperative processes received a major boost in July 2010 when it adopted 'the ASEAN-New Zealand Joint Declaration on Comprehensive Partnership for 2010-2015 and the Plan of Action to Implement the Joint Declaration. The basic objective of the Declaration is 'to broaden and deepen the ASEAN-New Zealand partnership in political and security, economic, and socio-cultural cooperation that is pro-active and responsive to future developments.'[27]

South Pacific Remains the focus Area

South Pacific continues to remain the core area of New Zealand's strategic worldview. The focus, however, is not limited to developing regional cooperation and greater aid distribution alone, rather also includes regional integration, and promotion of state-building, democracy, human rights, peace and stability in the region. Calling upon New Zealand's greater role in the conflict resolution in the Pacific region, New Zealand's the then Cabinet Minister, Phil Goff, declared in 2008, "New Zealand has a reputation as a country which thinks independently and makes a strong contribution in areas like peacekeeping, disarmament, inter-faith dialogue and development assistance. We can leverage off this to expand our contribution to conflict resolution."[28] The National government under the leadership of John Key has identified South Pacific as a priority area primarily for its regional and cultural affinity. The largest Pacific city is located in New Zealand, which also has a large segment of Pacific population and more than 50 per cent of New Zealand's aid goes to the region.[29] The country will host the 40th summit of Pacific Island Forum in 2012. The New Zealand Prime Minister, John Key has identified two important objectives of regional cooperation in the South Pacific. First, "we look to use our economic strength to help the Pacific nations, particularly around their fisheries, which is a big resource for them and one that is underdeveloped. Second, we can assist their over-dependence on oil by developing renewable energies."[30]

New Zealand has also raised the amount of its aid-budget from NZ$440 million in 2008-09 to NZ$600 million in 2011-12.[31] The bulk of this aid goes to the Pacific Island countries, especially the Polynesian countries. New Zealand has set up the Pacific Island Countries Participation Fund (PICPF) that regulates its Overseas Development Assistance to the region. The basic objective of the funding is to 'to increase attendance by Pacific islanders at regional and international conferences, where their attendance will strengthen ownership of regional and international development processes.'[32]

Australia and the USA are Principal Strategic Partners

Australia remains New Zealand's largest and closest neighbour, largest source of foreign investment, largest trading partner, and the largest source of foreign tourists. Moreover, Australia, on occasions, also offers the most reliable external perspective about changing realities of the global politics. While outlining New Zealand's foreign policy priorities, its Prime Minister, John Key has identified Australia as 'the largest and arguably the most important relationship.'[33] With the total trade of NZ$17 billion, Australia continues to enjoy the number one position of New Zealand's trading partner. An Australia-New Zealand FTA is operational since 1983, initiated by the National party-led government. New Zealand foreign policy makers continue to rely on the strategic worldview, predominantly constructed by the Australians. ANZAC/Canberra Pact is viewed as an important pillar of New Zealand's foreign policy.

The two countries have been working towards developing a coordinated approach towards the immediate neighbourhood of South Pacific, regional cooperative processes in the Asia-Pacific and issues of common defence and security. In a move towards developing a common defence forces, New Zealand and Australia declared in August 2009 their intent to develop a new ANZAC contingent that would draw on defence personnel from both the countries.[34]

There has been a consistent effort on the part of New Zealand to bring the New Zealand-US relations out of the chill emanating from New Zealand's suspension from the ANZUS.[35] Over the years, these efforts have borne positive results. The two countries have begun ignoring the irritating aspects of relationships, and discussing and cooperating on more positive aspects of relationships. For example, the United States and New Zealand are engaging with each other in the newly-floated exclusive cooperative initiative within APEC (Asia Pacific Economic Cooperation), known as Trans-Pacific Partnership (TPP). The initiative aims at developing greater economic integration with select economies within the region. TPP was launched in 2005 as a modest initiative between Singapore, Brunei, Chile and New Zealand. In the recently concluded APEC meeting in November 2011, the TPP has agreed to bring into its ambit five new members—Australia, Malaysia, Peru, the USA, and Vietnam. They have agreed on the broad terms for a Trans-Pacific Partnership (TPP) and set an ambitious target of eight months to finalise it.

The US Secretary of State, Hillary Clinton visited New Zealand in November 2010 and signed the 'Wellington Declaration' that affirms stronger politico, economic and security relations between the two countries.[36] The Declaration provides for an open-ended framework for the US-New Zealand strategic partnership. The Declaration calls for joint US-New Zealand efforts in resolving global and regional challenges with two-pronged focus on (a) 'practical cooperation in the Pacific region, and (b) enhanced political and subject-matter expert dialogue—including regular Foreign Ministers' meetings and political-military discussions.'[37]

Conclusion

New Zealand's foreign policy during the 21st century represents an interesting mix of normative posturing and practical necessities. While the fundamentals of the foreign policy remains more or less the same, new global and regional developments continue to reflect in its changing strategic priorities. Economics continues to remain one of the most important drivers and Australia remains the most important external factor of New Zealand's foreign policy. South Pacific continues to attract maximum attention from Wellington. Amidst all these elements of continuities, New Zealand exhibits three important changes—growing prominence of the eastern Asian hemisphere in New Zealand's foreign policy, China's growing influence within the country's policy makers and sustained effort to mend its fences with the world's most powerful player—the United States of America.

End Notes

1. David J. McCraw, "New Zealand's Foreign Policy under National and Labour Governments: Variations on the "Small State" Theme?," *Pacific Affairs,* vol. 67, no. 1 (Spring, 1994), p. 7
2. "Security Treaty between Australia, New Zealand, and the United States Of America," *Australia Treaty Series,* 1952, no. 2, http://www.austlii.edu.au/au/other/dfat/treaties/1952/2.html (accessed on 2 November 2011)
3. Jim Rolfe, "New Zealand's Security: Alliances and other Military Relationships," *CSS Working Paper*, no. 10/97, Victoria University of Wellington, 1997, http://www.victoria.ac.nz/css/docs/Working_Papers/WP10.pdf
4. David McCraw, "From Kirk to Muldoon: Change and Continuity in New Zealand's Foreign-Policy Priorities," *Pacific Affairs,* vol. 55, no. 4 (Winter, 1982-1983), p. 644
5. Ibid., pp. 641-642.
6. David Lange, "New Zealand's Security Policy," *Foreign Affairs*, vol. 63, no. 5 (Summer, 1985), p. 1019
7. Ibid., p. 1011
8. Dora Alves, "The Changing New Zealand Defense Posture," Asian Survey, vol. 29, no. 4 (Apr., 1989), p. 364
9. "New Zealand in Brief," *The Encyclopedia of New Zealand,* www.teara.govt.nz/en/nation-and-government/10 (accessed on 08 November 2011)
10. John Henderson, "New Zealand and the Oceania," in Roderic Alley (ed.) *New Zealand in World Affairs IV, 1990-2005,* (Wellington, Victoria University Press, 2007), p. 232
11. Ibid.
12. Ibid.
13. Kevin P. Clements, "New Zealand's Role in Promoting a Nuclear-free Pacific," *Journal of Peace Research*, vol. 25, no. 4, 1988, p. 395.
14. Thomas J. Christensen, "Fostering Stability or Creating a Monster?: The Rise of China and U.S. Policy toward East Asia," *International Security*, vol. 31, no. 1, (Summer 2006), pp. 81-126
15. C. Raja Mohan, "India in East Asia," *Australia-India Strategic Lecture Series 2007*, Lowy Institute for International Policy, Melbourne, 21 February, 2007. http://www.lowyinstitute.org/Publication.asp?pid=548 (Accessed on 09 October 2011)
16. Mohan Malik, "The East Asia Community and the Role of External Powers: Ensuring Asian Multilateralism is not Shanghaied," *Korean Journal of Defense Analysis*, vol. 19, no. 4, (Winter 2007), p. 34.
17. "New Zealand Must Find Shared Values with Asia's Rising Powers: Experts," *The Philippines News Agency,* Manila, 11 July 2011.
18. "Our Future with Asia," *New Zealand White Paper on Asia,* Ministry of Foreign Affairs and Trade, (Wellington 2007), p. 5
19. Helen Clark, "Towards a more pro-active role," *New Zealand International Review,* vol. 23, no. 4 (July-August) 1998, p. 6
20. New Zealand's Ministry of Foreign Affairs and Trade, "Foreign Relations with Asia," http://www.mfat.govt.nz/Foreign-Relations/Asia/index.php#documents
21. John Beaglehole had used the phrase in 1938 while explaining New Zealand's relations with Great Britain during the first half of 20th century.
22. "Our Future with Asia," p. 5.
23. Ibid.
24. K R Bolton, "New Zealand's Path to China Stems from Cold War Era," *Foreign Policy*

Journal, 07 July 2010, http://www.foreignpolicyjournal.com/2010/07/07/new-zealands-path-to-china-stems-from-cold-war-era/

25. John Key, "New Zealand in the World," *New Zealand International Review,* 2011, p. 1
26. K R Bolton, *op cit.*
27. "ASEAN-New Zealand Relations," *ASEAN Secretariat,* http://www.asean.org/5826.htm
28. Labour Sees Role for New Zealand in Conflict Resolution," *The New Zealand Herald,* 31 October 2008, http://www.nzherald.co.nz/politics/news/article.cfm?c_id=280&objectid=10540433
29. John Key, "New Zealand in the World," *op. cit.,* 2011, p. 1.
30. Ibid.,
31. Ibid.,
32. "Pacific Island Countries Participation Fund," New Zealand Aid Programme, Ministry of Foreign Affairs and Trade, http://www.aid.govt.nz/pic/ (accessed on 09 November 2011)
33. John Key, *op. cit.*
34. "Rudd, Key work on joint ANZAC force," *The New Zealand Herald,* 20 August 2009, http://www.nzherald.co.nz/nz/news/article.cfm?c_id=1&objectid=10592080
35. James M. McCormick, "Healing the American Rift with New Zealand," *Pacific Affairs,* vol. 68, no. 3 (Autumn, 1995), pp. 392-410.
36. "Background Note: New Zealand," *US Department of State,* 19 August 2011, http://www.state.gov/r/pa/ei/bgn/35852.htm
37. "The Wellington Declaration," *The New Zealand Herald,* 04 November 2010, http://www.nzherald.co.nz/nz/news/article.cfm?c_id=1&objectid=10685348

3

Does the FTA Really Matter? Trends in India-New Zealand Economic Relations

Nabeel A Mancheri

Free trade is a market model in which trade in goods and services between or within countries flow unhindered by government-imposed restrictions. Restrictions to trade include taxes and other legislation, such as tariff and non-tariff trade barriers. Governments often call managed international trade agreements "free trade", and although this is not really free trade, such treaties may result in freer trade. Preferential Trade Agreements (PTAs) are agreements among a set of countries involving preferential treatment of bilateral trade between any two parties to the agreement relative to their trade with the rest of the world. Preferences, however, need not extend to all trade between the two, and the coverage could depend on the type of PTAs. For this reason, at the urging of Bhagwati (1997), economists have increasingly adopted the term PTA to refer to Free Trade Areas.[1]

There has been much discussion in recent years concerning the FTAs and the presumed advantages and disadvantages of enacting trade agreement designed to permit freer trade among countries. India and New Zealand are no exception, pursuing negotiations for different trade agreements at different levels. India and New Zealand are expected to finalize a comprehensive economic partnership agreement (CEPA) by next year. Four rounds of negotiations have already been completed. The deal expects to facilitate trade and enable both parties to reach the target of NZ$ 5billion worth of bilateral trade by 2015 from its present NZ$1.26 billion. The deal also expected to help India to fix its trade imbalance of 533 million with New Zealand. India is already one of the fastest growing markets, with New Zealand exports having tripled over the last decade. A free trade agreement will lead to greater economic cooperation, and would increase trade and investment opportunities for both sides. According to India-New Zealand Business Council, bilateral trade would get boost with the FTA, as happened between New Zealand and China after they opened trade through a similar pact. At present, Sino-New Zealand trade amounts to $ 10 billion.

Under such circumstances, the present study explores the trade flows between India and New Zealand and provides an empirical analysis of emerging patterns of trade in order to assess the implications of CEPA. This paper focuses on the features of trade in commodities and analyses at a more comprehensive way using the trade data from UN Comtrade at SITC 1 digit level for India and New Zealand. The purpose is to establish empirically the basis for a closer economic relationship in the dimension of international trade, focusing primarily on merchandise trade and tariff levels. The paper explores an understanding of the current status of "revealed comparative advantage" indices (RCAs) among the goods traded between these countries in order to understand whether the countries have complementary or competitive export structures.

Economic and Trade Profile of India and New Zealand

The following table is a brief sketch of economic and trade characteristic of India and New Zealand. A comparative examination of the basic economic features is intended to give a better insight and a proper structure to the following analysis.

There is a growing perception that in the last 20 years the world has lived through an accelerated globalisation process. From an economic perspective, this can be explained by the rapid increase in the degree of integration through international trade and investment flows. While a closer look at the above figure reveals that these are the most dynamic economies of the world their development path has been different and they are highly integrated with other countries in the post-globalisation world. The population of New Zealand is approximately 4.4 million and is a predominantly urban country, with 72 percent of the population living in 16 main urban areas. New Zealand is a prosperous and developed market economy with an estimated gross domestic product (GDP) of USD 126.67 billion in 2009. Though it is 51st largest economy in the world, it still carries economic weight with very high levels of per capita GDP of USD 28993 compared to India's USD3296 in purchasing power parity. New Zealand is ranked 3rd in HDI ranks by UNDP in 2010. This means that the absolute *magnitude* of growth in the economy is very large even when growth *rates* are low, as has been the case in the recent past.

Being the most populous country after China, India is considered as the fourth largest economy in the world in ppp terms and 10th largest in nominal terms. India's economy grew faster than any other country along with China by a growth rate around 9 percent in 2009, even though there was a slowdown in 2008-09 because of global economic meltdown. New Zealand was one of the most affected countries during the crisis as its economy shrank by minus 0.43 in 2009. The trajectory of the deceleration in global measures of trade, industrial

Table 1: Economic and Trade Indicators of India and New Zealand (2005-09)

Indicators	India		New Zealand		World	
	2005	2009	2005	2009	2005	2009
GDP Current (US$ bn)	834.03	1377.26	110.97	126.67	45630.7	58259.7
GDP, PPP (current US $ bn)	2517.28	3808.44	104.60	12512	57093.6	72398.3
GDP Growth (Annual %)	9.3	9.1	3.15	-0.43	3.57	-1.92
Population (Mn)	1094.58	1155.34	4.133	4.315	6467.3.	6775.2
GDP Per Capita PPP (US$)	2299.7	3296.3	25304.8	28993.4	8828.02	10685.72
Merchandise Exports, US$ bn	99.61	162.61	21.73	24.93	10490.1	12492.1
Merchandise Imports, US$ bn	142.87	249.59	26.21	25.54	10766.3	12595.5
Service Exports (US$ bn)	52.52	90.59	8.69	7.87	2550.7	3436.1
Service imports (US$ bn)	47.28	80.99	8.23	7.93	2421.7	3220.1
Trade/GDP (%)	41.31	43.60	56.95	54.73	53.67	48.49

Trade to GDP ratio is estimated as an economy's total trade of goods and commercial services (exports + imports, balance of payments basis) divided by GDP, on the basis of data for the three latest years available.

Source: World Bank WDI, (2011).

production and financial flows has been extraordinarily rapid in the developed world including New Zealand compared to the emerging market like India and China during the crisis.

New Zealand is heavily dependent on international trade particularly in agricultural products, making New Zealand vulnerable to international commodity prices and global economic slowdowns. The country exported USD 21.73 billion worth of commodities in 2005 which rose to USD 24.93 billion in 2009 and imports were equal to USD 26.21 billion in 2005 which declined to 25.54 billion 2009. New Zealand has the highest trade as proportion to GDP, with around 56.9 percent in 2005 which declined to 54.7percent in 2009, only few other countries have such a high proportion of trade to GDP like Singapore. New Zealand is greatly dependent on international trade, mainly with Australia, the European Union, the United States and China. It has only small manufacturing and high-tech sectors, being strongly focused on tourism and primary industries like agriculture. New Zealand's economy has traditionally been based on a foundation of exports from its very efficient agricultural system. Leading agricultural exports include meat, dairy products, forest products, fruit and vegetables, fish, and wool.

Its principal export industries are agriculture, horticulture, fishing, forestry and mining, which make up about half of the country's exports. Tourism plays a significant role in New Zealand's economy, contributing $15.0 billion to New Zealand's total GDP and supporting 9.6 percent of the total workforce in 2010. Wool has historically been one of New Zealand's major exports. Even as late as the 1960s it made up over a third of all export revenues. But since then its price has steadily dropped relative to other commodities. In contrast, dairy farming increased, with the number of dairy cows doubling between 1990 and 2007, to become New Zealand's largest export earner. In the year to June 2009, dairy products accounted for 21 percent ($9.1 billion) of total merchandise exports. Other agricultural exports in 2009 were meat 13.2 percent, wool 6.3 percent, fruit 3.5 percent and fishing 3.3 percent. New Zealand's wine industry has followed a similar trend to dairy, the number of vineyards doubling over the same period.

Trade as proportion to GDP for India stood at 41 percent in 2005 which rose to 43 percent in 2009. The latest data reveals an upward trend as India's export and import have grown at a much faster rate. India has long had a much lower share of trade in GDP and the expansion is of a more recent origin, beginning after 2003. India's merchandise exports reached $162 billion in 2009, growing at an annual average of 19 per cent since 2000. During 2010-11 exports stood at $ 245.6 billion and recorded a growth of 37.8 per cent as against a decline of 2.5 per cent during 2009-10 reflecting higher growth in global income and trade. More than 26 per cent of its exports go to Asia, with Europe being the second-largest trading region (15 per cent). In 2009, India's imports reached $249 billion which rose to $ 350.5 billion in 2010-11, registered an increase of 21.9 per cent as the latest data from RBI shows. Furthermore, India has also had a consistent trade deficit, financed by private remittances and capital inflows. While exports have outperformed imports in terms of growth rates, this has been insufficient to significantly dent India's trade deficit, particularly in merchandise trade.

India's recent economic dynamism has led many to compare it with China and to expect a similar dramatic insertion in world markets. However, India's development path thus far has been considerably different from China's, and it is also very different from the paths followed in earlier decades either by New Zealand or Korea and the other Asian tigers. Remarkably, the recent growth in India's trade has been led by services rather than manufacturing and which is the only sector where India is quite close to the Chinese figures. Despite India's specialisation in skill and capital intensive activities, its manufacturing trade is highly concentrated in low-technology goods and the share of high-technology manufactured goods in its total exports has barely changed since the mid-1990s and remains under 10 percent, as compared to 30 percent for China.

India-New Zealand Trade Relations

According to the foreign ministry of New Zealand, its relations with South Asia are dominated by close relationship with India. 'India's growing political and economic influence, supported by its 'Look East' policy, has led to increasing interaction and India has become a priority relationship for New Zealand'. The New Zealand Government has developed the inter-agency, NZ Inc India Strategy that envisages India to be a core trade, economic and political partner for New Zealand by 2015. New Zealand and India had a lot in common sharing democratic traditions, being multi-cultural, shared aspirations and having similar regional interests. India and New Zealand were engaged in a relationship which is "special and important" in terms of its bilateral, regional and global context.

Despite their long record of friendly relations, their economic scale and their mutually complementary ties, New Zealand and India continue to be characterized by a relatively small bilateral flow of goods, services, human resources, capital, and information. As mentioned earlier, the two ways trade between India and New Zealand was around NZ$1.26 billion with a 533 million trade balance in favour of New Zealand in 2010. India exported 368 million NZ$ worth of commodities to New Zealand, while imported 901 million worth of commodities. India has become New Zealand's 7th largest export market in 2010. New Zealand's export to India constituted 2.1 percent of her total exports, while import was equal to 0.9 percent of total imports in 2010. India's export to New Zealand was about 0.14 percent of India's total export to the rest of the world while India imported about 0.17 percent of its total imports. India's export to New Zealand grew at rate of 35.28 percent in 2009-10 compare to the previous fiscal year while import growth rate was 17.81 percent in 2009-10 compare to the 26.14 percent of 2008-09. New Zealand's exports to India were valued at NZ$630 million in 2009, a 280 per cent increase on its 2001 exports to India and overall bilateral trade between India and New Zealand grew 180 per cent between 2001 and 2009 from NZ$353 million to NZ$985 million. Though the current level of trade between India and New Zealand is very meager compare to their other trading partners, the economic relation is unquestionably destined to evolve into one of the most important strategic partnerships.

India's Export and Import Relations with New Zealand

The type of goods imported and exported is analysed in the following sections in a more comprehensive way using the trade data from UN Comtrade. The commodities are classified on the basis of standard international trade classification (SITC rev-2) at one digit level. It is hoped that the two countries will strive for mutually beneficial and sustainable economic growth by cultivating stronger levels of bilateral economic exchange. The New Zealand business community has displayed increased interest in India in recent years. In fact, the number of New Zealand companies doing business in India have remarkably increased.

Table 2: India's Export and Import from New Zealand 2005 and 2010

(In US$ million)

Commodities, SITC rev-2	Exports		Imports	
	2005	2010	2005	2010
0. Food and Live Animals	12.241	24.435	5.123	123.956
1. Beverages and Tobacco	785,512	1.180	144,609	479,408
2. Crude materials, inedible, except fuel	4.762	7.463	72.997	178.643
3. Mineral Fuels, lubricants and related materials	134,198	1.886	61.312	7.129
4. Animal and vegetable oils, fats and waxes	201,351	737,443	897,424	1.863
5. Chemicals and related products, n.e.s	18.060	62.202	1.330	4.540
6. Manufactured goods, classified chiefly by materials	72.359	70.345	10.584	25.255
7. Machinery and transport equipment	13.644	27.714	9.293	64.437
8. Miscellaneous manufactured articles	31.491	57.676	2.889	7.395
9. Commodities and Transactions not classified elsewhere in the SITC	3.480	8.400	1.317	226.422
Total	157.160	262.038	165.886	640.117

Source: UN Comtrade database.

New Zealand has taken note of the fact that India's economy is registering an average growth rate of 8 per cent and its GDP is projected at $1.6 trillion for 2010-11. New Zealand, therefore, is seizing the opportunity to increase its bilateral trade with India as shown in the table 2. Its merchandise exports to India went up from $ 262 million in 2005 to $ 640 million in 2010. The table 2 represents India's bilateral trade of major commodities with New Zealand on the basis of merchandise trade disintegrated with SITC rev-2 for the year 2005 and 2010.[2] In 2006, according to India's Ministry of Commerce data, petroleum products have overtaken the jewellery and gemstones sector to become the top export product as India's top export product to the world. This is due to the rapid development of domestic refining capacity. In 1996, India imported both crude and refined petrol (around 2/3 crude and 1/3 refined) and exported only negligible quantities. In 2005 its imports of crude petrol have more than tripled (in quantity), its imports of refined petrol have considerably declined, and refined petrol has become a key export. It is yet unclear whether this export boom is sustainable or it was due to an incipient excess domestic refining capacity and lately the importance of engineering products including auto pars and components to India's export basket have increased. In general the latest trend on commodity-wise merchandise export reveals that engineering goods, oil, gems and jewellery contributed around 70 per cent of the overall growth in exports (RBI, 2011).

The major commodity items India exported to New Zealand constituted manufactured goods (SITC 6), classified chiefly by materials worth of $ 72.35 million in 2005, which marginally declined to $ 70.34 in 2010.[3] Miscellaneous manufactured articles (SITC 8) were the second largest item in value terms India exported to New Zealand that was equal to $ 31.49 million in 2005 which increased to $ 57.67 million in 2010.[4] Cemicals and related products (SITC 5), equal to $ 18.06 million in 2005 which considerably rose to $ 62.20 million in 2010 and machinery and transport equipment (SITC 7) equal to $ 13.64 in 2005 which rose to $ 27.71 million in 2010 were the third and fourth largest commodity items of India's exports. The other major export items included food and live animals (SITC 0) equal to $ 12.24 million, which valued 24.43 million in 2010, crude materials, inedible, except fuel (SITC 2) worth of $ 7.46 million in 2010 followed commodities and transactions not classified elsewhere in the SITC i.e., (SITC 9) worth equal to $ 8.40 million in 2010. India also exports items such as mineral fuels, lubricants and related materials (SITC 3) and beverages and tobacco products worth of less than three million in 2010.

The data at a more disaggregated level on the basis of harmonized system (HS) classification, reveals that the individual items that India exported the most to New Zealand were medicaments; in measured doses worth of NZ$ 46.554 million, jewellery articles for NZ$ 24.658 million, bed linen, table linen for NZ$ 14.270 million and diamonds worth of NZ$13.758 million in 2010 (Statistics New Zealand, 2011).

The major items India imported from New Zealand include commodities and transactions not classified elsewhere in the SITC i.e., (SITC 9) worth equal to $ 226.42 million in 2010, which was just over one million in 2005 with a spectacular growth rate of 287 percent over five years.[5] Crude materials, inedible, except fuel (SITC 2) which grown at rate of 147 percent from $ 73 million in 2005 to $178.64 million in 2010 was second largest followed by food and live animals (SITC 0) which grown from just $ 5.12 million in 2005 to 123.95 million in 2010 was the third largest commodity item India imported from New Zealand. The major items of import include machinery and transport equipment (SITC 7) worth of $ 64.43 million, manufactured goods, classified chiefly by materials (SITC 6) worth of $ 25.25 million and miscellaneous manufactured articles (SITC 8) equal to $ 7.39 million in 2010.[6] These items constituted more than 90 percent of India's import from New Zealand.

Again at a more disaggregated level data on the basis of harmonized system (HS) classification reveals the individual items that India imported from New

Zealand constituted, confidential items (HS 9809) worth of NZD 318.40 million in 2010 which grew 9.2 percent from previous year, logs worth of NZD146.286 million with a growth rate of 75.4 percent, butter equal to 87.477 million with a growth rate of 31.7, milk powder for 63.701 million followed by wool for 44.207 million with a 12.4 percent increase compare to previous year and machinery worth of 37.36 million in 2010 (Statistics New Zealand, 2011).

Trade Specialisation Index

Empirical research on international trade uses a wide array of statistical tools, ranging from simple descriptive indicators to complex econometric techniques, continuously experimented with and refined, thanks to the ever growing availability of detailed data. The methodological literature on these analytical instruments is rapidly expanding and spreading out in manifold directions of research.[7] The classic trade theory suggests that when a country starts trading with other countries, its economy tends to specialize in product or products where it has comparative advantages. However, specialization is not the only possibility that arises from an economic integration.

Krugman (1979, 1981) developed a model where trade is driven by economies of scale. The model essentially argues that trade occurs even between countries with identical tastes, technology and factor endowments because consumers have a taste for a variety of differentiated products. The model also shows that as countries become more similar, the trade between them becoming more intra industry in nature. Imbs and Wacziarg (2003) argue that specialization depends on level of development of the country; low income countries tend to diversify their production to reduce risk associated with idiosyncratic (sector-specific) shocks. One possible explanation is that smaller countries are driven toward intra-industry trade by economies of scale. That the companies in the smaller countries are unable to take advantage of the prevailing economies of scale on their own, and, hence engage in intra-industry trade with companies from other countries.

The study uses an indicator proposed by Lafay G (1992) to assess specialization between India and New Zealand. Trade Specialisation index (TSI) enables us to examine whether a country is either export oriented or import oriented in the international trade of a particular commodity. The normalized trade balance measures the country's performance in international trade for the given product. It can be shown easily that the indicator will rise if the export increases faster than the import, and vice versa. To measure specialization, the indicator is compared to the distribution of normalized trade balance of various products in the country. The index is calculated as,

$$\text{TS of a commodity k} = (X_{ik} - M_{ik}) / (X_{ik} + M_{ik}) \times 100$$

Where X_{ik} and M_{ik} denote exports and imports of commodity k of county i's international trade. If a country is relatively export-oriented in a commodity, the index should be close to 100. Similarly, the closer the index is to –100, the more import oriented a country is in the commodity and if the index value comes in between 20 and minus 20, then it is considered as intra industry trade. At a more comprehensive way, the specialization level of a particular product can be measured as the difference between its normalized trade balance, zik, and the overall trade balance of the country, Zi. The Lafay index for this product can be calculated by taking into account its contribution to total trade of the country W_{ik}

$$L_{ik} = z_{ik} - Z_i)\ W_{ix}$$

where

$$Z_i = \frac{\sum_k (X_{ik} - M_{ik})}{\sum_k (X_{ik} + M_{ik})} \qquad W_{ik} = \frac{(X_{ik} + M_{ik})}{\sum_k (X_{ik} + M_{ik})}$$

This specialization index of a product k in country i is thus related to the deviation of the product normalized trade balance and the country's overall trade balance and its share of trade. Trade Specialisation Index summarised for SITC one digit commodities, for India, and New Zealand are listed in Table 3.

Table 3: Trade Specialisation Index: For Total Trade and India's Bilateral Trade with New Zealand (2010)

Commodities, SITC 1 Digit level	Total trade of		India's bilateral trade with New Zealand
	India	New Zealand	
0. Food and live animals	42.00	68.68	-67.06
1. Beverages and tobacco	74.03	41.00	42.18
2. Crude materials, inedible, except fuel	-9.47	71.14	-91.98
3. Mineral fuels, lubricants and related materials	-55.00	-51.63	-58.00
4. Animal and vegetable oils, fats and waxes	-79.30	-19.00	-43.27
5. Chemicals and related products, n.e.s.	-18.11	-37.13	86.39
6. Manufactured goods, classified chiefly by materials	7.83	-14.78	47.16
7. Machinery and transport equipment	-36.64	-59.27	-39.85
8. Miscellaneous manufactured articles	52.14	-54.54	77.27
9. Commodities and transactions not classified elsewhere in the SITC	-56.52	73.92	-92.84

Source: Calculated using data from the UN COMTRADE database for the year 2010.

The chosen indicator must be able to measure specialization rather than trade performance. While specialization is closely associated with trade performance, one should be able to distinguish between the two. An indicator for international specialization should be able to reveal the country's comparative advantages (or disadvantages) in the different production sectors. The focus of comparison here is between the different products of the same country, rather than those of the rest of the world. Indicators to measure trade performance, on the other hand, focus more on comparing different countries in terms of their trade competitiveness.

The results from the above depicted table reveal that India and New Zealand have very different trade structures in terms of SITC one digit TSI's. In some commodities India has quite similar trade structure with New Zealand. However, if we consider it in total value terms it may become less relevant. On the basis of above calculated index, India is export-oriented in food and live animals (SITC 0), beverages and tobacco (SITC 1), miscellaneous manufactured articles (SITC 8) and moderately export oriented in manufactured goods, chiefly classified by articles (SITC 6). India has the highest index value of 74.03 for SITC 1 followed by 52.14 for SITC 8 and 42.00 for SITC 0. Index also exposes that India is highly import oriented in animal and vegetable oils, fats and waxes (SITC 4) with a value of -79.30, followed by commodities and transactions not classified elsewhere (SITC 9) with an index value of -56.52, mineral fuels, lubricants and related materials (SITC 3) having an index of minus 55.00, and machinery and transport equipment (SITC 7) with an index equal to -36.64. Also India is moderately import oriented in chemicals and related products, n.e.s. (SITC 5) with an index of -18.11 and crude materials, inedible, except fuel (SITC 2) with an index of -9.47. Table also reveals India having an intra- industry trade in the commodity items such as crude materials, inedible, except fuel, chemicals and related products, n.e.s. and manufactured goods, classified chiefly by materials in its global trade.

New Zealand is specialised in agriculture, diary products and material commodities and has different trade structure as compared to India. New Zealand is highly export-oriented in commodities and transactions not classified elsewhere (SITC 9) with an index value of 73.92, crude materials, inedible, except fuel (SITC 2) with an index of 71.14 followed by food and live animals (SITC 0) with value of 68.68 and beverages and tobacco (SITC 1) with an index of 41.00. New Zealand is import-oriented in rest of the commodities where the country is highly dependent on import of machinery and transport equipment (SITC 7) having an index of -59.27, miscellaneous manufactured articles (SITC 8) with an index of -54.54 followed by mineral fuels, lubricants and related materials (SITC 3) with an index of -51.63 and chemicals and related products, n.e.s. (SITC 5) with an index of -37.13. New Zealand also has a moderate intra-industry trade in manufactured goods classified chiefly by materials (SITC 6) and in animal and vegetable oils, fats and waxes (SITC 4) with an index value of -14.78 and -19.00 respectively.

In India's bilateral trade with New Zealand, each country has a complementary trade structure. In fact India's bilateral trade with New Zealand reveals a relatively strong complementarity and India is highly export oriented in chemicals and related products, n.e.s (SITC 5), miscellaneous manufactured articles (SITC 8), manufactured goods, classified chiefly by materials (SITC 6) and beverages and tobacco (SITC 1). India's bilateral trade with New Zealand shows a strong import orientation in commodities and transactions not classified elsewhere (SITC 9), crude materials, inedible, except fuel machinery (SITC 2) food and live animals (SITC 0) and moderate import specialization in mineral fuels, lubricants and related materials (SITC 3) and animal and vegetable oils, fats and waxes (SITC 4). Interestingly both countries don't have an intra- industry trade in any commodities at a considerable level.

The findings confirm some recent concerns about the quality of the pattern of specialization of Indian trade. The sectors in which India specializes still tend to be characterized by a relatively low technological content. Furthermore, the manufacturing sectors in which India does not specialize tend on average to possess a high technological content. This could limit the potential for trade to generate positive technological externalities. On the other hand, there is increasing evidence of specialization in a number of selected high-tech sectors. Furthermore, India's index of specialization has increased precisely in those sectors that have exhibited the fastest growth in world demand, and could therefore be regarded as the most dynamic sectors in world trade. These results confirm and match an earlier study by Alessandrini M et al, (2007) on the changing pattern of foreign trade specialization in Indian manufacturing.

The present analysis indicates better prospects for Indian merchandise trade with New Zealand where trade prospects remain very favourable. For goods, the two most favourable sectors are chemicals and related products, n.e.s., particularly medicinal and pharmaceutical products and miscellaneous manufactured articles, where India seems well placed to respond to the New Zealand market. However, sectors such as chemicals, metal–based manufacturing, engineering goods and motor vehicle are also well-positioned to expand. There are, therefore, strong grounds for expecting that the relationship will remain of huge importance for the foreseeable future. In some areas, there are clearly some items in which New Zealand has a comparative advantage and huge potential for increasing its share in Indian markets in products such as crude materials, inedible, except fuel particularly wool items and food and live animals especially diary and butter products. Potential areas of cooperation include capital markets, energy, biotechnology, pharmaceuticals, information technology (IT), healthcare, nursing, science, research and development.

Barriers to Trade and Prospects of Bilateral FTA between India, and New Zealand

Liberalisation with an emphasis on FTAs has been the key ingredient of recent economic policies of India and New Zealand, based upon the notion that removing trade restrictions such as tariff and non tariff measures have a beneficial impact on the domestic economy. This section analyses tariff levels of India and New Zealand and critically examine the average MFN applied tariff on major product categories. Exploration of the theoretical basis for the link between trade liberalization and trade growth demonstrate a well established positive relationship, with openness leading to higher trade. Empirical studies for different countries have thrown up mixed results. While some studies point to a strong association between trade openness and trade performance. On this given context the section analyses the trade barriers particularly the tariff levels imposed by India and New Zealand on import of various commodities. Even though the section gives some details of tariff levels imposed on commodities traded between them, it is beyond the scope of the study to link the tariff levels of these countries with their respective trade.

Trade agreements typically involve a lengthy staging of tariff reductions and because trade patterns take time to reflect changes in trade barriers in any event, there will inevitably be a lag between the conclusion of negotiations and ratifications of the agreement on the one hand, and final changes in trading patterns reflecting the fully implemented regional agreement on the other (Bagwell and Staiger, 1993). Dismantling of the high trade barriers are considered to be the fundamental aspects of opening up of an economy. India and New Zealand have been trying to reduce their trade barriers especially import duties in response to the commitment offered in various FTAs as well as on the basis of WTO agreements.

Trade barriers play a central role in the models of international specialization and trade. Much of the theory concerns the effects of barriers on trade and trade costs figure prominently in recent work that extends our understanding of the nature of specialization. Goto (2001) found that by liberalizing the economy, the welfare of Asian developing economies would improve substantially within an Asian trading block. A gravity model of bilateral trade involving 11 trading blocs, mostly in the Asia Pacific region, found that the impacts of preferential trade agreements vary remarkably across the region (Clarete et al. 2002).

Import duties are among India's main trade instruments as well as an important source of tax revenues, accounting for around 17.5 per cent of Central Government tax revenue. Applied MFN tariffs, especially for non agricultural products, have continued to fall steadily, with the overall average currently at 15.8 per cent. At 12.1 per cent (14.1 per cent including advalorem equivalents), the average for non agricultural products is considerably lower than the average

Table 4: Tariff Rate of India and New Zealand on MFN Applied Basis by Product Groups 2008-09

Product groups	MFN applied duties Average (India)	MFN applied duties Average (New Zealand)
Animal products	33.1	1.5
Dairy products	33.7	1.4
Fruit, vegetables, plants	30.4	1.2
Coffee, tea	56.3	2.3
Cereals & preparations	32.2	2.9
Oilseeds, fats & oils	18.2	0.6
Sugars and confectionery	34.4	1.5
Beverages & tobacco	70.8	3.0
Cotton	12.0	0.0
Other agricultural products	21.7	0.7
Fish & fish products	29.8	0.4
Minerals & metals	7.5	1.8
Petroleum	3.8	0.2
Chemicals	7.9	0.8
Wood, paper, etc.	9.1	1.3
Textiles	13.6	1.9
Clothing	16.1	9.6
Leather, footwear, etc.	10.2	3.1
Non-electrical machinery	7.3	3.0
Electrical machinery	7.2	2.6
Transport equipment	20.7	3.1
Manufactures, n.e.s.	8.9	1.7

Source: WTO, 2011, World Tariff Profile, 2010.

for agricultural products, which is 40.8 per cent. The growing gap between agricultural and non agricultural tariffs has also raised dispersion in the tariff and the escalation pattern shows increasing de escalation between unprocessed and semi processed and in some cases between semi processed and final products (WTO, 2007).

Average final bound duties are higher for agricultural products such as, oil seeds, fats and oils, coffee, tea, cereals & preparations and cotton ranging for 168 per cent to 100 per cent. These high rates of average bound duties reflect in MFN applied duties where beverages and tobacco have the maximum rate equal to 70.8 percent followed by coffee and tea have average applied rate equal to 56.3 per cent and oil seeds, fats and oils equal to 18.8. The applied tariff for cotton is relatively less among agricultural products which have a rate of 12 per cent (Table 4). As mentioned above the tariff rates, both bound and applied are lower for the manufactured items where average bound duties for clothing, textiles, chemicals, minerals and metals and leather, footwear etc have the highest rates, while other manufactured items such as electrical machinery and non electrical machinery have comparatively lower bound tariffs. In case MFN applied duties, the average tariff for chemicals, leather, footwear, wood and paper etc, minerals and metals, petroleum electrical and non electrical machinery are varied between 5 per cent and 10 per cent. However the applied rates for textiles, clothing, and transport equipment have the rate of 13.6, 16.1 and 20.7 per cent respectively.

New Zealand has much lower tariff rate than India, particularly, the simple average MFN applied duty for New Zealand is 2.1 percent where as India has a rate of 31.8 percent in 2009. In disaggregate level, New Zealand imposes 1.4 per cent duty for agricultural products and 2.3 per cent for non-agricultural products. This is substantially higher than India's agricultural duty of 32 per cent. As revealed in the above section, New Zealand's export to India is skewed towards agricultural and other raw material commodities where India has the highest tariff rates. So it is expected that an FTA with substantial reduction in agricultural tariff, especially from Indian side will benefit both countries in uneven terms. The majority of items India exports to New Zealand only face a duty about 3 percent on an average except cloths which has the highest duty of 9.6 percent on MFN basis in 2009.

So for India, the FTA with New Zealand doesn't make any sense until the country is able to increase its industrial competitiveness, particularly in New Zealand market which is presently dominated by China, U.S and some ASEAN countries. Moreover the deal will have a bigger impact when both countries finalise a comprehensive agreement involving goods, services, investments, movement of natural persons and technology. A broader agreement will definitely help to diversify their present trade structure. Two-thirds of India's goods exports in 2009 were manufactured goods, while agricultural goods accounted for only a tenth of the total. In contrast, about three-fourths of New Zealand's total exports were agricultural products while only one-fourth was manufactured goods. While New Zealand's exports are dominated by coal, unprocessed logs, wool and sheepskin leather, India's export basket comprises of medicines, diamonds, jewellery and bed linen. This needs to be diversified. Import of agricultural goods is a sensitive issue in India and therefore tariff reduction could be a touchy issue. New Zealand could stress its technological expertise in these industries and look for promoting partnerships and technological collaborations between the two countries.

Conclusion

New Zealand's gains from entering into a FTA with India, an economy whose GDP is projected at $ 1.6 trillion for 2010-11, growing at an average real rate of around 8 per cent, are well understood. And the opportunity to expand the relatively small bilateral trade between the two countries is a welcome development. As well as the strong case for export diversification and expansion which is currently dominated by coal, unprocessed logs, wool and sheep skin leather—all vital resources in New Zealand's exports and India's exports basket is narrowly based on diamonds, jewellery and bed linen, would indeed make the FTA a win-win deal.

Though the analysis of trade in services is beyond the scope of present study, the trade data reveals that there are complementarities between the two countries in services trade. The available data shows that India's trade in services is mainly in Information and Communication Technology (ICT)-enabled and professional services (76 per cent in 2009), while New Zealand's services exports are concentrated in the areas of tourism, education and recreation. Partnership of Indian companies with New Zealand organisations could be facilitated by a broader FTA, involving liberalisation of ICT-enabled services. In a similar way, partnership by New Zealand organisations with India's education industry could provide significant market potential for them and help address major constraints in India's progress toward a knowledge-based economy. According to a study by Asher M and Sen R in 2011, 'India is already among the fastest growing education markets for New Zealand, with nearly 9,000 Indian students contributing around NZ$100 million (US$72 million) to its economy'.

There are huge potential for tourism and related services. Indian visitors to New Zealand in 2009 were 26,000, constituting the ninth-largest group. Measures such as visa on arrival, multiple entry longer-term business visas, and greater cultural exchanges, negotiated as part of the FTA, could assist in facilitating deeper engagement. New Zealand also have a considerable population of Indian diaspora of over 100,000, they could play an important role in helping to expand bilateral investment flows between the two countries. It is a welcome step that both countries discussing a 'working holiday scheme' for young Indians, preferably graduates, that will allow Indians to stay in New Zealand for a short period of about six months and work to pay for their holiday. Two countries can cooperate in several segments including agriculture, pharmaceuticals, dairy products, research and development, tourism and films. India, which has an investment potential of $ 200 billion in the agro-processing and cold chain sectors, can utilise the expertise of New Zealand in the area.

There are many opportunities and have a huge potential for increasing the trade and investment. The proposed CEPA is a great step towards this realization. It is hoped that the two countries will strive for mutually beneficial and sustainable economic growth by cultivating stronger levels of bilateral economic exchange. The New Zealand's business community has displayed increased interest in India in recent years, which is evident in a survey report by the Ministry of Foreign Affairs and Trade, New Zealand. The Comprehensive Economic Partnership Agreement (EPA/CEPA) reflect a shared interest on the part of both countries to seek an even-stronger bilateral relationship. The conclusion of EPA/CEPA effectively removes or reduces tariff as well as non-tariff barriers and will increase both exports and imports.

End Notes

1. The term Preferential Trade Agreement is used in this paper to cover different types of integration agreements ranging from Free Trade Agreements to Economic and Monetary Unions as well as present day Comprehensive Economic Partnership Agreements. They may not be 'Regional' in nature like EU, ASEAN or NAAFTA and in case of India and New Zealand; it is completely a process of bilateral trade agreements between them. So the study basically focuses on the bilateral agreements between India- New Zealand implying any of the above mentioned terms.
2. Please refer UN Comtrade website for more information on commodity classification at SITC rev-2 Website, http://comtrade.un.org/db/mr/rfCommoditiesList.aspx
3. SITC 6, constitutes the products such as such as leather, leather manufactures, n.e.s., and dressed fur skins, rubber manufactures, n.e.s.; cork and wood manufactures (excluding furniture), paper, paperboard and articles of paper pulp, of paper or of paperboard, textile yarn, fabrics, made-up articles, n.e.s., and related products, non-metallic mineral manufactures, n.e.s. iron and steel, non-ferrous metals, manufactures of metals, n.e.s.
4. SITC 8, includes prefabricated buildings; sanitary, plumbing, heating and lighting fixtures and fittings, n.e.s. furniture, and parts thereof; bedding, mattresses, mattress supports, cushions and similar stuffed furnishings, travel goods, handbags and similar containers, articles of apparel and clothing accessories, footwear, professional, scientific and controlling instruments and apparatus, n.e.s. and photographic apparatus, equipment and supplies and optical goods, n.e.s.; watches and clocks.
5. SITC 9 basically consists of postal packages not classified according to kind special transactions and commodities not classified according to kind, coin (other than gold coin), not being legal tender and gold, non-monetary (excluding gold ores and concentrates).
6. SITC 7, comprises power-generating machinery and equipment, machinery specialized for particular industries, metalworking machinery, general industrial machinery and equipment, and machine parts, n.e.s, office machines and automatic data-processing machines, telecommunications, sound-recording and reproducing apparatus and equipment electrical machinery, apparatus and appliances, n.e.s., and electrical parts thereof (including non-electrical counterparts, n.e.s., of electrical household-type equipment), road vehicles (including air-cushion vehicles) and other transport equipment which makes almost half of total imports.
7. Some useful surveys can be found in Martincus and Sanguinetti (2005, Leamer and Stern (1970), Baldwin (1988), Feenstra (1988), Hooper and Richardson (1991), Dagenais and Muet (1992) and, Greenaway and Winters (1994).

References

Alessandrini M, Bassam Fattouh, and Pasquale, S. (2007), "The Changing Pattern of Foreign Trade Specialization in Indian Manufacturing", *Oxford Review of Economic Policy*, 23 (2): 270–91.

Asher M. and Sen Rahul (201), "India-New Zealand PTA: Broaden it for balanced gains" East Asia Forum, April 1st, 2011 .

Bagwell K. and Staiger R.W. (1998), "Will Preferential Agreements Undermine the Multilateral Trading System?" *The Economic Journal,* 108 (July): 1162-82.

Baldwin, R. E (1988), (eds.) *Trade Policy Issues and Empirical Analysis,* Chicago, IL: University of Chicago Press.

Clarete, R., Edmonds, C. and Wallack, J.S. (2002), "Asian Regionalism and its Effects on Trade in the 1980s and 1990s", *Economics and Research Department Working Paper 30,* ADB, Manila.

Feenstra, R.C. (1988), *Empirical Methods for International Trade,* Cambridge, MA: MIT Press.

Goto, J. (2001), "FTAs and Their Economic Implications with Reference to Asia", Paper presented to Capacity Building Workshop on Trade Policy Issues organized by Asian Development Bank Institute and Ministry of Foreign Affairs, Singapore, 16–24 April.

Greenaway, D.; Winters, L.A. (eds.) (1994), *Surveys in International Trade,* Oxford, United Kingdom: Blackwell.

Hooper, P.; Richardson, J.D. (eds.) (1991), *International Economic Transactions: Issues in Measurement and Empirical Research,* Chicago, IL: University of Chicago Press.

Imbs, J. and R. Wacziarg (2003), "Stages of Diversification", *The American Economic Review,* 93 (1): 63-86.

Krugman, P. (1981), "Intra-industry Specialization and the Gains from Trade", *Journal of Political Economy,* 89(5): 959-73.

Krugman, P. (1979), "Increasing Returns, Monopolistic Competition, and International Trade", *Journal of International Economics,* (9) (November): 469-79.

Lafay, G (1992), "The Measurement of Revealed Comparative Advantages", in M.G. Dagenais and P.A. Muet (eds.), *International Trade Modelling,* Chapman & Hill, London.

Leamer, E.E.; Stern R.M. (1970), *Quantitative International Economics,* Chicago, IL: Aldine.

Martincus, C.V. and P. Sanguinetti (2005), "South-South Integration Agreements and the Dynamics of Regional Specialization: Do Preferential Tariffs Matter?" http://ww.utdt.edu/~sanguine/South South_RIAs_andthe_Dynamics_Regional_Specialization3.pdf

Ministry of Foreign Affairs and Trade (2009), "FTA Exporter Survey Report", December 2009.

http://www.mfat.govt.nz/downloads/trade/fta-exporter-survey-report-(public).pdf

Reserve Bank of India (2011), "India's Foreign Trade: 2010-11 (April-March)", Reserve Bank of India Bulletin, June, p. 893. http://rbidocs.rbi.org.in/rdocs/Bulletin/PDFs/BLS100611FL.pdf, Accessed on June 12, 2011.

Statistics New Zealand (2011), Global New Zealand: Year ended December 2010. Wellington: Statistics New Zealand, p. 38.

WTO (2007), "Trade Policy Review of India" Geneva.

WTO (2010), "World Tariffs profiles 2010" Accessed April 12 2011. http://www.wto.org/english/tratop_e/tariffs_e/tariffs_e.htm

4

India's Engagement with New Zealand: What Ails the Relationship?

Dr. Rupakjyoti Borah

The relations between India and New Zealand have a long and chequered history. When New Zealander Edmund Hillary and Sherpa Tenzing Norgay scaled Mount Everest on May 23, 1959, they conquered one of the most formidable challenges known to mankind. Soldiers from the two countries fought together in the two World Wars and many other wars. Besides, the two countries share a common language, a strong democratic setup, similar judicial system, membership of the Commonwealth and a love for cricket.

India's foreign relations after independence were based on anti-colonialism and non-alignment as India had experienced the effects of colonialism with all its manifestations of exploitation and brutality. It decided to keep out of alliances and military pacts and refused to be drawn into the power politics between the USA and its allies and the erstwhile USSR and its allies. The main objectives of Indian foreign policy were listed by India's first Prime Minister, Jawaharlal Nehru as

> ... the pursuit of peace, not through alignment with any power or group of powers, but through an independent approach to each controversial and disputed issue; the liberation of subject peoples , the maintenance of freedom, both national and individual; thc climination of racial discrimination; and the elimination of want, disease and ignorance which affect the greater part of the world's population.[1]

Nehru had described colonialism as 'obsolete in the modern world'.[2] He had taken the initiative to convene the Asian Relations Conference at New Delhi in 1947 where he remarked, 'we do not intend to be the playthings of others'.[3]

As opposed to this, New Zealand's foreign policy followed a different trajectory. In September 1954, Britain, Australia, New Zealand, France, Thailand, Pakistan and the Philippines formed the South East Asia Treaty Organisation (SEATO), an alliance of nations for defence and economic co-operation in South East Asia and the South Pacific. Like the North Atlantic Treaty Organization (NATO), SEATO was intended to prevent the spread of Communism; but unlike NATO, the SEATO agreement did not obligate any member to assist another against a military threat. Nehru showed his unease within a month of its establishment. He went on record in the Lok Sabha (The Lower House of the Indian Parliament)

> It seems to me this particular Manila Treaty is looking dangerously in his direction of spheres of influence to be exercised by powerful countries. It is the big and powerful countries that will decide and not the two or three weak and small Asian countries that may be allied to them … this Manila Treaty is not only a wrong approach but a dangerous one from the point of view of any Asian country.[4]

The Colombo plan, many Indian students studied in New Zealand. It also helped to make New Zealanders aware of Asian cultures. However, after this, the relations between the two countries remained lukewarm to say the least. The then Indian Prime Minister Indira Gandhi visited New Zealand in 1968 while Rajiv Gandhi visited New Zealand in 1986 respectively.

The end of the Cold War forced India, like most other countries, to reconsider its position in the world. The collapse of the Soviet Union eliminated India's security umbrella and economic and defence cushion. Clearly, the end of the Cold War brought an end both to alliance diplomacy and to non-alignment, at least in the form in which they were originally conceived. In India's case, the collapse of the Soviet Union in 1991 meant the loss of a political, military and economic counterweight to China. This was accompanied by other developments like the end of the bipolar world order, the ascendancy of geo-economics over geopolitics, India's economic crisis of mid-1991, the loss of Soviet-bloc markets and the emergence of economic 'tigers' in the East. After decades of looking towards the West, India turned its attention eastwards and announced its desire to 'dance with the tigers in the east'.[5]

Though contacts between India and New Zealand have been few and far between in the period after India's independence, it changed with the enunciation of India's "Look East Policy", whereby India began to pay renewed attention to the countries of East Asia and Southeast Asia. New Zealand has close ties with many countries in the region. This was also the same time when India liberalised its economy, which brought in private enterprise and foreign direct investment in many sectors.

The first phase of India's "Look-East policy" focused on renewing contact with a region from which India had drifted due to the logic of the Cold War and its own insular economic policies. India's *de facto* alliance with the Soviet Union had left its ties with the other major Asian powers stunted. It had also hampered its relations with regional groupings such as the Association of South East Asian Nations (ASEAN). India had been kept apart from the economic dynamism of East Asia and by the turn of the 1990's, had been marginalized in Asia.[6] In late 1995, India was granted full dialogue partner status with ASEAN and was admitted as a member of the ASEAN Regional Forum in July 1996.

It is only since 1991 that India's growth potential was widely represented as promising. According to the *Economist*, 'till 1991 India was one of the most mismanaged and inward looking economics of the world—an economy whose immense potential has been squandered for decades'.[7] In 2002, India participated in its first summit meeting with ASEAN. At the second summit meeting in 2003, India signed three significant agreements with ASEAN: the Framework Agreement on Comprehensive Economic Cooperation, involving pledges to remove trade barriers progressively; a joint Declaration on Cooperation for Combating International Terrorism; and ASEAN's Treaty of Amity and Cooperation.

Multilateral Links

India and New Zealand share platforms on many multilateral fora like the United Nations, Commonwealth, World Trade Organisation (WTO). Besides, they are also partners in the East Asia Summit (EAS) and ASEAN Regional Forum (ARF). In 2003, India became a dialogue partner of the Pacific Islands Forum. The common membership of international forums gives India and New Zealand the chance to discuss key issues like climate change and the Global Research Alliance on Agricultural Greenhouse Gases, international trade, United Nations reform, human rights, counter-terrorism and other transnational issues.[8]

Improving Indo-US Ties

India's ties with the United States have seen a tremendous improvement in the post-Cold-War era, especially after the signing of the Indo-US civil nuclear deal. Meanwhile, New Zealand's ties with the United States have also seen a marked progress, more so after the signing of the Wellington Declaration last year. The Wellington Declaration has provided for a new strategic partnership between the United States and New Zealand and was signed when the American Secretary of State Hillary Clinton visited New Zealand in November 2010.[9]

Divergences

However, there are a couple of areas where India and New Zealand have divergent viewpoints as well. New Zealand strongly condemned India's nuclear tests in May 1998. This resulted in a temporary downturn in the relations, but the relations soon bounced back.

There was no clear-cut support from New Zealand during the process of granting a NSG (Nuclear Suppliers Group)-waiver to India. Differences also prevail over domestic support for agriculture, market access for agriculture and non-agriculture market access. New Zealand has raised concerns over high tariffs on items of interest to it like processed products and India's sanitary and phytosanitary (quarantine) barriers to agricultural and forestry exports.

Common Interests

However, there are a host of areas where India and New Zealand share common concerns. China's aggressive posturing in Asia is an area of concern for both India and New Zealand. Islamic extremism in countries of Southeast Asia is another area of worry since both India and New Zealand share an obvious interest in the stability of this region.[10] The two countries also share an interest in combating threats like piracy, human trafficking, narcotics trafficking and environmental pollution.

India's population is expanding and hence it will need to increase its food output. It is here that India could make use of New Zealand's expertise in areas like agri-business/agri-technology.[11] Another area of cooperation is the Indian Ocean region. The Indian Navy is the predominant power in the region between the Straits of Hormuz and the Straits of Malacca, home to some of the world's most important and vulnerable sea lanes of communication. The Indian Navy in the post 9/11 period has participated in escort and joint patrolling activities in this region. India's location places it adjacent to some of the most vital sea-lanes of the world stretching from the Suez Canal and the Persian Gulf to the Straits of Malacca through which around 55,000 ships and much of the oil from the Gulf region transit each year.[12]

Even though New Zealand does not face any direct threat from any country, it still faces threats from trans-national security threats like terrorism, proliferation of weapons of mass destruction and trans-national organised crime. Cooperation between India and New Zealand can help them protect sea lanes, control piracy, drug trafficking and illegal human smuggling. New Zealand also has close ties with Fiji, given their geographical proximity. This is yet another reason why New Zealand is important for India given the fact that a significant chunk of Fiji's population is of Indian descent.

High-Level Visits

From the Indian side, the then Prime Minister of India Indira Gandhi visited New Zealand in 1968 while Rajiv Gandhi visited New Zealand in 1986 respectively. New Zealand's Prime Minister Helen Clark paid an official visit to India from October 16-20, 2004. New Zealand's Prime Minister, H.E. John Key accompanied by his wife Bronagh Key paid a state visit to India from June 26-

30, 2011. In this visit, he was accompanied by Trade Minister Tim Groser and Member of Parliament, Kanwaljit Singh Bakshi, senior officials and a business and media delegation.

Earlier, the then Governor General of New Zealand Sir Anand Satyanand accompanied by Lady Susan Satyanand visited New Delhi in October 2010 to represent the New Zealand Government at the Delhi Commonwealth Games. The Governor General accompanied by Lady Susan Satyanand again visited New Delhi in January 2011 for the Pravasi Bharatiya Convention where he was Chief Guest and was also honoured with the Pravasi Bharatiya Samman award.

Defence and Strategic Ties

Troops from the two countries fought together in the two World Wars. Besides, New Zealand defence officers served with the United Nations Military Observer Group in India and Pakistan in 1952 while the then New Zealand Chief of Navy visited India to coincide with the ship visit by *HMNZS Te Mana* to Mumbai and Kochi in 2006.

India and New Zealand also have a long history of contributing men and material to UN peacekeeping operations in countries and regions ranging from Solomon Islands, Timor Leste, Afghanistan, Korea, the Middle East, Sudan, Bosnia-Herzegovina and Kosovo. Troops from the two countries have worked together in the UN missions in East Timor, Sudan, Lebanon and Kosovo.

The two countries are members of the ASEAN Regional Forum (ARF) and the ASEAN Plus Defence Ministerial Meeting (ADMM+). In May 2011, a delegation from the Indian National Defence College visited New Zealand, while the former Chief of the New Zealand Defence Force (CDF), Lieutenant General Mateparae, visited India in November 2009 (which was incidentally the first visit of its kind). From the Indian side too, there have been a series of visits to New Zealand. Chief of the Indian Navy, Admiral Nirmal Verma, visited New Zealand in November 2010. There has been a flurry of ship visits too. While HMNZS Te Mana visited Mumbai in August 2008, HMNZS Te Mana and Endeavour visited Port Blair in May 2007. HMNZS Te Mana visited Kochi and Mumbai ports in June 2006. From the Indian side, INS Tabar visited Auckland in 2006.[13]

Educational Ties

An increasing number of Indian students are making their way to New Zealand. At present, India is the fourth largest source of foreign students in New Zealand (after China, South Korea, and Japan). Last year, there were 9065 international fee-paying students from India in New Zealand, contributing about NZ$100 million to the local economy.

The New Zealand-India Education Cooperation Arrangement was first signed in 2005, which is a broad framework for bilateral cooperation on

Table 1: Enrolments of International Fee-paying Students by Education Sector and by main Source Countries, 2009

Source country	Education provider group (%)					Total (%)
	School	ITP(2)	University	PTE(3)	Subsidiary(4)	
China	10.4	12.8	29.3	44.4	3.0	100.0
South Korea	35.3	4.8	8.0	47.7	4.2	100.0
Japan	16.7	7.3	8.7	59.6	7.6	100.0
India	0.8	32.4	13.0	53.7	0.1	100.0
Saudi Arabia	5.3	4.5	22.3	58.3	9.6	100.0
All others	17.3	10.2	25.2	44.0	3.3	100.0
Total row (%)	16.5	11.3	20.2	48.1	3.9	100.0

Note: Due to rounding, percentages may not sum to 100.
(1) Ordered by descending number of enrolments in 2009.
(2) ITP = institute of technology and polytechnic.
(3) PTE = private training establishment, including English language provider.
(4) The subsidiary group comprises mainly the English language training affiliates of some universities and high schools.
Source: Ministry of Education.(http://dol.govt.nz/publications/research/life-after-study/life-after-study_06.asp accessed September 20, 2011)

education. The Arrangement led to an Education Joint Working Group of senior officials, which has met once in New Zealand in 2008 and once in India in 2010.[14]

Tourism and Bollywood

The number of Indian tourists visiting New Zealand has registered a constant increase. In terms of visitor arrivals, India is the 10th largest market for New Zealand (around 30,000 annually). New Zealand is a popular destination among honeymooners from India while most Indians prefer to visit New Zealand during April to June.[15]

The Bollywood has played a major role in promoting interest in New Zealand. Hit Hindi movies like *Kaho Na Pyaar Hai* have popularised New Zealand and its locales. Last year, another popular Bollywood movie *I Hate Luv Stories,* was shot in New Zealand. However, the lack of direct air connectivity between India and New Zealand is an impediment to increasing tourist arrivals from India in New Zealand, though in 2006, a bilateral air services agreement was signed which provides for direct aircraft services between Mumbai and Auckland.

The Recent Relationship

India is rising in New Zealand's scheme of things given India's fast-growing economy, which has managed to avoid the pitfalls of the global economic downturn. The increasing importance being given to India can be seen from the fact that the New Zealand Government has developed the inter-agency NZ Inc India Strategy that envisages India being a core trade, economic and political partner for New Zealand by 2015.[16] In May 2010, New Zealand opened a Consulate-General in Mumbai.

Trade and Economic Relations

Trade and economic relations between India and New Zealand have also picked up. It was in October 1986 during the then Prime Minister Rajiv Gandhi's visit that India and New Zealand agreed to have a Joint Trade Committee which was set up under the New Zealand/India Trade Agreement. Meanwhile, negotiations have started on a bilateral free trade agreement (FTA) in April 2010 after a joint feasibility study had come to the conclusion that the two economies are largely complementary, and an FTA would be mutually beneficial. One area of contention in the proposed FTA with New Zealand is the import of agricultural goods from New Zealand to India.[17]

The bilateral trade between India and New Zealand has reached nearly $1.268 billion last year. While India's main imports from New Zealand include coking coal, wool, logs, sheep skin leather, raw hides and skins, it exports diamond, jewellery articles, bed linen, table linen, garments and footwear to New Zealand.[18]

During the visit of the Commerce Minister Anand Sharma to New Zealand in May 2011, several areas of co-operation were looked at—these include post-harvest technologies/logistic management for the agriculture sector, renewable energy sector, (wind and geo-thermal energy) tourism, films (including animation films), pharmaceuticals, education, IT enabled services; and financial services.[19]

Indian companies like Mahindra, Satyam, HCL Technologies, CMC, WIPRO, Infosys, TCS, Tata Steel, New India Assurance Co. Ltd and Bank of Baroda and Bank of India are present in New Zealand while companies like Saurashtra World Holdings Pvt Ltd and Gujarat NRE Coke Ltd have invested US$ 20 million each in Pike River coal Ltd.[20]

India is one of the fastest growing economies of the world. The economic potential of China and India is aptly illustrated by a Carnegie Endowment report "The G-20 in 2050" which says "by 2050, the United States and Europe will be joined in economic size by emerging markets in Asia and Latin America. China will become the world's largest economy in 2032, and grow to be 20 per cent larger than the United States by 2050."[21]

People-to-People Links

The Indian community in New Zealand is over 100,000 strong as per the 2006 census. They constitute around 2.5 per cent of the population and are a very successful community. The previous Governor General of New Zealand was of India origin. The Indian community in New Zealand has excelled in public life, business, medicine, education, arts and other walks of life.

Indian festivals like Diwali have become famous in New Zealand, thanks to the patronage it has received from both the official and non-official organisations in New Zealand. In May 2003, the famous mountaineer Sir Edmund Hillary was honoured by the Indian government and two roads in front of the New Zealand High Commission in New Delhi were named after Sir Edmund Hillary and Tenzing Norgay. Later on in 2008, Sir Edmund was posthumously awarded the "Padma Vibhushan", one of India's highest civilian honours.

Sports are another arena where India and New Zealand have forged close bonds. Many New Zealand cricketers are part of the Indian Premier League (IPL) while the Indian and the New Zealand cricket teams have played lot of matches against each other at various venues across the world. New Zealander John Wright was formerly a coach of the Indian cricket team.[22]

The Indian Council for Cultural Relations (ICCR) has been sending cultural troupes of musicians, dancers and other artists to New Zealand. In October 2007, a life size statute of Mahatma Gandhi was unveiled in Wellington by the Governor General and the Mayor underlining the commitment of the people of India and New Zealand to shared values of peace, non-violence and international cooperation.[23]

What Ails the Relationship?

- The Indian diaspora in New Zealand have not been sufficiently involved by both the governments of India and New Zealand in the strengthening of the bilateral relations, as has been the case in some other countries like the US. The Indian community in the US is almost 2.7 million strong, and an increasing number of Indian Americans occupy high-level posts in the US federal government and the private sector, which augurs well for the bilateral relationship. Although the numbers of the Indian diaspora are quite less in New Zealand, they have to be roped in by both the Indian and New Zealand governments.
- New Zealand had taken a very strong stand on the NSG-waiver that was granted to India. Prior to the India-specific NSG-waiver granted in September 2008, the then New Zealand Disarmament and Arms Control Minister Phil Goff had said "what we would like to see ideally are a range of conditions which would apply to India if the exemption is given",[24] though both the US and India did not want any conditions to be written into the agreement.
- The items of trade have not moved beyond a few traditional ones, especially from the Indian side, although India's strengths in sectors like I-T are now recognized across the world

The Way Forward

- New Zealand should understand India's security situation given that India has two nuclear powers in its immediate neighbourhood. India has also been a responsible nuclear power and has never indulged in the proliferation of nuclear weaponry.
- There should be greater cooperation between the armed forces of the two countries in working together to promote international security. These include cooperation in disaster relief, peacekeeping and sea lane protection roles such as countering piracy. The Indian Navy played an important role in the relief and rescue efforts in the aftermath of the 2004 Indian Ocean Tsunami and has been playing an active role in countering pirates off the coast of Somalia.
- New Zealand should devote more resources to the study of India and Indian languages. It should also train some of its diplomats in the Indian languages. India should also endeavour to develop expertise on New Zealand.
- Sharing of real-time intelligence and information, especially regarding terrorism and the Indian Ocean is crucial. India has been facing the problem of terrorism for a long time and has a rich experience in countering terrorism, which could prove beneficial to New Zealand. India and New Zealand have much information and expertise that can be of assistance to each other, whether in Southeast Asia, South Asia or the South Pacific. Besides, there are possibilities of developing interoperability with armed forces of other countries like the United States, Australia, Singapore, besides New Zealand and India. New Zealand has been providing support to countries in the Pacific and Southeast Asia to counter terrorism and radicalisation. In May 2011, New Zealand co-hosted *Exercise Ready Pasifika 2* which successfully tested the region's capacity to counter a host of terrorist threats.[25]
- There is scope for more collaboration between India and New Zealand in regions like Southeast Asia. India has already reached out to this region through its "Look-East Policy". Southeast Asia has three of New Zealand's top 10 trading partners (Singapore, Malaysia and Indonesia) and accounts for around 11 per cent of New Zealand's merchandise exports (NZ $4.7 billion) and 16 per cent of its imports (NZ $7.6 billion).[26]
- A readiness to work with third countries on regional security, like with Indonesia. The three countries have contiguous maritime zones of interest as well as shared challenges of maritime security, terrorism, Islamist radicalism, people smuggling and other transnational threats.
- From the Indian side there have been no Prime Ministerial visits since 1986, when the then Prime Minister Rajiv Gandhi had visited New

Zealand. A Prime Ministerial visit from India to New Zealand is much overdue.

Conclusion

A very significant aspect of New Zealand-India bilateral ties is the commitment shown to the bilateral relationship in spite of divergent viewpoints on many issues. But there is still a long way to go. The next few years will see increasing interaction between the two countries. Both the countries have realised that they have not paid enough attention to each other in the past and have woken up to the potential of their bilateral relationship. There is tremendous scope for increasing cooperation between India and New Zealand in all fields-whether it is economic, political, security or people-to-people links. However, to take their bilateral relationship to the next level, a strong commitment from both India and New Zealand is a *sine qua non.*

End Notes

1. Quoted in T.M.P. Mahadevan (1967), 'Indian Philosophy and the Quest for Peace', in Paul F. Power, *India's Non-alignment Policy*, Boston: D.C. Heath, pp. 2-3.
2. S. Gopal (1980), ed., *Jawaharlal Nehru: An Anthology*, New Delhi: Oxford University Press, p. 64.
3. Millar, T.B. (1991), Australia in Peace and War: External Relations since 1788, Canberra: Australian National University Press, p. 258.
4. Lok Sabha Debates, 29 September 1954, Col. 3680 as quoted in Nihal Henry Kuruppu, *Non-Alignment and Peace versus Military Alignment and War* (2004), New Delhi: Academic Foundation, p. 179.
5. A.L. Handoo (1994), "Dancing at Last with Tigers in the East", *New Straits Times*, 28 September 1994.
6. C. Raja Mohan (2002), "Looking East: Phase Two", *The Hindu* (Chennai) April 11, 2002.
7. "A Tiger Stir (1933)", *Economist*, 6 March 1993, p. 12.
8. *Republic of India, Ministry of Foreign Affairs and Trade, Government of New Zealand*, http://www.mfat.govt.nz/Countries/Asia-South-and-Southeast/India.php accessed on July 20, 2011.
9. Ministry of Foreign Affairs and Trade, Government of New Zealand, Annual Report, p. 20.
10. Pankaj Jha (2010), "Reconfiguring India- New Zealand Relations" in Rajaram Panda, Pankaj Jha eds. *India and New Zealand: Emerging Challenges*, Institute for Defence Studies and Analyses, New Delhi, September 20.
11. Rupert Holborow (2010), "India-New Zealand Relations: Perspectives from New Zealand" in Rajaram Panda and Pankaj Jha eds. India and New Zealand: Emerging Challenges, Institute for Defence Studies and Analyses, New Delhi, September 2010.
12. Ministry of Defence, Government of India, Annual Report, 2009-10, p. 2.
13. *Republic of India, New Zealand Ministry of Foreign Affairs and Trade*, http://www.mfat.govt.nz/Countries/Asia-South-and-Southeast/India.php accessed on May 10, 2011.
14. Ibid.

15. India: Visitor Arrivals September 2011- http://www.tourismnewzealand.com/markets-and-stats/south-east-asia/india accessed on September 20, 2011.
16. New Zealand Ministry of Foreign Affairs and Trade (2010), Annual Report (for the year ended June 2011), p. 20.
17. *Rajaram Panda (2011), India and New Zealand aim to boost ties through FTA*, http://www.idsa.in/idsacomments/IndiaandNewZealandaimtoboosttiesthroughFTA_RajaramPanda_200511
18. *Ministry of External Affairs, Government of India (2011), India-New Zealand Relations*, http://www.mea.gov.in/mystart.php?id=50044506
19. *High Commission of India in New Zealand, India-New Zealand bilateral relations*, http://www.hicomind.org.nz/index.php/india-and-new-zealand/ accessed September 27, 2011.
20. Ibid.
21. Uri Dadush (2009), *Bennett Stancil, The G20 in 2050*, November 2009, <http://carnegieendowment.org/publications/index.cfm?fa=view&id=24195>, accessed June 17, 2011.
22. Ministry of Foreign Affairs and Trade (2011), http://www.mfat.govt.nz/Countries/Asia-South-and-Southeast/India.php accessed October 10, 2011.
23. *High Commission of India to New Zealand, India-New Zealand Bilateral Relations*, http://www.hicomind.org.nz/index.php/india-and-new-zealand/ accessed August 20, 2011.
24. *NZ wants conditions written into nuclear agreement*, http://www.nbr.co.nz/article/nz-wants-conditions-written-nuclear-agreement-34210 accessed on 20 July 2011.
25. *New Zealand Ministry of Foreign Affairs and Trade*, http://www.mfat.govt.nz/downloads/media-and-publications/annual-report/annualreport10-11.pdf, p. 28.
26. *New Zealand Ministry of Foreign Affairs and Trade, New Zealand and Southeast Asia*, http://www.mfat.govt.nz/Foreign-Relations/Asia/2-South-East-Asia.php accessed October 7, 2011.

5

Role of Diaspora in India's Relations with New Zealand

Ganganath Jha

The Indian community in New Zealand is skilful and influential. According to 2006 census, Indians are about 105,000 in the total population of 4.2 million.[1] The Singhvi committee had earlier in 2001 estimated that the number of Indian origin population in New Zealand was merely 55000 out of which 10,000 were migrants from Fiji.[2] Indians are engaged in all types of professions but they are influential in domestic retail trade, hospitality, medical, engineering and information technology (IT) sectors.[3] Although their social integration with Maories and Europeans has not been possible so far, but there is mutual respect and also no legal hindrances to prevent it. Indians value the cultural moorings of others and express faith in "Unity in diversity." The Singhvi Committee on Indian Diaspora has noted that the "Indian community has mostly adapted itself well to local conditions and is regarded as a law-abiding, educated and responsible community in New Zealand.[4] They continue to have strong links with India through family ties and frequent visits. As they feel empowered, they may facilitate stronger cultural, economic and strategic linkages with India, which will benefit both.

Needless to emphasize that this is the age of globalization and the distance between one nation and another is shrinking. The US President Barack Obama has recently remarked that "America needs to adapt to a changing world as-countries like China and India are rising; areas like the Middle East becoming less stable; the world shrinking because of technology; and so I think we understand that we were going to have to adapt in some fundamental way in order to make sure that our kids and grandkids end up inheriting the kind of America that we inherited".[5]

As the United States is ready to change its perspective and mindset to forge closer ties with India, as they find relations with India complimenting their national interests, it will have wider ramifications. New Zealand cannot ignore those developments especially in this age of globalization. India is a country of more than one billion people and the number of middle class population is rising. India has given special attention to Millennium Development Goals and its literacy rates are rising. The quality of higher studies in science, technology and IT are well recognized and the old cold war mindset have withered away. The projection of a buoyant and vibrant economy is on threshold. Indians are trying to make their mark in the global arena through strategic and economic linkages in a big way. India is being projected as the next Asian super power, along with China. Its soft power potentials are immense. As explained by Joseph Nye, there are three ways to influence the behaviour of others first by means of coercion and threats, second by inducement and payment, and third by attraction or in other words getting others to want what you want.[6] Soft power is of the third type.

Both India and New Zealand are important in their respective regions and it is complimentary to use soft power to attract each other for mutual benefits. In that context, it has been observed that diaspora are huge sources of soft power. They represent their countries of origin more than the diplomats do.[7] The Indian community in the United States has a very organized lobby group to facilitate Indo-US relations. Indian diaspora in New Zealand are not as strong as in the US, but they do carry substantial influence in the society and politics of the country. They are in forefront of the dairy business, and made innovations in the cookery, confectionary, IT, medical and engineering sectors. Their performance is admirable and they are respected in their respective areas. Indians feel proud to be a citizen of New Zealand and they admire the environmental concerns of the government. They had ardently supported anti-nuclear stances of the Labour Party in 1980s. In July 1985, when the ship Rainbow Warrior, the flagship of the anti-nuclear environmentalist group, Greenpeace was blown up and sunk in Auckland harbour for protesting against the French nuclear testing in the Pacific, there were reactions in India. This event had triggered greater protests and the French government subsequently had to seek a formal apology from New Zealand. The French government also paid NZ$7 million in compensation for the damage of the ship. Prime Minister David Lange was determined to oppose nuclear experimentation in the region for protecting the ecology and environment of South Pacific.

In that year, the Lange government upheld its election manifesto by imposing a ban on the entry of any nuclear-capable ships into New Zealand ports at the cost of offending the United States. New Zealand's access to intelligence sharing and military cooperation was withheld by the United States in retaliation. In August 1986 security guarantees to New Zealand under the ANZUS Treaty were suspended and the Christchurch base was closed for ANZUS exercises. But New Zealand did not change its stand and began to evolve new defence strategy based on self-reliance. Indian media gave a substantial coverage to all these developments and appreciated the heroic role of Lange. However, the objective of this paper is to analyse the role of Indian diaspora in India-New Zealand relations, and in that connection the reference to diasporic activities, multiculturalism and "Pacific way of life" are necessary.

Indian Diaspora

Brij V. Lal has written that the existence of Indian diaspora can be traced back in the 19th Century. They came from Gujarat and Punjab initially and their journey to New Zealand were arduous. Travelling to Calcutta to Fiji and from there to New Zealand were difficult in those days. Most of the Gujaratis migrated from villages in the Navasari and Bardoli of Surat district, while Punjabis migrated from Jullundur and Hoshiarpur districts.[8] He further writes that Gujaratis have been involved in retail at various periods, including hawking or running fruit or grocery shops and also supermarkets. They have established fruit and vegetable businesses and general stores in remote rural areas. On the other hand, the common occupations for Panjabis have been flax cutting, farm work, drain digging and the arduous clearing of scrub and weeds on remote hilly farms on the North Island. Several Panjabis have established successful dairy farms in the Waikato and Thames Valleys. Mangal Singh developed the acclaimed Mount Cosy Jersey Stud farm about a century ago and Indians are active in business at Auckland, Wellington and Hamilton.[9]

It has been further observed that from 1970s a growing number of Indians are employed in clerical, professional and technical positions. The 2001 census revealed occupational changes and also continuation of traditional work patterns. About 24 per cent of Indians in New Zealand were employed in retail but 44 per cent were in the white collar occupations.[10] The performance of Indians in New Zealand has been impressive and while illustrating this aspect Jacqueling Leckie has termed them 'Indian Pioneers" and devoted a full chapter in her book, entitled, Indian Settlers: The story of New Zealand South Asian Community.[11] She has narrated the story of Bir Singh Gill and Phuman Singh Gill who arrived at New Zealand in 1890 and initially worked as a hawker but later displayed entrepreneurial skills. Phuman Singh moved to Wellington and married Margaret, an English nurse, and established confectionary business in the name of Abraham Singh and company. He subsequently established Indian Lolly Manufacturers also and opened a shop, named Eureka.[12]

On the other hand, Bir Singh Gill married a Maori girl, but he died too young to display any entrepreneurial skills. Another Indian migrant Ganda Singh and Daya Kaur started dairy business in 1913 when they built a small cottage in Seddon Terrace in Runanga. Similarly, there are other success stories of Harnam Singh, Sham Singh, Keshavbhai Parshottam, Edward Peters, Keshaw Daji, J.K. Natali, which have been recollected by Leckie. She has written that Edward Peters from Goa, rather than the celebrated Gabriel Reed, was the first to discover gold in Otego. This discovery was foundational not only to Dunedin's emergence as a wealthy city during the 19th century, but also to the worth of New Zealand as a nation.[13]

The developments in New Zealand suggest that Indians have a low profile and accommodative nature. They are trying to preserve their culture and identity through cultural activities and they celebrate Holi, Deepawali and other festivals as in India. The various associations, for example New Zealand Tamil Society, Telugu Association, Fiji Indian Satsang Mandal, Marathi association, New Zealand Kannada Koota, Goan Overseas association, Probasee Bengalee association, and the Ramayana Sanstha have kept their ethnic and Indian identity alive. These organizations provide social and cultural networks while others offer support to new migrants and contacts with the host community.

The Indian communities have sought to preserve their native language in New Zealand. The government has allowed facilities in that direction. Gujarati language classes are available in Wellington and Auckland. There are arrangements for Panjabi, Hindi, Tamil, Telugu, Bengali, Kannada and Malayalam language classes. Besides, new cultural centres have come into existence to make the activities of diasporic communities vibrant. Mahatma Gandhi centre (MGC) in Auckland and Bharat Bhavan Indian cultural centre (BBICC) in Wellington are important centres for cultural activities. BBICC was inaugurated by Governor General Dame Kith Tizard in 1992. The centre has supported both religious and social activities, including sports and Indian language classes. Again Pukekohe Indian association community centre has been built by Magan Ranchhod and is considered an important place to understand the essence of indigeneous and Indian culture. Again some temples, Gurudwaras and mosques are built for congregation of the devout, for religious sermons or get together.

The government is keen to provide equal opportunities to its people. New Zealand's Bill of Rights (1990) clearly indicates its determination to treat all the sections of its people on equal footing. The Bill of Rights indicates that New Zealand is one of the most progressive societies in the Asia-Pacific. This is an act to affirm, protect and promote human rights and fundamental freedoms, and also its commitment to the International Covenant on Civil and Political rights. Article 20 deals with the rights of minorities which says, "A person who belongs to an ethnic, religious or linguistic minority in New Zealand shall not be denied the right, in community with other members of that minority, to enjoy the culture, to profess and practice the religion, or to use the language, of that minority."[14] Another provision which is worth mentioning is article 27 which has defined right to justice in the following words:

"(a) Every person has right to the observance of the principles of natural justice by any tribunal or other public authority which has power to make a determination in respect of that person's rights, obligations, or interests protected or recognized by law;

(b) Every person whose rights, obligations or interests protected or recognized by law have been affected by a determination of any tribunal or other public authority has the right to apply, in accordance with law, for judicial review of that determination, and

(c) Every person has the right to bring civil proceedings against, and to defend civil proceedings brought by the crown, and to have those proceedings heard, according to law, in the same way as civil proceedings between individuals.[15]

Thus we find clear constitutional arrangements to address the grievances of all the sections of the people and to make the system fair, transparent and effective. The act is aimed at not only to protect right to life, liberty and property, but also to protect the thriving of multiculturalism and the "Pacific Way of life".

Multiculturalism

It is understood that to be an equal member of any society, providing equal rights may be necessary, but it is also important that the identities of all sections of society should be attached equal importance. As ethnic background forms distinct identity, their cultural heritage cannot be ignored. D. Gopal and A.S. Narang, in this context, have cited that "the demands of multiculturalism build on the already established principles of the politics of equal respect. If withholding the presumption is tantamount to a denial of equality, and if important consequences flow for people's identity from the absence of recognition, then a case can be made for insisting on the universalization of the presumption as a logical extension of the politics of dignity. Just as all must have equal rights, and equal voting rights, regardless of race or culture, so all should enjoy the presumption that their traditional culture has value.[16]

Multiculturalism is an integral part of pluralist ideology, and a basic principle of cultural relativism. Contrary to ethnocentricisms, it holds that we should not evaluate other cultures by standards of our own. Instead we should recognize the right of individuals and groups to self-identification and promotion of their own culture, regardless of cultural distance.[17] New Zealand has pursued the policy of multiculturalism without much fanfare and provided equal rights and opportunities to all its citizens. Whether a person is migrant from Uganda, South Africa, Mauritius, Britain, France, Holland or Tonga, Fiji, Nauru or Kiribati, they find New Zealand hospitable and safe. A number of IT professionals from India have migrated to New Zealand in recent years and a number of students are keen to go to New Zealand for advanced level managerial, management and medical studies. Similarly, thousands of Chinese are going there to seek their fortunes. Manmohini Kaul, Professor of South Pacific affairs in Jawaharlal Nehru University has stated that the increase in the number of Asians in New Zealand is changing its insular character and noted the personal interview with a New Zealand diplomat, Christopher Laidlaw, who said, "we are of course a much more multicultural society now than ever before. Large waves of immigrants particularly from Asia, have transformed the cultural landscape. That is a reality and it is a stimulating one. Multiculturalism is alive and acceptable. A decade ago, it was beyond imagination that Sir Anand Satyanand will be the Governor General of New Zealand, but it became a reality in 2006."[18]

Appointing Sir Anand Satyanand is a matter of symbolic importance for people of Asian origin in New Zealand. This event demonstrates New Zealand's commitment to multiculturalism. New Zealand, like Australia, was considered a bastion of white culture in Asia-Pacific for centuries. The appointment of a person of Indian Origin as head of the state has shown that New Zealand is ready to accept equal rights of all ethnic groups in governance matters as well. It is indeed open minded to understand the differences between white culture and Asian culture and is searching a middle path to adjust and accommodate the interests of all the people.

It is understood that the adoption of multicultural policy is a critical part of new thinking and diplomacy of New Zealand in theory and practice. The White Paper of May 1991 is indicative of the new course of action especially in relation to Asia. The creation of Asia Foundation (2000) is geared to promote relationship with Asia and efforts are made to create better environment and harmonious living.

It is necessary to indicate that Indians feel safer in New Zealand and they have every right to protect their cultural identity. Although New Zealand and Australia were colonized by the Britishers and both had been given similar values of governance and security, perspective and policies of the two countries differ. It was under the British rule that there had been demographic transformations. The people of European origin came to Australia and New Zealand in large numbers and outnumbered the size of the indigeneous population, but their approaches were qualitatively different from one another. In contrast with the accommodative approach of the European immigrants towards indigenous Maoris of New Zealand, the attitude of the initial migrants towards the aborigines in Australia were violent and brutish.

The white population in New Zealand was more benign towards indigenous Maories. They survived in the new dispensation under British rule. Presently, the Maories comprise 16 percent of the total population of the country. Their rights are constitutionally protected and they are beneficiaries of the affirmative action.

It is understood that the Maories had a positive image of the Britishers before the advent of the colonial era. It was this reason that they were tempted to sign the Treaty of Waitangi (1840) and ceded sovereignty to Great Britain. Signed on 6th February by the British lieutenant Governor, Capt. William Hobson and many Maori chiefs, the treaty acknowledged Maori ownership of land. The treaty had also accorded Tangata Whenua (the status of British subjects) to New Zealanders. Jeanine Graham has written that early Europeans, were in fact heavily dependent on Maori cooperation and goodwill.[19] However the interpretation of the Treaty of Waitangi continued to differ as the texts in Maori language and English were not the same.

There were continuous disputes over land rights of Maories. An important initiative to resolve the dispute between Maories and non-Maories (Pakeha) was taken in 1975 when Waitangi Tribunal was established to consider the grievances of Maories retrospectively dating back to 1840. However before analyzing various steps towards addressing the rights of minorities, a few words about pacific way of life will be discussed for better understanding of the policy of multiculturalism.

Pacific Way of Life

According to Bhagwan Singh, India's reputed expert on South Pacific, the 'Pacific Way' of life, said that it is gaining ground and respectability in the region. The cornerstone of the 'Pacific Way' is dialogue and discussion, not in a hurry, not by majority, but by unanimity. This has become an ideal to live with and even to live for.[20] Pacific way' is a tantalizing all-purpose expression which, in the broad sense, implies a unique approach to things and suggests a community of interests, regional solidarity, collective outlook and direction.[21] This concept has been further analysed by Ron Crocombe. He says that the 'Pacific Way' has been used from 1970 onwards to summarize some common values, practices and sentiments in the region which differed from Europeans. These include emphasis on distribution and consumption as against saving and investment, priority for extensive Kinship networks, spending a high proportion of time and resources on ceremonies associated with initiation, marriage, death, accession to chiefly titles and other community events, a lower priority for work time and output.[22] Western ways in contrast, are characterized by higher priority to efficient use of time and money, to savings and investment, a narrower range of obligations to kin but a wider commitment to community through taxation and government and other formal institutions, and to legal processes rather than customary ones.[23]

Ron Crocombe has further noted that everyone values change. Many of the dominant values in Europe in the historical past had similar values as the Asian today but they started changing AFTER INDUSTRIAL REVOLUTION. Again much of what islanders in South Pacific consider to be the 'Pacific way' is similar to patterns in Europe and Asia in earlier phases of history. Kinship was as binding for older generations as it is for most Pacific islanders today. So was religion, the emphasis on informal consultations rather than legalistic relations, long-term loyalties to kin and localities of origin and nostalgia for them when away, the subordinate role of women, and the coherence of families.[24]

Thus we find multiculturalism and 'Pacific Way' are reflecting in the perspective and policies of New Zealand. The government has tried to address the grievances of Maories and Pakeha objectively and the attitude of white supremacy have been diluted. When David Lange became the Prime Minster of New Zealand in 1984 he displayed dynamism in domestic and international affairs. He enabled Waitangi Tribunal to be active to exercise its responsibilities. The representation and evidence presented by the claimants to the tribunal were considered to be important for the nation. Under his stewardship, Maori language was adopted the official language of the government in 1987. The government felt the need of affirmative action to redress educational and social disadvantage, much of which was regarded as the unforeseen consequence of the past politics.

The government of New Zealand has become liberal in comparison with Australia. In 2002, old grievances of the Chinese minority was assuaged by the Labour government, when Prime Minister Helen Clark officially apologized to the Chinese community for the legislative discriminations regarding the imposition of a poll tax that the first wave of the Chinese immigrants had to pay in the late 19th Century. In February 2004, following a reconciliation and consultation process with the Chinese community, the government provided a NZ$5 million grant to establish a Chinese Heritage Trust Fund, for the welfare of that community.

New Zealand has shown sensitivities towards Muslims also, whose activities have come under surveillance especially after 9/11. The Muslims of New Zealand understood the compulsions and opened their mosques to the general public to dispel any misconceptions. This step was appreciated and the government was kind to allow the schools and tertiary institutions to make a provision to provide prayer rooms for Muslim students in their campuses.

Another step in the direction of multiculturalism was taken when Maori Queen Te Arikinui died in 2006. She was a popular leader to articulate the grievances of the Maori population. She was critical of the Treaty of *Waitangi* (1840) and was emphatic that the Treaty had not been signed by all the Maori Chiefs, and therefore its imposition on the entire country was arbitrary. She was responsible for negotiations and settlement with the British crown in 1996, regarding the grievances arising from the raupatu (unjust confiscation of the land) after the treaty of *Waitangi*. She was the undisputed leader of *Kingitanga* movement and respected, adored and obeyed by the Maories.

The death of Queen Arikinui was mourned not only by the Maories but also by Pakeha and the Pacific islanders. The government had declared the mourning period for six days. According to *Kingitanga* custom, her eldest son Tuheitia Paki was to be crowned before the funeral rites of her mother. Prime Minister Helen Clarke and Chief justice Sian Elias took interests and attended the coronation. The wide coverage of the function at the national level evoked enthusiastic response of the public as it gave a glimpse of Maori *tikanga* (custom) to the people.

In fact, the government of New Zealand has been bestowing similar weightage to adherents of all religion and culture. Whether it is Maori, Melanesian, Chinese, Indians or Micronesians, they are provided equal opportunities. The Bill of Rights has taken care to address the grievances of all the sections of the society, including people of Indian origin. As stated earlier, their cultural associations are recognized and they view the appointment of Sir Anand Satyanand as the success of their contribution to affluence and prosperity of New Zealand. The bilateral relations between the two countries are growing and it is yet to touch new heights. Now that the two countries are partners in East Asia Summit (EAS), ASEAN Regional Forum (ARF) and other groupings, fruitful dialogues are taking place.

Bilateral Relations

India and New Zealand have senior officials meeting held regularly. India-New Zealand Joint Business council (JBC) meetings are taking place in both the countries. In 1998, New Zealand reacted strongly to India's nuclear tests and announced a temporary recall of its High Commissioner from New Delhi. But efforts were simultaneously made to improve trade relations. New Zealand's Minister for International Trade, Lockwood Smith visited India from 10 to 15 October 1998 to attend 8th JBC Meeting in New Delhi. India's exports to New Zealand were US$63 million and imports US$6 million[25] , which needed to be improved. Thereafter New Zealand Foreign Minister, Phil Goff visited India in 2001, which was reciprocated by the visit of India's External Affairs minister. Again, India's Minister of Information Technology, Pramod Mahajan visited New Zealand and held meetings for collaborative ventures.[26] Indian exports to New Zealand reached US$181.7 million and imports were valued at US$163.8 million.[27]

New Zealand Trade Minister, Tim Groser visited India twice in 2009 during the Doha Round of WTO negotiations. He announced that New Zealand would open a consulate-general office in Mumbai to promote bilateral trade and investment relations.[28] India-New Zealand Foreign office consulations were held in Wellington on 30 March 2009. The Council for Leather Exports organized a Buyer-Seller Meet in Auckland from 31 August to 1 September 2009 and Bank of Baroda was granted a license by the Reserve Bank of New Zealand to open a subsidiary in Auckland. In 2010, Human Resource Minister Kapil Sibal and Minister for Overseas Indians, Vyalar Ravi visited New Zealand and signed agreements to promote relations. On the other hand, Sir Anand Satyanand, Governor General of New Zealand visited India.[29] Thereafter, negotiations for free trade between New Zealand and India started in Wellington in April 2010. New Zealand is displaying active interest in the changed economic climate in India and several companies from New Zealand are doing business with India with the active facilitation of India-New Zealand Joint Business Council. Kiwi fruits especially apples are easily available and the names of New Zealand cricketers- Daniel Vettori, Jessy Rider, Stephen Fleming, Styris, etc—are known to the cricket lovers in India.

Conclusion

Diaspora by definition is a transborder phenomenon. The increased pace of globalization and trans-nationalism has caused diasporas to integrate themselves horizontally as well as vertically with their respective homelands. Indian diaspora in New Zealand are also attached to their homeland through family ties, cultural association and business networking. The volunteers of Swaminarayan sect, Ramakrishna Mission, Chinmay Mission, International Society for Krishna Consciousness, Sai Baba cult are active at the international level. On the other hand, the Indian Council of Cultural Relations (ICCR) is sponsoring the visit of intellectuals and think tanks to promote cultural relations. At the same time, India's overall image is changing as its growth rates are high and economy is buoyant. The United States and the European Union are attaching importance to security and business ties and India's substantial rise as a powerful force in the Asia-Pacific is a reality to be reckoned with. Hence, Indian diaspora are also feeling empowered and their contacts with their homeland through business networking, remittances, political lobbying, marriage relations, pilgrimages, tourism, and socio-cultural exchange programmes have increased.

Again, globalization and new information technologies and communication have served as catalyst in promoting new transnational kin-based networks and groupings. It is understood that the Global Organisation of people of Indian Origin (GOPIO) is working to preserve and promote their identities and cultures uniting India with their diaspora at the global level. The GOPIO activities are complimented by the programmes of Sindhi, Malayalee, Tamil, Sikh and Bengali associations of India's diasporic community.

How Indian diaspora can play a role in promoting India-New Zealand relations depend on how they are used by the government. There are several areas of cooperation, which may prove mutually profitable. An important area of cooperation is the tourism sector. Indian diaspora have played a pioneering role in innovating food and cuisines in New Zealand and their role in hotel industries are appreciated. Most of the pioneers in the hotel industries who thrived in New Zealand in the 20th century were from Punjab. Although they are in New Zealand, but they are nostalgic about their place of origin, and can facilitate better relations in the tourism sector. Pilgrimage to Darbar Sahib will be an incentive for them and business through tourism will benefit India-New Zealand relations. Secondly, Ayurvedic medicine and yogas are to be explored. Baba Ramadev has made several innovations in this area in India and the craze for naturopathy are increasing. Ayurvedic herbs and therapies can cure serious diseases and it does not have side effects. Thirdly, IT sector in India are quite advanced and the new wave of Indian migrants are mostly IT professionals. This area is suitable for joint ventures. Fourthly, New Zealand has a large section of Gujarati diaspora, who are proficient in general merchandise, food stuffs, and textile business. On the other hand, New Zealand has sophisticated woollen products. Gujaratis have a good network with their counterparts at the global level. Gujarat is one of the most developed states in India and with the facilitation of Gujarati diaspora, business relations with New Zealand can be strengthened. Lastly, New Zealand is famous for its dairy products and may get a ready market in India, if proper incentives are given to the dealers in the Indian market. In fact, the objective conditions for business and trade are so favourable that the two countries are negotiating the conditions of free-trade.

To conclude, it can be stated that Indian diaspora in New Zealand are educated, affluent and sophisticated. As L.M. Singhvi has stated (2001), they are always interestd to maintain their cultural links with India. Their associations including Sikh Society, Brahma Kumari Raj Yoga Centre, Satya Sai Organization and Ramayana Mandalis are mostly based in Auckland and they are interested in cultural discourses. Their expectations are that they should be considered a respected community. The demands from the Indian diaspora as noted by L.M. Singhvi are few concessions, for example, the removal of difficulties at the immigration counter at Indian airports, abolition of the dual tariff structure and removal of the difficulties in remitting charity funds from New Zealand to India. As they are prudent, the Indian diaspora would like to facilitate better relations between India and New Zealand. However, they require suitable guidance and direction at the government level. If an Indian helped New Zealand in the discovery of gold centuries ago, they can repeat that feat in finding out precious treasure by exploring tourism and joint ventures.

End notes

1. http://www.teara.govt.nz/New Zealand Peoples/Indian/4/en.
2. L.M. Singhvi (2001), Report of the High level committee on the Indian Diaspora, ICWA, December, p. xxii.
3. Ibid.
4. Ibid.
5. Barack Obama, (2011), It is a changing world with India, China Rising", The Asian Age, 23 April.
6. Petras Shelton–Zumpano, (2011), "Cultural Politics in South Asia: Soft Power and Hard Prowers," *Link Times*, Beijing, 1 February, p.22,
7. Ibid.
8. Brij V. Lal (2006), The Encyclopaedia of the Indian Diaspora, Singapore, Editions Didier Millet, p. 389.
9. Ibid, pp. 390-91.
10. Ibid, p. 391.

11. Jacqueline Leckie (2007), Indian Settlers: The Story of a New Zealand South Asian Community, Dunedin, Otago University Press, p. 17.
12. Ibid, pp. 17-18.
13. Ibid, p. 21
14. See the text of New Zealand's Bill of Rights (1990), http.//www legislation. Govt. nz/ act/public/1990/0109/latest/DML 225521.html; and for better understanding of the act see, Susan Glazebrook (2004), "The New Zealand Bill of Rights Act, 1990: its operation and effectiveness", the paper presented at the South Australian State Legal convention, 22-23 July, pp.1-46.
15. Ibid.
16. A.S. Narang and D. Gopal, (2002), "Multiculturalism in Australia: Perspective and Problems", in D. Gopal, ed. Australia in the Emerging Global order, New Delhi, Shipra, pp. 40-41.
17. Ibid.
18. Manmohini Kaul's interview with Christopher Laoidlaw at India International Centre, New Delhi, 12 April 2006.
19. Jeanine Graham (2008), "New Zealand: History", Far East and Australasia, Hong Kong, p. 842.
20. Bhagwan Singh (1978), "The South Pacific: A new regional entity", *India Quarterly*, New Delhi, Vol. 34, No. 3, July-September p. 372.
21. Ganganath Jha (1987), "Politics and Society in South Pacific", Foreign Affairs Reports, Vol. 36, Nos. 11&12, November-December, p.263.
22. Ron Crocombe (2001), "The South Pacific, Suva, the University of South Pacific, p. 159.
23. Ibid.
24. Ibid, pp. 159-60.
25. Ministry of External Affairs, Annual Reports, 1997-98, New Delhi, pp. 35-36.
26. Ibid, 1998-99, p. 29.
27. Ibid, 2001-02, p. 19.
28. Ibid, 2009-10, p. 22.
29. Ibid, 2010-11, p. 22.

6

Multiculturalism in New Zealand: Reality or Rhetoric?

G. Vijay Kumar Reddy and P. Krishna Mohan Reddy

Multiculturalism, as distinct from the adjective multicultural ["pertaining to a society of varied cultural groups"], first came into wide circulation in the 1970s in Canada and Australia as a key plank of government policy to assist in the management of ethnic pluralism within the national polity. Coined by a Canadian Royal Commission in 1965, this governmental use of 'multiculturalism' is widely supported and endorsed by its proponents and importantly is an official article of faith—a term associated in principle with the values of equality, tolerance, and inclusiveness toward migrants of ethnically different backgrounds. The Canadian government enacted Canadian Multiculturalism Act in 1985 which is described as "An Act for the preservation and enhancement of multiculturalism in Canada". Canada's multicultural policy is also incorporated in the act as "3. (1) It is hereby declared to be the policy of the Government of Canada to—

(a) recognize and promote the understanding that multiculturalism reflects the cultural and racial diversity of Canadian society and acknowledges the freedom of all members of Canadian society to preserve, enhance and share their cultural heritage;

(b) promote the full and equitable participation of individuals and communities of all origins in the continuing evolution and shaping of all aspects of Canadian society and assist them in the elimination of any barrier to that participation;

(c) recognize the existence of communities whose members share a common origin and their historic contribution to Canadian society, and enhance their development;

(d) ensure that all individuals receive equal treatment and equal protection under the law, while respecting and valuing their diversity;

(e) encourage and assist the social, cultural, economic and political institutions of Canada to be both respectful and inclusive of Canada's multicultural character;

(f) promote the understanding and creativity that arise from the interaction between individuals and communities of different origins;

(g) foster the recognition and appreciation of the diverse cultures of Canadian society and promote the reflection and the evolving expressions of those cultures;

(2) It is further declared to be the policy of the Government of Canada that all federal institutions shall

(a) ensure that Canadians of all origins have an equal opportunity to obtain employment and advancement in those institutions."[1]

A little later it became commonplace for western liberal democracies to describe themselves as multicultural societies, even though only a few had embraced official policies of multiculturalism. Even nation states, which had traditionally been known as fiercely homogeneous, such as Germany and Japan, could no longer avoid acknowledging the ethnic and racial diversification of their populations. As a result of intensifying global migrations, 'the world becomes increasingly a place of multi ethnic states, with up to 30 per cent of the population coming from other societies'.[2] 'Multicultural' is thus often equated with multiethnic in public discourse, which in turn is conflated with multiracial, indicating the extent to which debates on multiculturalism are concerned predominantly with the presence of non-white migrant communities in white, western societies. Some scholars like Vincent, Andrew and Grilo[3] opine that multiculturalism is a freely ill-defined and nebulous idea, and its manifestations display a great deal of variation, dependent on the particulars of the society in question.

Even in Canada, Multiculturalism emerged as an explicit government policy, in the 1970s in response to complex variety of issues, including demands for greater autonomy or independence by Francophone Canadians; assertions of indigenous rights by various first nations groups; and political pressure from migrants for explicit recognition of their own cultural traditions in their new country.[4] In addition to this, multiculturalism came to play an important role in the creation of national identity in Canada, the conception of the nation being composed of a unique, multicultural society, embracing the related value of tolerance which became an emblem of national identity and could serve to distinguish Canada from both the United States and various European countries.[5] From Canada, government policies of multiculturalism, either *de jure* or *de facto* spread to a number of countries, principally the United States, Australia, Great Britain and, somewhat belatedly and in an ambiguous form, New Zealand.[6]

Multiculturalism permits the maintenance of cultural difference of ethnic minorities within the state, in explicit contrast to the assimilative ideal formerly associated with the nation-state. Rather than requiring assimilation into the mainstream culture, and the repression and the denial of cultural difference, multiculturalism purports to allow and encourage the different cultural features of ethnic minorities, while extending to them the full rights of citizenship of the state.[7] In a related manner, it is generally regarded as both natural and desirable that recognized culturally distinct groups should generate civil society organizations to represent their legitimate culturally specific concerns. Thus, multiculturalism encourages ethnic groups to maintain a distinctive identity and engage in the politics of recognition within a single society. In this way particular ethnic identities may be preserved, while common citizenship provides a countervailing identity that unites the different groups in a common polity.[8]

It is interesting and somewhat perplexing to note that in a number of developing nations like India, Indonesia or Eritrea there is no mention of 'multiculturalism' as an official or national policy though they have been multicultural societies as far back as we can remember. It appears as though the 'West' is reluctant to learn multiculturalism from the 'developing', 'non-white' nations. But when immigrants from these nations go to the West, the immigrants who went there legally are discriminated in spite of the 'West' being multicultural.

The researchers and policy makers in the US have been debating whether 'treating' the immigrants and minorities [evidently meaning all the non-whites though 'Hispanic' was still a separate category though being white] 'equally' will help them 'assimilate' or 'integrate' into the 'host' society. Though it was assumed that through the 'melting bowl' theory all the minority, non-white communities will eventually be absorbed into the 'host society', it was also believed that if the host society recognizes and encourages the immigrants and the minorities to protect their cultures, their integration will be much healthier .

In another, more activist, context, "multiculturalism" stands for an attempt to overturn dominant, monocultural conceptions of history and society, which were considered ethnocentric or even racist. In the early 1980s, in the USA, multiculturalism came into wide public use in the context of public/state school curriculum reform. School curricula were criticized for their so called Eurocentric bias and their failure to acknowledge the achievements of women, people of colour, or people from outside the tradition of western civilization.

To discuss multiculturalism in New Zealand is a challenge not only because it is complex but also because New Zealand is the only country which is officially committed to bi-culturalism through its founding document in 1840, *Te Tiriti o Waitangi* (the Treaty of Waitangi) enacted between the Maori, the indigenous and an unconquered people, and the British Crown established the signatories as equal partners holding equal rights and privileges. Despite this treaty and some evidence of paternalistic and humanitarian attitudes, assimilation was overtly and covertly the prevailing policy.[9] In the 1970s, the national and international social movements created possibilities for Maori resistance. In a climate of liberal humanism, fostered by economic prosperity, the seeds of biculturalism were planted.[10] In 1975, as a consequence of Maori pressure for affirmation of rights, the Treaty of *Waitangi* Act was passed by Parliament and the *Waitangi* Tribunal established to consider grievances arising from Maori relationships with the Crown.[11] Although the precise interpretation of this declaration of equality and its legal status has been argued ever since, and the issues involved continue to create tensions in Maori European relations, *Te Tiriti o Waitangi* remains the defining document of New Zealand's nationhood.[12]

In the 1970s while the other former British colonies were introducing multiculturalism as national policy, cross-cultural understanding in New Zealand was advocated in terms of biculturalism, with multiculturalism a hoped-for future outcome.[13] It is argued that early attempts to promote multiculturalism were "rightly discarded for their potential to undermine prior and pre-eminent bicultural commitments to Maori as *tangata whenua*".[14] This emphasis contrasts with the position of other colonized peoples such as the indigenous Aboriginal in Canada and Australia. However, Maoris, a minority group in New Zealand, are protected by bicultural policy. For example, in 1986 the Waitangi Tribunal stated:

> We do not accept that Maori is just another one of a number of ethnic groups in our community. It must be remembered that of all minority groups the Maori alone is party to a solemn treaty made with the Crown. None of the other migrant groups who have come to live in this country in recent years can claim the rights that were given to the Maori people by the Treaty of Waitangi.[15]

This policy and position of the *Waitangi* Tribunal vis-à-vis the Maoris seems to be not only discriminatory towards other immigrant groups in New Zealand but also somewhat obsolete in the present era of globalization. Hill[16] suggests that multiculturalism can be "fitted into" biculturalism. In the new millennium the voices have become more optimistic about ways of "accommodating multiculturalism" within a bicultural framework.[17] This optimism seems to be an illusion in the case of New Zealand because biculturalism is an obligation while multiculturalism is a vague idea.

Among a group of scholars, who are impressed, Christian Staerkle appreciates the bicultural policy of New Zealand when he says 'in particular, the role of Maoris' in creating a national and cultural identity based on a positive and complimentary relationship between the majority (NZ Europeans) and the minority group (Indigenous Maoris) could have far reaching consequences'.[18] He is also impressed that 'a national majority builds its identity on a positive relationship with the national minority. Rather, the general tendency seems to go in the opposite direction in the sense that minorities are a "problem" for majorities, representing symbolic and material threat to the majority identity'.[19] It must however be emphasized that, in practice, now or never in the past the "NZ Europeans" seem to have built up "their identity" based on Maori's culture or identity. The concept of "New Zealander" itself is so complex and vague.

The following paragraphs describe the evolution of the concept of "New Zealander" historically.

Mâori as New Zealanders

The first Europeans in New Zealand did not use these terms. Abel Tasman described the inhabitants as 'Indians', a European term for indigenous peoples of other places. But by the time of Cook's voyages the country had been given the Dutch name Nieuw Zeeland on European maps. From 1769 the local people, the Mâori, were called New Zealanders by the visitors; this continued for the next 80 years. Europeans in New Zealand did not wish to be considered 'New Zealanders'. In George Craik's 1830 book about Mâori, The New Zealanders, a Pâkehâ–Mâori man is introduced as 'a white New Zealander' and promptly responds that he is 'not a New Zealander, but an Englishman'.[20]

Until 1840, people in New Zealand other than Mâori were few in number and often on temporary visits, so there was little need to refine the distinction between New Zealanders (Mâori) and Europeans. But as the European population increased they realized that their interests and attitudes were different from those who were only visiting. New terms appeared. Those who came out on New Zealand Company ships to obtain land and settle were 'colonists' or 'settlers'. Hybrid names such as 'Anglo-Mâori' or 'Anglo-New Zealander' were occasionally used, but did not catch on.

From the 1830s Europeans had begun to call the indigenous people Mâori —or more often 'Mâoris'. This allowed a change of meaning for the term 'New Zealander'. So from the early 1850s people began to describe the European inhabitants as New Zealanders. As late as 1859 the historian A.S. Thomson still referred to Mâori by this name, but he was unusual. In 1854 for example, Thomas Cholmondeley, an English visitor, noted that 'the New Zealander will retain more of the Briton than any other colonist', a remark which suggests that for him Mâori were not even included in the concept. By the end of the 1850s, as the non-Mâori population rose to over 100,000, 'New Zealanders' were those with white faces, not brown.[21]

Pâkehâ identity

Other New Zealanders played with the idea of a distinct *Pâkehâ* culture. This was the culture of those whose families had inhabited the land for – in some cases—150 years or more, and had developed their own traditions and identities, such as a love of the beach and the bush, and the ritual of rugby games.

The historian Michael King wrote Being Pakeha to explore this idea. When first published in 1985 its subtitle was 'an encounter with New Zealand and the Maori renaissance'. On re-publication in 1999, the subtitle had changed, significantly, to 'reflections and recollections of a white native'. But the number of white natives who were really comfortable about being considered Pâkehâ was small. They preferred to think of themselves as 'real New Zealanders'.

At a popular level, however, the idea that non-Mâori New Zealanders did have a distinctive culture was reflected in a heightened interest in '*kiwiana*'—iconic objects such as Buzzy Bee toys, pavlova, Marmite and meat pies, or clothes like jandals and bush shirts.[22]

It is therefore impossible to define precisely who is a New Zealander. Biculturalism is framed as an equal partnership between Maori and Pakeha, with the later group seen as an essentially homogenous Anglo-White cultural community, with no room for other partners.[23] There is strong concern among Maori that a formal policy of multiculturalism could undermine their distinctive relationship with the state as the indigenous people of New Zealand, and reducing them to simply one ethnic minority among them.[24] Despite the lack of clear official policy of multiculturalism, a number of significant government policies reflecting the ideology of multiculturalism have been implemented which serve to create a *de facto* multiculturalism within New Zealand—though one which is particularly ambiguous and ill-defined. In particular, the 1986 Immigration Policy Review committed the government to encouraging migrants 'to participate fully in New Zealand's multicultural society while being able to maintain valued elements in their own heritage'.[25] Importantly, the Review also rejected 'the old notion of assimilation' and noted that 'our society clearly now sees a positive value in diversity and the retention of ethnic minorities of their cultural heritage'.[26]

The terms of 'multicultural' and 'multiculturalism' litter government documentation and official policy, though little or no attempt is made precisely to define the nature or limits of this multiculturalism. The term is used in general public discourse in a broadly positive manner, sometimes contrasted, but more often juxtaposed, with 'biculturalism', as meaning the tolerance and acceptance of a certain form and degree of cultural difference. This 'difference' is clearly perceived as a deviation from the majority, Anglo-Celtic cultural norm, though it is never explicitly defined as such.[27]

As in Canada, multiculturalism in New Zealand is often invoked as part of a mythology of identity of the Anglophone majority, in an attempt to differentiate themselves from the notionally homogenous European societies which had previously served as models for national identity.[28] However, "the fact that essentially the same features of multiculturalism are being used to make similar claims to uniqueness, in the very Anglophone-dominated countries that the New Zealand identity is seeking to distinguish itself from, and that New Zealand is simply following them down the multicultural road, is conveniently ignored".[29]

Significantly, in New Zealand multiculturalism is not made into any government act as a national policy while in Canada a specific act of multiculturalism as a government policy was enacted in 1985. In addition, since then the Canadian government has been continuously monitoring the operation of the Canadian Multiculturalism Act till this day.

The Multiculturalism Program in Canada supports the Department's mandate and the Canadian Multiculturalism Act by assisting the socio-economic integration of individuals and communities and their contributions to building an integrated and socially cohesive society. The Program promotes intercultural understanding through public education and outreach initiatives, Historical Recognition Programs and Canada's Action Plan Against Racism, and by supporting civil society organizations through the Grants and Contributions Program. Activities range from reaching out to the community through diversity education programs, such as the Mathieu Da Costa Challenge, to recognizing the contributions of individual Canadians through the Paul Yuzyk Award for Multiculturalism.

A key goal of the Act is to ensure that the government is sensitive and responsive to Canada's multicultural reality. The Multiculturalism Program assists federal and public institutions in their efforts to integrate multiculturalism into the development of their policies, programs and services through networks, partnerships and joint activities. The Program also coordinates the production of results-based reports submitted by federal institutions on the operation of the Canadian Multiculturalism Act and produces and disseminates multiculturalism research and other products.

The Program's activities extend beyond Canada's borders. By participating in international forums, hosting international delegations, and participating in international research initiatives, Canada learns from, and contributes to the international policy dialogue on diversity. Mervin Singham, the Director of the Office of Ethnic Affairs, New Zealand states that "New Zealand has ratified a number of international conventions based on elimination of discrimination and the assurance of fundamental rights for all citizens including minority groups.[30] In this context he mentions New Zealand's ratification of International Convention on the Elimination of All Forms of Racial Discrimination, International Covenant on Civil and Political Rights and International Covenant on Economic Social and Cultural Rights.[31] Among the examples involving disparity reduction he mentions that the Equal Employment Opportunity (EEO) targets set by the State Services Commission for State Sector Agencies is an initiative which seeks to ensure that ethnic minority people are represented in all levels of state services. It also helps achieve equality by ensuring that the ethnic minority views are manifested in policy development and service delivery.[32] In spite of the writings or statements by the government officials such as above, there is genuine fear and concern among the immigrants from Asia that there is indeed discrimination in employment. This pain is further complicated because the immigrants such as doctors, engineers, science graduates, pharmacists, management professionals, IT professionals, accountants were invited to New Zealand because New Zealand needs them.

This feeling is best illustrated by an article by Dr. Arvind Zodgekar, School of Social and Cultural Studies, Victoria University of Wellington, New Zealand, who is an immigrant himself. Many research studies and anecdotal reports in recent years have shown the immigrants' experiences of discrimination in the work place, housing and also socially. The overall pattern of inequality in average income clearly showed that immigrants from traditional sources (UK, USA/ Canada & Australia) achieve parity or exceed the incomes of New Zealand born person, but those from non-traditional sources do not perform as well.[33] Many of these migrants also have experienced barriers to gaining suitable employment in New Zealand. The recent migrants from non-traditional sources have experienced difficulties in getting their qualifications and overseas work experiences recognized in New Zealand and were unable to obtain suitable employment.[34] Spoonly[35] has argued that discrimination on racial and ethnic grounds results in many forms of inequality in New Zealand. Many studies also provide evidence of general discrimination on ethnic grounds in New Zealand.[36] Arvind makes an emphatic, rather an emotional statement that "if we do not want migrants and non-migrants to go to extremes, then the policy makers, politicians and others must examine the ways in which they portray the image of these immigrant groups. It is essential to advocate to the general public that a degree of adjustment would be necessary on the part of resident citizens. The concerns regarding immigrant integration and assimilation could be alleviated to a greater extent if more attention was given towards facilitating settlement at the early stages of their arrival in New Zealand".[37]

In a recent survey (in 2006), it was found that Indians in New Zealand face job discrimination up to 10 times or more compared to New Zealanders. Almost two in every three Indians (63 per cent) felt that they had been discriminated in the recruitment process or at work, according to the survey by the Global Indian magazine. Importantly, this survey revealed that three in four (72 per cent) Indians felt that their career has been adversely affected after migrating to New Zealand. One in two Indians said they have never been promoted in a job in New Zealand. Two in three Indians feel that their salary is not in line with their qualifications and skills. One said that he had not had a permanent job for the past 12 years. "I did not get one promotion in the last 10 years. I am in a Catch—22 situation because my kids are schooling in New Zealand. Now I am unable to go back to India as I have to wait for them to finish their schooling" another respondent said.[38] This sums up broadly the feelings of 'non-white, Asian immigrants and citizens' of New Zealand.

The problem of multiculturalism in New Zealand is primarily a manifestation of the *Treaty of Waitangi* which simply looks through the eyes of White New

Zealanders (overwhelmingly of British and Irish ancestry) and the Maoris, totally ignoring other minority groups and immigrants from Asia.

A researcher is perplexed at the frequent use of New Zealand culture and identity and an indirect pressure on the immigrants from non-white and Asian backgrounds to integrate into the so-called host New Zealand culture, while a vast majority of the white New Zealanders takes pride in their British ancestry. So are the Maoris who think that it is they who gave New Zealand its identity. The fact that New Zealand itself is a Commonwealth nation, taking pride to be under the 'Crown' and the Queen Elizabeth II being the official emblem on New Zealand currency doesn't seem to bother either the government or the people to force an artificial identity on the part of immigrants. It would be a mistake to treat white New Zealanders with multiple identities specially in comparison to the immigrants with the same multiple identities as Indian or Chinese as the case may be. Therefore, it cannot be said that white New Zealanders and Maoris are 'more New Zealanders' and the Asian immigrants as 'less New Zealanders'.

It is becoming increasingly clear that in future the immigrants are going to play a significant role in not only the economy but also in other fields in New Zealand. In 1986, 81.2 per cent of New Zealanders identified themselves as of European ethnicity (evidently 90 per cent of them British ancestry) and 12.5 per cent as Maori and only 6.3 per cent as others (Chinese, Indians, Pacific Islanders etc.). By 2001 this distribution has changed significantly and Europeans now account for only 67 per cent of the New Zealand population, Maori 15.5 per cent and others 17.5 per cent.[39] It is projected that by 2016 the percentage of others (Chinese, Indians etc.) will increase to 21.7 per cent and that of the European New Zealanders percentage will be 61.3 per cent. Then this group will become the largest minority group overtaking the Maoris who will be of 17 per cent of New Zealand's population.

A recent article by Roger Openshaw and Elizabeth Rata, faculty from University of Auckland puts into perspective some problems faced by biculturalism and the *Treaty of Waitangi*.[40] The New Zealand Universities have a statuary role to 'accept a role of critic and conscience of society'[41] and in theory should enable the universities and individual academics to express views unhindered by threats of external interference.[42] However, despite serious conceptual and interpretative problems, biculturalism was the main vehicle through which culturalism as an ideology has become embedded in New Zealand's tertiary institutions, including universities. Roger Openshaw's study in 2006 traces the beginnings of bicultural policy from the 1960's to the present to show how New Zealand's liberal educators became transformed into radical biculturalists to the point where it became unquestioning (and unquestionable) doctrine.

For example there is requirement that teacher training providers 'fulfill the obligations of Treaty of Waitangi as they relate to teaching and learning' and the auditing of this requirement by *Te Puni Kokiri* (TPK), the Ministry of Maori Development.[43] The newly created New Zealand Teachers Council which is responsible for Graduating Teacher Standards throughout the country also incorporates a strong bicultural strand that recognizes two distinct cultures in Aotearoa New Zealand and makes it mandatory for teacher education providers to give effect to 'Treaty of Waitangi Principles'.[44]

Such an obligation on the part of researchers in the university seems to have placed heavy burden when the applications in the Health research Council of New Zealand 'Partnership Programmee Request for Proposals' asks applicants to 'meet at least the minimum requirements for Maori Responsiveness' which includes whether Maori groups are consulted, any Maori participants are involved in the research, Maoris role in further development, and if any Maori researchers or research staff are named on the proposal.[45]

The further questions in the application include 'what are the plans within your research group or department to support the development of Maori capacity in this area? If Maori researchers are named on this proposal, how will their involvement contribute to the development of Maori Health research Workforce?; will this lead to Maori Specific Research Methods? ; and if data is collected from Maori participants, in what way has the research been designed to ensure that Maori tikanga/culture will not be compromised?.[46]

The above discussion indicates the amount of interference and the curtailing of academic freedom of the university researchers owing to the *Treaty of Waitangi.* Sometimes, the same research questions seem to have become political. Sometimes the Treaty gives a small group of Maori academics a degree of control, even a *de facto* veto over research. For example, the rapid growth of kaupapa Maori research (KMR) (research from a Maori worldview) and its influence over all research ignores Marie and Haig's caution in 2006 with respect to the development of Maori science, paradigms and methodologies. They argued that 'it should be of considerable concern that KMR is described as "world-class" when its methodology has not been subject to critical evaluation and that little of the research has been published in peer-reviewed journals.[47] As a consequence of Treaty compliance, there is an uncritical acceptance of kaupapa Maori knowledge: an acceptance that has led to kaupapa Maori knowledge being taken up as a legitimate form of science by government departments.[48]

In February 2000, at Wellington's Victoria University, Paul Dunmore, an Associate Professor in Accounting and Commercial Law, refused to attend a Maori blessing of Rutherford House arguing in an inter-departmental e-mail that an institution dedicated to the advancement of knowledge was inaugurating its new premises with 'an act of animist superstition', adding that he would have opposed other religious superstitions on similar grounds. Dunmore was denounced as 'bigoted' and 'ill-educated' in the editorial of Victoria Universities Student Magazine *Salient.* It was further ominously warned that 'academic freedom is not the right of academics to speak out on any issue, no matter who it might harm, embarrass, demean, belittle or ridicule' and calling for the recalcitrant professor to be disciplined by the university. When a senior academic and philosopher at the University of Canterbury compared this disciplinary call to those of Nazi Germany's brownshirts, there was a subsequent article by Peter Rochford, Maori Vice-President of the Association of University Staff, strongly upholding culturalist perspective which was also embraced by the University's management. Rochford condemned both dissenting academics and supported the call for disciplinary action on the grounds that New Zealand was a bicultural society within which each culture had the right to its own world-view, without denigration.

This kind of atmosphere in academic institutions does not augur well for the future of either biculturalism or multiculturalism.

Finally, the policy makers and politicians of New Zealand should realize that for the immigrants, especially from Asia, New Zealand is the least favoured destination. Obviously, they want to realise their 'American dream' in USA. It is fairly well known that the students and youth in Asia migrate to New Zealand only when they cannot get a USA visa, and utilize the New Zealand experience to gain entry into the USA. A decade or so back one consultancy in Hyderabad dealing with New Zealand immigration boldly advertised that 'New Zealand, Gateway to USA' causing much uproar in New Zealand Parliament. Further, the very small size and a very small size of the population of New Zealand cannot offer much employment, career or business opportunities for the immigrants in comparison to USA or Canada.

As Arvind Zodgekar analyses it is clear that 'we are experiencing a net loss of New Zealand Citizens and a net gain of New Zealand Citizens' in the last two decades.[49] During this entire period the outflow of New Zealand citizens exceeds returnees of New Zealand citizens especially during the peak outflow years of 1988 and 2001. This means that recent international migratory flows to and from New Zealand is increasingly resulting in New Zealand citizens being replaced by non New Zealand citizens.[50] Interestingly out migration of New Zealand citizens in their 20s and 30s has been the major feature of this migration trend.[51]

The above figure and table suggest that in the past two decades, the external migration from New Zealand has been gradually increasing while the internal migration to New Zealand has been gradually decreasing. It is interesting to note that the net PLT migration to Australia is on the rise according to the table above. It may not be an alarming situation for the New Zealand government but surely it is a cause for concern because the net migration of the Asians is on the rise and it is almost certain that percentage of Asians in the coming decades might cross the number of local Maori population.

Figure 1: PLT Total Arrivals, Departures, and Net Migration, 1986-2007

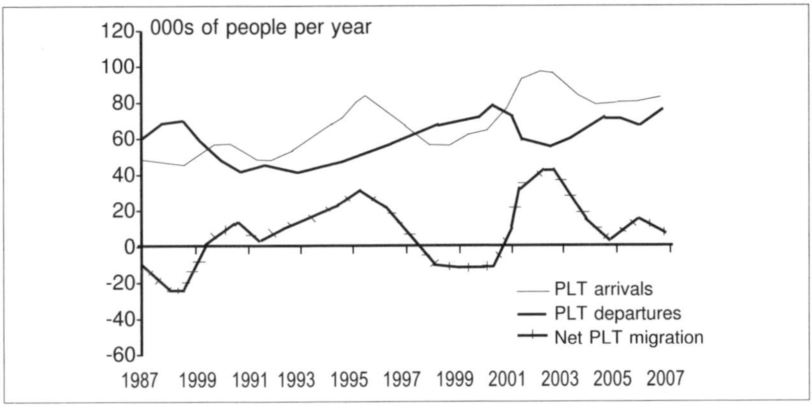

Source: http://www.dol.govt.nz/lmr/lmr-external-migration.asp

Table 1: Permanent and long-term migration by region and country of last/next permanent residence (number of people)

	PLT arrivals		PLT departures		Net PLT migration	
Years to December	**2006**	**2007**	**2006**	**2007**	**2006**	**2007**
Oceania	**19,499**	**19,548**	**35,790**	**43,436**	**-16,291**	**-23,888**
Australia	13,306	13,636	34,015	41,634	-20,709	-27,998
Fiji	2,590	2,786	333	276	2,257	2,510
Samoa	1,569	1,450	446	494	1,123	956
Tonga	921	711	229	194	692	517
Asia	**20,487**	**22,939**	**9,104**	**9,306**	**11,383**	**13,633**
China, PR	4,271	4,207	2,443	2,391	1,828	1,816
India	2,743	4,232	618	656	2,125	3,576
Japan	3,192	2,659	1,404	1,440	1,788	1,219
Korea, Republic of	1,896	2,068	1,825	1,861	71	207
Malaysia	1,413	1,547	462	524	951	1,048
Philippines	2,533	3,374	134	148	2,399	3,226
Singapore	612	631	383	437	229	194
Taiwan	818	902	326	321	492	581
Thailand	920	1,004	385	376	535	628
Europe	**30,262**	**26,888**	**15,627**	**16,448**	**14,635**	**10,440**
France	799	894	448	538	351	356
Germany	2,283	2,447	773	797	1,510	1,650
Ireland	1,227	1,214	970	898	257	316
United Kingdom	22,695	19,381	11,760	12,276	10,935	7,105
Americas	**6,422**	**6,550**	**4,758**	**4,769**	**1,664**	**1,781**
Canada	1,615	1,569	1,440	1,542	175	27
United States	3,636	3,540	2,596	2,494	1,040	1,046
Other[a]	**6,062**	**6,647**	**2,844**	**3,122**	**3,218**	**3,525**
South Africa	1,850	2,127	380	330	1,470	1,797
Total	**82,732**	**82,572**	**68,123**	**77,081**	**14,609**	**5,491**

Sources: External Migration, Statistics New Zealand. http://www.dol.govt.nz/lmr/lmr-external-migration.asp

Thus, multiculturalism in New Zealand cannot be compared with the multiculturalism in Canada, USA and Australia or for that matter with any other country because a country officially committed to biculturalism, strictly speaking, can never be a multicultural nation since biculturalism in any form covertly or overtly opposes multiculturalism. In case of New Zealand, it is really surprising that the office of the ethnic affairs has ratified almost all the international conventions on elimination of discrimination, racism, equal employment opportunity, equal economic, social and cultural rights and the assurance of fundamental rights for all citizens including minority groups. But no thought seems to have been applied how to achieve these objectives in the so called "multicultural New Zealand" committed to an official policy of biculturalism.

Acknowledgements: The authors are grateful to Prof. Dr. A. Lakshmana Chetty and Prof. Dr. Y. Yagama Reddy, both former Directors, Centre for Southeast Asian & Pacific Studies, Sri Venkateswara University, Tirupati for their comments, suggestions and support.

END NOTES

1. Canadian Multiculturalism Act R.S.C., 1985, c. 24 (4th Supp.), An Act for the preservation and enhancement of multiculturalism in Canada. [1988, c. 31, assented to 21st July, 1988], Act current to 2011-05-29 and last amended on 2003-04-01 [http://laws-lois.justice.gc.ca/eng/acts/C-18.7/page-1.html]]
2. Alistair Davidson, "Multiculturalism and Citizenship: Silencing the Migrant Voice", *Journal of International Studies*, Vol. 18, No. 2, 1997, pp. 72-99
3. Andrew Vincent, "What is so Different about Difference?" in Bruce Haddock and Peter Sutch (eds), *Multiculturalism, Identity and Rights*, London 2003, pp. 42-60 and also Ralph Grillo, *Pluralism and the Politics of Difference: State, Culture and Ethnicity in Comparative Perspective,* Oxford 1998, p. 176. Emphasis added.
4. Eva Mackey, *The House of Difference: Cultural Politics and National Identity in Canada*, Routledge, New York, 1999, p.70. Emphasis added
5. Alastair Bonnett, *Anti-Racism*, Rouletdge, New York and London, 2000, p. 63. Cited in Ian Clarke, "Essentialising Islam: Multiculturalism and Islamic Politics in New Zealand", *New Zealand Journal of Asian Studies*, Vol.8. No.2, December 2006, p. 63.
6. Ian Clarke, "Essentialising Islam: Multiculturalism and Islamic Politics in New Zealand", *New Zealand Journal of Asian Studies*, Vol.8, No.2, December 2006, p.72. Emphasis added.
7. Ralph Grillo, *Pluralism and the Politics of Difference: State, Culture and Ethnicity in Comparative Perspective*, Oxford, New York 1998, p. 178.
8. Peter Kivisto, *Multiculturalism in a Global Society*, Oxford 2002, p.36. Cited in in Ian Clarke, "Essentilising Islam: Multiculturalism and Islamic Politics in New Zealand", *New Zealand Journal of Asian Studies*, Vol. 8, No. 2, December 2006, p. 73.
9. R.S. Hill, *State Authority, Indigenous Autonomy: Crown-Maori Relations in New Zealand/ Aotearoa 1900-1950*, Wellington 2004. Cited in Jill Smith, "Biculturalism and Multiculturalism: Competing Tensions in Visual Arts Education in Aotearoa-New Zealand", *International Journal of Multiculturalism*, Vol. 12, No. 2, 2010, p. 4. R.S. Hill, "Fitting multiculturalism into biculturalism: Maori-Pasifika relations in New Zealand

from the 1960's", *Ethnohistory*, Vol. 57, No. 2, pp. 291-319. Cited in Jill Smith, *op cit*, pp. 1-17. Emphasis added.

10. Jill Smith, *op cit*, p. 2. Emphasis added.
11. See, Claudia Orange, *The Treaty of Waitangi*. Wellington: 1987.
12. *Ibid.* Emphasis added.
13. R.S. Hill, "Fitting multiculturalism into biculturalism: Maori-Pasifika relations in New Zealand from the 1960's", *Ethnohistory*, Vol. 57, No. 2, 2010, pp. 291-319. K. Irwin, "Multicultural education: The New Zealand response", *New Zealand Journal of Educational Studies*, Vol. 24, No. 1, 1989, pp. 3-18. Cited in Jill Smith, "Biculturalism and Multiculturalism: Competing Tensions in Visual Arts Education in Aotearoa-New Zealand", *International Journal of Multiculturalism*, Vol. 12, No. 2, 2010, pp. 1-17.
14. S. May, "Accommodating multiculturalism and biculturalism in Aotearoa/New Zealand: Implications for language teaching", *Waikato Journal of Education*, Vol. 8, 2002, p. 49. Emphasis added.
15. Ibid, p. 37.
16. R.S. Hill, "Fitting multiculturalism into biculturalism: Maori-Pasifika relations in New Zealand from the 1960's", *Ethnohistory*, Vol. 57, No. 2, 2010, pp. 291-319.
17. A. Bartley & P. Spoonley, "Constructing a workable multiculturalism in a bicultural society", in M. Belgrave, M. Kawharu & D.V. Williams (Eds), *Waitangi revisited: Perspectives on the Treaty of Waitangi*, 2nd ed., Auckland, 2004, pp. 136-148. E.T. Durie, "The rule of law, biculturalism and multiculturalism", Paper presented at the Australasian Law Teachers Association Conference (ALTA), July 2005, University of Waikato, Hamilton, New Zealand. Cited in Jill Smith, "Biculturalism and Multiculturalism: Competing Tensions in Visual Arts Education in Aotearoa-New Zealand", *International Journal of Multiculturalism*, Vol. 12, No. 2, 2010, pp. 1-17.
18. Christian Staerkle, "The individual as the source of progressive thinking: A comment on Liu and Sibley (2006)", *Papers on Social Representations*, Vol.15, 2006, pp.6.1-6.7.
19. E.G.T. Green, "Guarding the gates of Europe: A typological analysis of immigration attitudes across 21 countries", *International Journal of Psychology*, 2006. Cited in Christian Staerkle, *op cit* W.G. Stephan & C.L. Renfro, "The role threats in intergroup relations", in D. Mackie and E.R. Smith (Eds.) *From prejudice to intergroup emotions*, New York, 2002, pp. 191-208.
20. *http://www.teara.govt.nz/en/the-new-zealanders/1*
21. *http://www.teara.govt.nz/en/the-new-zealanders/2*
22. *http://www.teara.govt.nz/en/the-new-zealanders/12*
23. Ian Clarke, "Essentialising Islam: Multiculturalism and Islamic Politics in New Zealand", *New Zealand Journal of Asian Studies*, Vol. 8, No. 2, December 2006, p. 76. Emphasis added.
24. *Ibid.*
25. Ho Cheung Elsie, Bedford Eric, Charlotte and Polly Leung, *Settlement Assistance Needs of Recent Migrants*, Report for the New Zealand Immigration Service, Department of Labour, Wellington, 2000. Emphasis added.
26. *Ibid.*
27. Ian Clarke, *op cit*, p. 77.
28. Eva Mackey, *The House of Difference: Cultural Politics and National Identity in Canada*, Routledge, New York, 1999, p. 70.
29. Eva Mackey, *op cit*, p. 77.
30. Mervin Singham, "Multiculturalism in New Zealand—the need for a new paradigm", *Aotearoa Ethnic Network Journal*, Vol. 1, No. 1, June 2006, p. 34.

31. *Ibid*, note 64.
32. *Ibid*, p. 35.
33. Dr Arvind Zodgekar, "The Changing Face of New Zealand's Population and National Identity" Paper presented at the XXV International Population Conference, 18-23 July, Tours, France. Can be found at http://iussp2005.princeton.edu/download.aspx?submission1d=50179.
34. "High Hope: A Survey of Qualifications, Training and Employment Issues for recent immigrants to New Zealand", *Department of Internal Affairs*, 1996, Wellington. "Pilot Study Report: Longitudinal Immigration Survey New Zealand", *Department of Labour*, 2004, New Zealand, Cited in Dr Arvind Zodgekar, "The Changing Face of New Zealand's Population and National Identity" Paper presented at the XXV International Population Conference, 18-23 July, Tours, France.
35. See, P. Spoonley, *Racism and Ethnicity*, Auckland 1988.
36. C. Ward & A. Masgoret, "New Zealanders Attitudes Towards Immigrants and Immigration", Centre for Applied Cross Cultural Research (www.ac.nz/cacr), 2004. Cited in Dr Arvind Zodgekar, "The Changing Face of New Zealand's Population and National Identity" Paper presented at the XXV International Population Conference, 18-23 July, Tours, France.
37. Zodgekar, *op cit*, p. 13.
38. http://www.dnaindia.com/report.asp?NewsID=1056674. Emphasis added.
39. Dr Arvind Zodgekar, "The Changing Face of New Zealand's Population and National Identity" Paper to be presented at the XXV International Population Conference, 18-23 July, Tours, France.
40. Roger Openshaw & Elizabeth Rata, "The weight of inquiry: Conflicting cultures in New Zealand's tertiary institutions", *International Studies in Sociology of Education,* Vol. 17, No. 4, December 2007, pp. 407-425.
41. *Education Act*, New Zealand Government, 1989, Wellington New Zealand Government. Cited in Roger Openshaw & Elizabeth Rata, "The weight of inquiry: Conflicting cultures in New Zealand's tertiary institutions", *International Studies in Sociology of Education,* Vol. 17, No. 4, December 2007, pp. 407-425.
42. *Ibid.*
43. Roger Openshaw & Elizabeth Rata, "The weight of inquiry: Conflicting cultures in New Zealand's tertiary institutions", *International Studies in Sociology of Education,* Vol.17, No.4, December 2007, pp. 407-425.
44. *Ibid*, pp. 410-411. Emphasis added.
45. Roger Openshaw & Elizabeth Rata, *op.cit,* p.413.
46. *Health Research Council of New Zealand Partnership Programme Request for Proposals Expression of Interest Form (HRCREF) EO1204-OHS*, 2004. Available online at www.hrc.govt.nz, cited in Roger Openshaw, *op cit*, p.413. Emphasis added.
47. D. Marie, & B. Haig, "Kaupapa Maori research methodology: a critique and an alternative", *New Zealand Science Review,* Vol. 63, No. 1, 2006, pp. 17-21 cited in Roger Openshaw & Elizabeth Rata, "The weight of inquiry: Conflicting cultures in New Zealand's tertiary institutions", *International Studies in Sociology of Education,* Vol. 17, No. 4, December 2007, pp. 407-425.
48. Roger Openshaw, *op cit*, pp.415-416. Emphasis added.
49. Zodgekar, *op cit*, p. 6, fig. 2.
50. Zodgekar, *op cit,* p. 7.
51. *Ibid.*

7

Tackling Terrorism: The New Zealand Way

Renu Sharma

Globalization and revolution in communications technology have created a whole new set of opportunities and risks in today's interconnected and interdependent world. Today, terrorism has made its presence felt across the globe. The watershed event of 9/11 terrorist attacks in the United States shook the world and raised global concerns on terrorism. We all have a vague idea or notion of what terrorism constitutes but there is lack of a precise, tangible, and truly explanatory definition of the word. Majority of the policymakers and experts view terrorism as one of the gravest threats to international peace and security. Undoubtedly, the world is wedged in a complex quandary over combating terrorism which transcends boundaries.

Conceptualizing terrorism, however, is not a simple task as there is no consensus definition and it is also hugely problematic to classify every act of violence as terrorism. Terrorism has been described as "propaganda by deed,"[1] for a self-propagated raison d'être. Unlike 19th century terror acts which targeted specific leaders, the post-World War II and the 21st century anti-state terrorism was a protest and struggle against what was regarded as "systemic political-economic forces combined with the structural violence, caused by territorial divisions and governed by colonial or neo-colonial regimes."[2] Concomitantly, any abhorrent act of violence perceived as directed against society—whether it involves the activities of anti-government dissidents or governments themselves, organized-crime syndicates, common criminals, rioting mobs, people engaged in militant protests, individual psychotics, or lone extortionists—is often labeled as "terrorism."[3]

The nature of the terror threats has changed dramatically over the time. The challenge to governments whether internal to a country, foreign-based, or multinational in character, as Al Qaeda, is profound and consequently requires a spirit of enhanced cooperation against terrorism.[4] The world has witnessed the most virulent phenomenon embodied by various terror networks. Today, we face the reality of terrorism and the threat posed by the proliferation of weapons of mass destruction which inadvertently require concerted international response. The burgeoning wave of mass communication and internet has also increasingly diluted the state's ability to control the free flow of ideas within their borders adding to the advantage of the terror networks. The fundamental question for the 21st century global affairs is how readily the nations are inclined to nurture and uphold an international system to tackle these intricate problems.

Combating transnational terrorism requires multi-faceted policy responses from both the states and societies. Today, terrorism is dominated by different but intertwined trends often resulting in disturbing consequences. Local issues of contention in different regions of the world have also given a regional character to terrorism. In today's inter-connected world, the terror outfits have easier access to both support groups and financial aid that transcends national boundaries besides having sophisticated weapons and technology at its disposal. Furthermore, the prospect of terror networks gaining access to nuclear or biological weapons multiply arduous counter-terrorism challenges faced by the states, regions and societies. It has become abundantly clear that key global challenges for the 21st century-in environment, energy security or terrorism, to name a few, cannot be resolved by powerful countries acting alone or in alliance with one another.

Facing the Changed Realties

Though terrorism is not a new phenomenon, 9/11 attacks have manifested its global reach, level of organization, scale of attacks and the funds at its disposal.[5] No state, however powerful, can defend itself unilaterally against transnational terrorism. Counter terrorism strategies entail extensive coordinated cooperation on financial flows, intelligence, police action, and parallel action to curtail the social and political appeal of terrorism. Effective strategies to combat terrorism require states to (1) fulfill universal responsibilities not to sponsor, aid, or abet transnational terrorism; (2) take responsibility for the external impacts of conditions within their borders; (3) take responsibility for the well-being of their citizens, thereby diminishing the risk of terrorism; and (4) build adequate capacity to implement their responsibilities. [6] This can be achieved when powerful states driven by their self-interest also assist the weak states in building its capacity to shoulder the responsibility of promoting world peace and order. There must be "effective multilateralism, more shared responsibilities, less paranoia about sovereignty, more genuine acceptance of the idea of a global society and no more policies rooted in outdated concept of hegemonistic world order."[7] Thus, both individual and collective efforts by the nations are indispensable to counter the asymmetric and unpredictable character of this formidable menace.

New Zealand has strongly endorsed effective multilateralism and the rule of international law for long. Its foreign policy endeavours to maintain an essential mix of bilateral and multilateral diplomacy besides focusing on disarmament and non-proliferation. The sense of external threat in New Zealand is low owing to its strategic geographical location. However, geography cannot alone assure security in today's interconnected and globalized world. Today, the technology and communication revolution has cut down barriers for people. The nation is no longer shielded by the tyranny of its remoteness. Rules-based international system is crucial for New Zealand, as it lacks hard power and economic weight in the world. It is therefore more active in multilateral diplomacy, "seeking coalitions of like-minded interest and supporting even-handed negotiation where agendas and outcomes are fair to all involved."[8]

New Zealand government has strengthened its homeland security post 9/11 which includes the ability to deter, prevent and handle any acts of terrorism on its shore. It has significantly increased its intelligence, law enforcement, border and transport capabilities. The Bali bombings in October 2002 exposed the geographically insulated island to the reality and perils of terror threats in the neighbourhood. Undoubtedly, New Zealand's interests, values and world view will be determined by many factors like its demography, geopolitics, and the nature of collective responses to international threats regionally and globally. It continues to pursue foreign policy objectives through bilateral, regional and multilateral engagements. For instance, New Zealand's commitment to Asian multilateralism is also guided by a strong sense of self-interest. The building of strong, engaging and interactive forums like ASEAN, APEC, ADMM+, ASEAN Regional Forum and East Asia Summits will be advantageous to the country's interest.[9] The stakes for New Zealand, as it seeks to deepen its economic and political engagement with the world, have been high as it can't escape from proliferation of what have been described as 'problems without passports'.[10] The failure of the multilateral systems to address serious security and development challenges will affect New Zealand interests both directly, and indirectly.[11] The scope of the present article is to underscore the importance attached to multilateral governance system by New Zealand, in particular, to the United Nations.

The New Zealand Way

In New Zealand, terrorism was first legally defined in the 1977 Security Intelligence Service Act as: "planning, threatening, using or attempting to use violence to coerce, deter, or intimidate the lawful authority of the state of New Zealand; or the community throughout New Zealand or in any area in New Zealand with the purpose of furthering any political aim".[12] Following the 2001 attacks, New Zealand government implemented a number of legislative changes. It approved additional funding of almost $30 million for three years till June 2004 for initiatives at airports, increased provision of intelligence capacity and the establishment of a biochemical response capability.[13] The first police counter-terrorist squads came into being in 1977. Another Terrorist Emergency Group came into force in 1980s. The 1987 International Terrorism (Emergency Powers) Act brought censorship of local media in times of terrorist activity. Through the 1990s, New Zealand strived to reduce any possibility of chemical or biological threats or cyber attacks. In 2001, Terrorism (Bombing and Financing) Bill was passed to stem terrorist activities from the country. New Zealand's Ministry of Foreign Affairs and Trade, its principal aid agency NZAID, other government agencies, including the Police and border control agencies are also increasing their capacity to provide assistance to other countries in fighting global threats.

New Zealand has offered military assistance to the US-led 'War on Terror' by sending SAS troops to Afghanistan and by sending frigates to be part of the Maritime Interdiction Force in the Persian Gulf. In line with the UN Security Council resolution 1373 on counter-terrorism, New Zealand government enacted Terrorism Suppression Act (2001) which also highlighted the causes and targets of terrorism. Furthermore, the Counter Terrorism Act (2003) provided greater authority to the government agencies to detain, intercept and search goods and people to avert any act of terrorism. Besides, the New Zealand Provincial Reconstruction Team has helped in the nation building process of war-torn Afghanistan. New Zealand's significant contribution in the Bamyan province was to promote national resiliency to prevent re-emergence of terrorism.[14] Thus, individual state actions and multinational actions against terrorism are required to encourage greater anti-terrorism cooperation across the globe. New Zealand relied on United Nations' strong support for the early phase of 'War on Terror'. New Zealand has also relied on multilateral arms control and disarmament for long. It has advocated collective action to refashion the international security architecture.

As a strong advocate of multilateralism, New Zealand has also supported collaborative efforts in achieving progress on disarmament and non-proliferation issues. Though there is skepticism about the readiness, willingness and ability of the United Nations to deal with the global problems, the overwhelming challenges can be addressed by the United Nations done, provided it is unanimously given the requisite mandate and power to intervene for the world peace and order. The much-needed multiple reforms in the method of functioning, systems and priorities besides attitudes and policies of the member states will shape and determine the role of the international or global institutions in the 21st century. The multilateral organizations may not reflect the geopolitical realities and also do not offer the perfect forum for deliberations, yet, they represent a necessary high table of international affairs to discuss or settle any global crisis threatening world security and order. For instance, the Security Council can hold a government accountable for its action with respect to global peace and security.

New Zealand's bilateral, regional and multilateral engagements and its advocacy of rule-based environment through United Nations in particular are vital to its national interest. Prime Minister John Key, rightly noted in 2009 that during times of global uncertainty, small countries like New Zealand rely greatly on effective international rules to "help roll back protectionism, protect resources and deal with global challenges such as terrorism, weapons proliferation, climate change, the threat of pandemic and the effectiveness of international financial and economic institutions".[15] The successes against the menace of terror threats can only be achieved by multilateral, regional and bilateral engagements. There is a need to evolve an effective and collaborative way to combat these transnational threats. Thus, the coming years will witness an increasing engagement of the international community in responding to the challenges of terrorism.

Multilateralism Matters

Today, multilateralism operates at several levels both regionally and globally. The capitals of powerful, however, have exhibited little confidence in the capability of the UN system to operate effectively. Since its inception, the United Nations, grounded in a charter and accepted by all its members, constitutes a universal system to manage peace and prosperity. The international system provided the much needed safety valve by bringing the adversaries to a common discussion forum during the Cold War era. The issue of legitimacy vs. effectiveness of multilateral organizations in the realm of international governance has dominated the post Cold War era. For instance, the multilateral institutions were criticized for their responses during the 1997-98 East Asian economic crises. Nonetheless, one or more nations acting alone, no matter how powerful, cannot tackle multiple and complex challenges confronting the globalised and inter-connected world. Tackling issues like terrorism, proliferation of dangerous weapons, financial mismanagement, climate change etc. require collective action by governments acting in unison.

The 1990s and early 2000s crisis of multilateralism was triggered by the increasing assertiveness of rising regional and global powers which regarded the multilateral order as anachronistic. The BRIC countries i.e. Brazil, Russia, India and China and many other countries of the global South considered the contemporary world order as "frozen configurations of privilege and bias" which deprived them of their legitimate rights, denied them recognition as major powers and impeded their continued rise.[16] The emerging regional and global powers demanded an institutional order which catered to their aspirations and in which their past role as "rule takers" and their current role as "rule challengers" is increasingly substituted by the one in which they become partners in rule making.[17]

Divisive blocs have often impaired the functioning and efficiency of the United Nations. The five permanent members of the Security Council or the

P5 are often divided on issues. The 118 countries supporting the non-aligned movement and occupying two-third of the United Nation's membership have emerged as a powerful negotiating force within the system. Moreover, there is also a sort of coalition of the developing countries in the form of G-77. Though the blocs have sometimes facilitated faster solutions by engaging with a handful of negotiators, the fear of the reasonable voices being subsumed by a group position has loomed large. Scandals, bureaucratic problems, financial challenges and bloc politics have adversely affected the effective functioning of the United Nations over the years. Nonetheless, the United Nations has delivered comprehensive supervisory responsibilities at the request of its members, from nuclear activities to the conduct of elections and the observance of cease-fire agreements.

The emerging new world order and the changing geopolitics will dominate the international governance in the days ahead. The old bloc dynamics of the UN system will become increasingly outdated, as the new emerging multi-polar world unfolds itself, and more emerging economies will take a centre-stage place to assume the global challenges and responsibilities. China is swiftly gaining a central place in the world economy. Other regional players are also taking a centre-stage place in the 21st century geopolitical order. For the United States, reform of multilateralism has signified steps taken to invigorate its global leadership. Post 9/11 shock, the United States had resisted any idea of restraint upon its absolute autonomy to operate according to its perceived requirements and interests. Preventive wars of choice were declared, the aftermath of which remain in Afghanistan and the Middle East, as long-term tests for international governance.[18] President Obama, nonetheless, has recently maintained that the United States can no longer 'go it alone' in the ways of his predecessor, and wants to be involved with others in the management of international responsibility. [19] Thus, the geopolitical complexity of the 21st century created by the emergence of newly industrializing powers will continue to govern and shape the evolution of the multilateral forums.

The need to remodel and nourish the systems for international governance according to the changed global realities has become indispensable. It is important that the system of global multilateralism reflected in the United Nations is rehabilitated. For this to happen, the traditional managers like Britain, France and the United States will have to make the necessary concessions in the wake of the changing geopolitical realities. The alternatives, sometimes suggested in the form of G-20, or the adhoc coalitions of the willing or a globalised NATO may indeed provide a pragmatic solution to the impending problems, but will it be a be-fitting substitute for the global institutions in terms of providing collective safety and well-being still remains to be seen. The non-G-20 countries, New Zealand included, also known as 3G group view G-20 as a complement to, and not a substitute for, the United Nations.

New Zealand has a genuine stake in the effectiveness of the international institutions and legitimate interest in their future. Membership of regional groups like APEC, ASEAN, and Commonwealth gives New Zealand a platform to voice concerns over global security and development. New Zealand has benefited immensely by engaging with the multilateral forums. Under the UN Convention on the Law of the Sea (UNCLOS), New Zealand has a 4 million square kilometer exclusive economic zone (EEZ), the world's fourth largest. Under the United Nations' extended continental shelf regime, New Zealand's extended continental shelf covers 1.7 million square kilometers of seabed beyond the EEZ-six times the size of New Zealand—an outcome that could never have been achieved through bilateral negotiations.[20] For New Zealand, United Nations is the primary window through which most governments in the world view this country. The assistance given to New Zealand to recover from the grave crisis of the Christchurch earthquake underlines the importance of fighting intricate challenges together in an inter-connected world. Thus, the relevance of the multilateralism in the multi-polar 21st century is only likely to rise, as no single country can alone solve the complex problems confronting the world. The need of the hour is to make these institutions work effectively and efficiently.

Combating Terrorism Together

Terrorism demands deliberate, timely and effective responses from both the state and non-state actors. Addressing the Security Council of the United Nations in 2010, Secretary-General Ban Ki-Moon noted, "Terrorism may be gathering storm, but the international response is gathering steam. No cause or grievance can justify terrorism. Let me stress again the determination of the United Nations to rise to a global, cross-border challenge that seeks to do such harm to us all."[21] Two weeks after 9/11, the UN Security Council adopted Resolution 1373,[22] which obliges member states to enhance legislation, strengthen border controls, coordinate executive machinery, and increase cooperation in combating terrorism.[23] A task force on counter terrorism implementation was established in 2005 to ensure overall coordination and coherence in counter-terrorism efforts of the United Nations system. It was intended to enhance national, regional and international efforts to counter terrorism by strengthening state capacity to better coordinating United Nations system's counter-terrorism activities.

The United Nations General Assembly adopted resolution 64/297 in 2010 on the Global Counter-Terrorism Strategy which reaffirmed its' earlier Counter-Terrorism Strategies besides condemning terrorism in all its forms and manifestations, committed by whomever, wherever and for whatever purposes, posing one of the most serious threats to international peace and security. It reaffirmed the United Nations Global Counter-Terrorism Strategy and its four pillars, which constitute an ongoing effort, and calls upon member states, the United Nations and other appropriate international, regional and sub-regional organizations to step up their efforts to implement the Strategy in an integrated manner and in all its aspects.[24] The United Nations has also elaborated eighteen universal instruments (fourteen instruments and four amendments) against international terrorism relating to specific terrorist activities. The global strategy to counter terrorism strategy, in the form of a resolution and an annexed Plan of Action (A/RES/60/288), is a unique global instrument that will enhance national, regional and international efforts to counter terrorism. This is the first time that all member states have agreed to a common strategic approach to fight terrorism, not only sending a clear message that terrorism is unacceptable in all its forms and manifestation but also resolving to take practical steps individually and collectively to prevent and combat it.[25]

The horrific shock of 9/11 attacks and the resulting initiation of a US-led 'War on Terror' has undoubtedly changed the world view on the transnational threats. The tenth world Summit on Counter-Terrorism held in Herzliya, Israel in 2010 reiterated the Al-Qaeda threat to national, regional and international security. The Counter Terrorism Group (CTAG) set up by the G8 grouping makes resources available for meeting anti-terrorism requirements of the international community. The International Civil Aviation Organization has endorsed a new airline security strategy after 9/11 which includes mandatory audit on airport security and implementation of a comprehensive Aviation Security Plan of Action. The International Maritime Organization has similarly developed an extensive framework for maritime security. The Financial Action Task Force set up by G7 and operates out of the OECD in Paris has set new monitors against terrorist funding. Multilateral counter-terrorism strategies have been greatly supplemented by the regional initiatives. For instance, various forums like APEC has set up a Counter-Terrorism Task Force to deter the destructive threats posed to its goal of free trade and investment in the region. Besides these initiatives, there is also Malaysia based South-East Asia Regional Centre for Counter-Terrorism. In 2002, the Pacific Islands Forum adopted the Nasonini Declaration on Regional Security to counter security challenges in the region. Thus, a wide range of measures have been put in place since 11 September 2001. However, all effective action to counter terrorism has not always taken multilaterally.

Terrorism has widely been defined as an act or threat of violence undertaken for political purposes. The United Nations had passed resolutions and sanctions against Sudan's regime and the Taliban for providing safe haven to Al-Qaeda. Financial sanctions and terrorist deterrence with economic tools is one of the preferred forms of UN's counter-terrorism strategy. For instance, a Convention for the Suppression of Financing of Terrorism came into force in 2002 which defines terrorism as 'criminal and unjustifiable'. The initiatives taken by G-8, G-20 and other forums have also helped in articulating the responsibilities of states in dealing with terrorism at the regional level. Groups such as the

Organization of American States (OAS), the Organization for Security and Cooperation in Europe (OSCE), and the Asia Pacific Economic Cooperation (APEC) forum have adopted summit declarations, joint statements, or similar commitments to tackle terrorism.

NATO's role since the 9/11 attacks has also undergone a reappraisal. NATO controls an international force made up of 48 countries, 20 of which are not members of the alliance. The argument given in favour of NATO is that a broad international coalition with modern military capabilities is required to tackle the new security challenges. Its chemical, Biological, Radiological and Nuclear Defence Battalion and the NATO Response Force have been put in place to tackle specifically pressing requirements.[26] Recently, the U.N. Security Council mandated NATO forces for military intervention in Libya to protect civilians targeted during anti-regime protests. The Security Council adopted Resolution 1973, which imposed a no-fly zone in the country's airspace and authorized member states to take measures to protect civilians.[27] NATO helicopters and fighter jets also attacked two military border posts in northwest Pakistan on November 26, 2011. This latest incident provided the Pakistani army some breathing room which had faced strong criticism from both the Pakistani public and the United States after Osama bin Laden was killed in a secret raid by U.S. Special Forces in May. U.S. Secretary of State Hillary Clinton had asked Pakistan to bring all militant groups to the negotiating table in order to stabilize Afghanistan.[28]

The 2010 Lisbon summit of NATO confirmed that it will maintain an appropriate mix of conventional, nuclear and missile defence forces and bolster deterrence as a core element of the collective defence.[29] The alliance's engagements in Iraq and Afghanistan and more recently during the Arab uprising were backed by the United Nations. The United Nations and its array of experienced and specialized agencies have a track record of engaging in social and economic reconstruction programmes for years. They have an understanding of the global challenges and are equipped to tackle the crisis. Nonetheless, an integrated response is now needed to address the global threats with much greater co-operation between states, international organizations, international financial organizations, the private sector and non-governmental organizations.[30]

Conclusion

Multilateralism is one of the few viable ways to address complex issues in an emerging multi-polar world. There is a need for wider acceptance of the relevance of collective security based on the United Nations for world peace and security. Since 9/11, often people have argued over the relevance and efficacy of multilateralism. But, most of the effective actions to counter terrorism have been taken multilaterally. Threats of transnational terrorism have undoubtedly introduced new security challenges. Terrorism has to be fought continually with diplomatic, economic, political and legal instruments. The international campaign against terrorism can succeed only if it is sustained on a long-term basis and targets terrorist cells and networks.

Though the threat perception of direct attack is low in New Zealand, it has taken measures to comply with international obligations applicable to counter-terrorism. New Zealand has relied more on multilateral arms control and disarmament and the United Nations' strong support for counter-terrorism policies. The common desire of India and New Zealand to fight terrorism could be the imperative that would establish foundations for mutually beneficial partnerships both in their economic and security relations. There is a need for greater cooperation among the nations in the region and better engagement with extra-regional partners through multilateral arrangements. Terrorism is a direct challenge to the state's authority and legitimacy and merits forceful response. It can be stemmed only through concerted and sustained international effort. Thus, the persistent issue of international security and development challenges and the uncertain progress towards making the multilateral institutions more effective will continue to govern the world affairs in the future.

End Notes

1. Steve Coll, Ghost Wars: *The Secret History of the CIA, Afghanistan and Bin Laden, from the Soviet Invasion to September 10, 2001* (New York: Penguin Press, 2004), p. 51.
2. Hall Gardner, *American Global Strategy and the 'War on Terrorism'* (Brookfield: Ashgate Publishing Group, 2007), p. 53.
3. Bruce Hoffman, *Inside Terrorism*, (New York: Columbia University Press, 2006), p. 1.
4. Christopher C Harmon, *Terrorism Today*, (New York & London: Routledge, 2000), p. 128.
5. Dell Higgie, "Combating Terrorism," *New Zealand International Review*, 30.1 (2005), 3.
6. Bruce Jones et al., *Power and Responsibility: Building International Order in an Era of Transnational Threat* (Washington, DC: Brookings Institution Press, 2009), pp. 204-205
7. Shridath Ramphal, "Can Multilateralism Recover?" *New Zealand International Review,* 29.4 (2004), 4.
8. Terence O'Brien, "Facing the world the New Zealand Way", *New Zealand International Review,* 30.1 (January-February 2005), 25.
9. Robert Ayson, "New Zealand, Australia and the Asia-Pacific strategic balance: from trade agreements to defence white papers," *New Zealand International Review*, Vol. 36 (1), Jan-Feb. 2011, p. 2.
10. Winston Peters, "New Zealand Foreign Policy: the next five years," *New Zealand International Review,* 31.3 (2006), 2.
11. Ibid, pp. 2-3.
12. New Zealand Law Commission, Report No. 22: Final Report on Emergencies (Wellington, 1991), p. 189; as quoted in B.K Greener Barcham, "Combating Terrorism," *New Zealand International Review,* 29.3 (2004), p. 12.

13. Garth Den Heyer, "Anti-Terrorism: The Police Approach," *New Zealand International Review*, 31.2 (2006), 6.
14. Peter Nicholas, "Fighting Terrorism in Afghanistan," *New Zealand International Review*, 31.2 (2006), 3.
15. John Key, "Making a Difference in International Affairs," *New Zealand International Review*, 34.5 (2009), 6.
16. Barnett I. and Raymond Duvall, "Power in International Politics", *International Organization,* 59.1 (2005), 39-77.
17. Jurgen Ruland, "Southeast Asian Regionalism and Global Governance: 'multilateral utility' or 'hedging utility'?" *Contemporary Southeast Asia,* 33.1 (2011), 83.
18. Terence O'Brien, "Adjusting to a changing world," *New Zealand International Review,* 35.6 (2010), 18.
19. Terence O'Brien, "What is the true value of the United Nations? *New Zealand International Review*, 36.4, (2011), 18.
20. Jim McLay, "Tracing Our Un Footsteps," *New Zealand International Review*, 36.1, (2011), 15.
21. See "Efforts by Secretary-General to Counter Terrorism," Accessed 20 January, 2012, URL: http://www.un.org/terrorism/sg.shtml
22. See "UN action to Counter Terrorism" Accessed 21 January, 2012, URL: http://www.un.org/terrorism/
23. Bruce Jones et al., *Power and Responsibility: Building International Order in an Era of Transnational Threat* (Washington, DC: Brookings Institution Press, 2009), p. 215.
24. See "General Assembly Resolution A/RES/64/297 on the Global Counter Terrorism Strategy (2010),", Accessed 22 January, 2012, URL: http://daccess-dds-ny.un.org/doc/UNDO C/GEN/N09/479/65/PDF/N 0947965.pdf?OpenElement
25. See "United Nations General Assembly Adopts Global Counter-Terrorism Strategy," Accessed 22 January, 2012, URL:http://www.un.org/terrorism/strategy-counter-terrorism.shtm
26. Jaap de Hoop Scheffer, "NATO: A Forward Looking Alliance," *New Zealand International Review*, 30.3 (2005), 15.
27. NATO ends Libya mission, CNN Wire November 3, 2011, Accessed 25 November 2011, URL: http://edition.cnn.com/2011/10/31/world/africa/libya-nato-mission/index.html)
28. Chris Allbritton and Zeeshan Haider, "Enraged Pakistan says NATO attack threatens war on terror," Reuters.com, December 1, 2011, Accessed 2 December 2011, URL: http://www.reuters.com/article/2011/12/01/us-islamabad-idUSTRE7B00UH20111201
29. See "Lisbon Summit Declaration," November 20, 2010, Accessed 22 January, 2012, URL: http://www.nato.int/cps/en/natolive/official_texts_68828.htm
30. Claudia Bisogniero, NATO in a Globalised World, *New Zealand International Review*, 36.3 (2011), pp. 10-12.

8

New Zealand-China Relations in the 21st Century: NZ Perspective on Rising China

Anushree Chakraborty

New Zealand is a country distinguished for its geographical location in the world map. The country, far removed from the rest of the continental landmasses, is peacefully situated about 1,000 miles southeast of Australia in the South Pacific. The geographical isolation and the general prosperity in the country because of its primary activity-based economy account for its previous reticence and limited presence in the world affairs. However, the international politics has changed considerably since the post-Cold War period and so has New Zealand's conduct of foreign policy. According to Spykman, with the advancement of navigation and technology, geographical insularity no longer provides the almost perfect defense it once offered.[1] New Zealand therefore, is fully aware that its future prosperity and security is no longer separated from Asia despite the long nautical distance.

New Zealand's foreign relations have gradually expanded from its earlier focus on South Pacific and Australia to the Asia Pacific over the last two decades. Without any pretense of becoming a medium power unlike its' bigger and powerful neighbour Australia, New Zealand is presently seeking deeper linkages with the key partners in Asia and European Union.[2] Its' growing international trade and commitment to global issues makes it a valuable participant in the international affairs. Over the past two decades, New Zealand has transformed from an agrarian economy dependent on concessionary British market access to a more industrialized, free market economy that can compete globally.[3] Accordingly, in order to benefit from the economic dynamism in the Asia Pacific and to escape the strategic isolation as a result of its geography, New Zealand's foreign policy is investing a great deal in the evolving architecture of regional relationships in Asia.[4]

Wellington's inclusion in the East Asia Summit (EAS) meetings since 2005 highlights its growing profile in the Asia Pacific economic and strategic theatre. It realizes that the future of the country lies with Asia. The future course of the Asian regional architecture is expected to bear profound implications for its foreign and defence policies. In the Annual Report of 2003-04 published by the New Zealand Ministry of Foreign Affairs and Trade (MFAT), for the first time it is mentioned that closer engagement with the countries of Asia has become a priority in the country's foreign and trade policy.[5] Since the centre of gravity in the Asia Pacific affairs is shifting towards East Asia, more precisely, China; New Zealand has accordingly stepped up its high-level visits in Beijing and seeking closeness for deeper trade and cooperation. Therefore, it is pertinent to have a closer look at the present state of New Zealand's relation with the Asian superpower—China. This will provide a nuanced understanding of New Zealand's long-term position in the Asia Pacific and more broadly, in the Indo-Pacific architecture. India's increasing presence in the ASEAN affairs and its ambition to play a vital role in the security and stability of Asia Pacific region makes it imperative for New Delhi to analyse China's ties with the remaining EAS members, including New Zealand. Given the strengthening of bilateral ties between India and New Zealand and their growing interactions at the multilateral podium such as EAS, it is of considerable interest to understand New Zealand's links with the sole superpower in the Asia Pacific.

With this background, the current chapter aims to examine the evolving relation of New Zealand with China over the years. The primary aim of the chapter is to understand New Zealand's perspective of the Asian superpower – China, considering the fact that Wellington is currently an active participant of the Asia Pacific regional architecture. The study underlines that in addition to the traditional western allies including the US, Britain and Australia, over the last three decades, China has become the primary focus in New Zealand's foreign policy priority.

Historical Overview

Since 1792, New Zealand and China shared linkages through trade. The contact between the two became distinctive with the Chinese immigrant to New Zealand. The Chinese being first non-Maori, non-European migrated population in New Zealand came in large number as a result of two Otago invitations to Cantonese goldseekers in 1865. In the 1996 census, the Chinese population in New Zealand numbered 81,309 and was still the most numerous Asian group (40.8 per cent), comprising 2.25 per cent in all Asians of 5.5 per cent.[6] On the other hand, the New Zealanders came in direct contact with China through Christian missionary work. It was as early as 1898, when the New Zealand Presbyterian Church built the Canton Villages Mission in Guangdong, China. The missionary work carried out by individual New Zealanders in China expanded the health care services into rural Guangdong and provided educational opportunities to the poor Chinese. The work of these individuals brought awareness of China to their countrymen and created the much needed interest to understand the middle kingdom before its pre-1949 communist takeover.

New Zealand's early contact with China had less to do with their respective governments. The relationship between the two countries was established and carried forward by the common man in search for livelihood, trade, religious and political goals and adventures. Anne-Marie Brady cites example of Rewi Alley, the New Zealander who first went to China in 1927 to join a war (he hoped to get a job as a foreign mercenary fighting against the Northern Expedition) and eventually ended up as a world-renowned figure—first for his involvement in implementing industrial safety standards in Shanghai, and then for his key role in relief efforts in the Chinese cooperative movement.[7] Similarly, there are other figures such as, Iris Wilkinson, James Bertram and others, who contributed to New Zealanders' awareness, sympathy, and understanding of the problems China faced in the pre-1949 era.[8]

Despite the strong sympathies and willingness within the New Zealand government quarters towards People's Republic of China (PRC) since the late 1949, the relation between the two countries was not formally established before 1972. The delayed diplomatic ties were the result of New Zealand government's public pronouncement and diplomatic commitment to the US position contrary to the Beijing government during the Korean War in particular and the Cold War era in general. Nevertheless, there was much public pressure and considerable debate in New Zealand to recognize China. In 1956, a Prime Minister's Department memo commented that the New Zealand public seemed ready to recognise China "at any time the government wishes to accord it." The diplomatic community, however, was wary of such view considering that New Zealand could not recognise the PRC until its most important ally did so; otherwise it risked jeopardising the hard-won ties established between New Zealand and the US since Second World War.[9] Nevertheless, the absence of diplomatic relation neither hindered New Zealand citizens from visiting China nor disturbed the early resumption of New Zealand-China trade and the home official attitude towards the Chinese living in New Zealand. In fact, New Zealand became the first western country to lift its economic embargo on China in 1956.[10]

Political and Diplomatic Links

Notwithstanding the Cold War hiatus, there has been much political goodwill between China and New Zealand. New Zealand is in fact credited for having many "firsts" initiatives with China among the western world. In 2005, Prime Minister Helen Clark told *People's Daily* that New Zealand was "the first developed country to conclude a bilateral market access agreement with China for its entry to the World Trade Organization; the first to recognise China's status as a market economy and the first country to enter FTA negotiations with China." Ms Clark also noted that New Zealand was hoping to conclude a fourth first; to be the first developed country to conclude a FTA agreement with China.[11]

New Zealand has been sensitive to China's political overtures. As a result, it severed ties with Taiwan thereby diligently subscribing to the 'One China Policy' since 1972. During the Cold War, unlike its allies - the US and Australia, New Zealand government was positive about China's role in the security of the Asia Pacific. Wellington was rather skeptical about the moves of Soviet Union in the Asia Pacific region, and shared the Chinese opposition towards the encroachment of the former in the region. This made the two countries members of the same camp with their close proximity towards the US on the one hand and opposition to Soviet Union on the other.

Nonetheless, the political relation between China and New Zealand during the Cold War period was sluggish given that Cultural Revolution was gripping China domestically in the early years of Sino-New Zealand diplomatic ties. Initially, the relationship failed to go beyond formal contact. New Zealand's denunciation of China's nuclear testing and the latter's support to the Southeast Asian insurgent groups were the primary irritants. Despite these differences, in 1980 when New Zealand Prime Minister Robert Muldoon visited China, Wellington sought China's presence in the South Pacific claiming that the latter's presence would deter Soviet Union from penetrating this part of the world. Therefore, irrespective of the ups and downs between China and the western allies such as the US and Australia in the 1970s and thereafter during the Cambodian crisis, New Zealand maintained a stable relationship with the Beijing.

The political bonhomie between China and New Zealand continued during their more than three decades of diplomatic ties and in 2007, New Zealand and China celebrated 35 years of diplomatic relations. From New Zealand's perspective, China is an important country to engage considering it is the second-largest trading partner, and a major source of migrants, students and tourists, in addition to their partnership in regional and multilateral fora.[12] On the other hand, China valued New Zealand's ties with the Southeast Asian countries during the Cold War period when it failed to draw its southeastern neighbours under its influence. Moreover, it considers New Zealand an important partner in the multilateral fora in the present age of globalization. For example in 1997, New Zealand became the first western country to sign off on the bilateral paperwork which led to China being accepted into the WTO.[13] The diplomatic link between China and New Zealand enabled the relationship to forge cooperation into various fields including, education, cultural, scientific, sporting, art, medicines, journalism, mountaineering and trade-related contacts.[14]

The political ties between New Zealand and China accelerated during the

1980s when the governments of the two countries underlined their "special relationship" by drawing from past nostalgia. The convergence between their interests during this phase rested with their ambition to play an important role in the Asia Pacific architecture. Beijing sought a leadership role while having the confidence that its relationship with Wellington will draw the latter's support. Towards the end of the 1980s, the New Zealand – PRC bilateral relations reached the third phase, wherein pragmatism ruled thereby shedding the earlier rhetoric. This was the result of economic linkages getting the primary focus in response to the expanding Chinese market for the New Zealand exporters. In addition, the changing world order with the collapse of Soviet Union and the revelation of human rights abuses following the Tiananmen Square incident made New Zealand government prudent in forging its ties with the Beijing government. Notably, it was less critical as compared to its western allies such as the US and Australia in denouncing China's human rights issues, nevertheless, it raised human rights issues if not publicly but privately at bilateral meetings. However, recognizing the unprecedented opportunity coming from China's opening up of the economy, New Zealand began to focus more on trade rather than political issues during its interaction with Beijing. As a result, in the nineties, New Zealand's trade and other commercial linkages grew deeper with China.

The New Zealand government realized that a strong political foundation is required to build a lucrative economic relationship. As a result, greater emphasis was laid on regular high level visits by the two governments. In 2006, Chinese Premier Wen Jiabao visited New Zealand. The visit followed Cultural Agreement between New Zealand and the PRC, in addition to the Treaty on Mutual Legal Assistance in Criminal Matters. In 2007, New Zealand's Foreign Minister visited China, followed by the visit by the Trade Minister. In the same year, another landmark event was the opening of New Zealand's newest consular post in Guangzhou (southern China), taking the country's network of overseas posts to fourteen in the region. The cooperation between the two countries witnessed another exchange of notes for the agreement on Reciprocal Access for Airline Crew Members.

The relationship between the two countries reached its pinnacle with the signing of Free Trade Agreement (FTA) in April 2008. The FTA provided for comprehensive liberalisation of bilateral trade in goods and services as well as investment. Separate instruments also covered labour and environment cooperation between them. The MFAT initiated Track II dialogue in order to facilitate NZ Inc. activities in trade, tourism, education, science and technology and cultural promotion. Moreover, New Zealand's aid provided humanitarian responses during key global crisis areas, which includes earthquake in Sichuan, China in May 2008, thereby earning substantial goodwill among the Chinese populace. In this background, the visit of the Kiwi Premier John Key to China in April 2009 provided the necessary political momentum to accelerate the FTA between the two countries. During this visit, China described the relationship as being "at its best ever".[15] The unprecedented high level dialogue between the two sides encouraged them to seek common ground. For example, China was the first nuclear-weapon state to support the UN resolution led by New Zealand to de-alerting nuclear weapons, which is a key measure to reduce the risk of a nuclear exchange. Similarly, both countries opposed the US invasion of Iraq.[16]

Nevertheless, there are pitfalls in the relationship. One particular domestic concern of New Zealand involves the activities of the Chinese Diaspora in the Pacific. The social anxiety about issues such as violent crimes involving Chinese overseas students and drug smuggling often traced back to China complicates New Zealand's relationship with Beijing.[17] Moreover, New Zealand has raised human rights issues from time to time in bilateral interactions with the Chinese government, despite causing discomfort to the latter.[18] Most notably, New Zealand realizes that it is insignificant and small from the Chinese perspective. Beijing is too big and powerful to depend upon New Zealand's diplomatic support or trade linkages. If New Zealand challenges China on an issue that it regards as crucial, Beijing is likely to respond by removing trade and other privileges. Because of this realization, of late, New Zealand officials are cautious to avoid offending Chinese sensibilities.[19] Unlike its ties with the traditional allies wherein Wellington took steps independent of its allies' stand, relations with China appear timid and less independent.

China-New Zealand Economic Interaction

Given the island economy status and the associated locational hazards, trade promotion has been an integral part of New Zealand's foreign policy. Accordingly, the New Zealand government renamed the Ministry of Foreign Affairs to Ministry of Foreign Affairs and Trade. One of the stated objectives of New Zealand's foreign policy is developing relationships and trade access that will improve New Zealand's economic performance. As a result, New Zealand focuses its energy in building ties with the Asia Pacific countries. The economic dynamism and the regional economic institutions in the Asia Pacific region are enabling an environment of greater trade facilitation and New Zealand is keen to gain from the current dynamism. Asia is presently home to ten of the top twenty export markets. Almost forty per cent of New Zealand's total trade is with the region.[20] Therefore, the continent gets special attention in New Zealand foreign policy. China being the growth engine of the current ongoing economic dynamism in the Asia Pacific region holds a special position for New Zealand in this context. The political ease in the Sino-New Zealand relationship has provided the necessary impetus in boosting their economic ties as well. In fact, the strategic perceptions of the two countries shape their commercial engagement. The New Zealand-China relationship reached a higher plane after the visit by President Hu in 2003 and the decisions to strengthen consular, trade and economic cooperation followed subsequently.[21]

China and New Zealand signed the FTA in 2008, and the FTA entered into force from 1 October 2008 onwards. China is expected to bring their tariff rate to zero in a significant number of commodities by 2012, while New Zealand has already done so for several product categories. The FTA intends to liberalise bilateral trade in goods and services and investment. It is expected to improve trade facilitation between the partners through a number of associated provisions on sanitary and phytosanitary (SPS) measures, technical barriers to trade (TBT), intellectual property etc. In addition, the FTA has provided greater impetus for cooperation in other areas as well. For instance, China / New Zealand Film Co-Production Agreement in July 2010 and New Zealand's first currency swap arrangement with China, agreed in 2011, deserve mention in this regard. The deeper engagement between the two sides has also led to the conclusion of arrangements on fruit access, live seafood access and meat premises with China.

The cross-sectoral trend in the bilateral trade between China and New Zealand is summarized in Table 1, which reveals an interesting picture. Since mid-nineties, New Zealand enjoyed a trade surplus with respect to China upto 2004. However, during 2005-08, the manufacturing export from China to New Zealand increased considerably and the balance of trade shifted in the former's favour. The scenario underwent another sea change in the aftermath of the FTA between two sides in 2008. From 2009 onward, the export of both primary and manufacturing products from New Zealand increased significantly. On the other hand, while the Chinese export of manufacturing products increased considerably to New Zeeland, the growth in their primary export in the post-FTA phase has been modest. The last column of Table 1 reveals that in 2010 New Zealand has a huge trade deficit in manufacturing segment vis-à-vis China, but the same is more than compensated with an even greater agricultural export surplus.

Table 1: Bilateral Trade between China and New Zealand (US$ Bn)

Year	China's Export to New Zealand		China's Import from New Zealand		Balance of Trade Overall
	Agriculture	Manufacturing	Agriculture	Manufacturing	
1996	0.16	2.15	0.77	3.26	-1.71
2000	0.10	4.06	2.20	4.17	-2.21
2005	0.46	13.08	5.31	7.95	0.27
2010	1.04	26.60	18.97	18.66	-9.99

Source: Calculated by the Author from WITS data.

The evolving nature of the trade basket between the two countries also reveals an interesting picture. Table 2 compares the major export items of China to New Zealand between 1996 and 2010. In general, a decline in the relative importance of primary products (e.g. cotton) and low value-added semi-skilled labour-intensive products (inorganic chemicals, leather, fabric, apparel and clothing etc.) in Chinese export basket can be noted from the table. On the other hand, sharp increase in the proportional presence of certain pollution-intensive low-tech product groups (plastic and rubber) and several high-value technology-intensive products (iron and steel, machinery and equipments, electrical machinery etc.) is witnessed. The observation is clearly in line with the growing diversified manufacturing base of China in recent years.

Table 2: China's Evolving Export Composition to New Zealand (per cent)

Commodity Group	1996	2010
Inorganic chemical	4.22	1.38
Organic chemicals	1.83	2.10
Fertilizers	0.04	2.51
Plastics and articles thereof	2.48	3.94
Rubber and articles thereof	0.55	1.71
Articles of leather etc.	1.88	1.13
Paper & paperboard etc.	0.36	2.11
Cotton	2.00	0.07
Knitted or crocheted fabrics	2.19	0.11
Articles of apparel & clothing accessories, knitted or crocheted	14.62	8.84
Articles of apparel & clothing accessories, not knitted or crocheted	16.91	5.73
Other made up textile articles	6.30	2.88
Footwear, gaiters and the like	3.71	2.55
Ceramic products	1.63	1.09
Articles of iron or steel	2.33	4.65
Nuclear reactors, boilers, machinery & equipments	4.33	15.21
Electrical machinery and equipments	7.58	13.78
Vehicles, auto-parts and components	1.56	2.03
Furniture; bedding, mattress etc.	1.91	6.70
Toys, games & sports requisites	3.45	2.12

Source: Calculated by the Author from WITS data.

On the other hand, the changing composition of New Zealand's export to China reveals an equally remarkable scenario. In 1996, more than fifty percent of New Zealand's export was explained by agricultural and processed primary products (e.g. marine products, animal fats, articles of wool etc.). While the importance of the primary products remains intact in New Zealand's export basket to China in the post-FTA phase, the proportional importance has not. Given the sharp increase in population in China, the importance of meat products, preparation of cereals, dairy products etc. has increased over this period. The proportional importance of wool, to be used as raw material in China's apparel export, has declined over the years, which partially signifies China's move towards synthetic fibre based product groups. On the other hand, within the manufacturing segment, the proportional importance of wooden articles has increased. Tables 2 and 3 jointly indicate that the export basket diversification has been limited for New Zealand vis-à-vis China.

Table 3: New Zealand's Evolving Export Composition to China (Per cent)

Commodity Group	1996	2010
Meat and edible meat offal	0.46	2.61
Fish & crustacean, mollusks & other marine products	4.92	2.57
Dairy products etc.	1.47	34.58
Animal/vegetable fats & oils	8.53	2.03
Preparations of cereal, flour, starch/milk	0.01	4.73
Residues & waste from food products	1.74	0.84
Ores, slag and ash	0.75	1.83
Mineral fuels, oils & processed products	4.47	2.92
Organic chemicals	4.74	1.13
Albuminoidal substances; modified starches etc.	0.09	1.78
Plastics and articles thereof	0.78	1.26
Raw hides and skins	8.82	2.02
Wood and articles of wood	4.63	24.93
Pulp of wood/of other fibrous celluloid etc.	2.50	3.79
Paper & paperboard etc.	4.61	1.19
Wool, fine/coarse animal hair etc.	41.61	5.21
Iron and steel	0.65	0.11
Nuclear reactors, boilers, machinery & equipments	3.87	0.72
Electrical machinery and equipments	0.97	1.06

Source: Calculated by the Author from WITS data.

The trade integration through the FTA has been crucial for New Zealand to maintain its presence in the Chinese market. For instance, in 2009 the discovery of melamine in dairy products produced by Fonterra's (a major dairy producer in New Zealand) partner in China could have led to serious problems. However, both sides were successful in managing the situation without damage to key political relationships in China or New Zealand's reputation as a producer. The official statement by the Chinese authorities strongly aired their unaltered regard for New Zealand, and Fonterra, as long-term dairy partners. As a result, New Zealand's access to the Chinese market on dairy sector did not suffer, which is reflected from Table 3 as well.

Despite the trade surplus enjoyed by New Zealand in the Chinese market, its economic relevance for the middle kingdom is still limited. It is observed from Diagram 1 that the country's share in China's export basket has increased from 0.15 percent in 1996 to a meager 0.18 percent in 2010. On the other hand, the corresponding figures for China's import basket has been 0.29 percent in 1996, but declined to 0.18 percent by 2007. The trade growth resulting from the FTA has increased the share of New Zealand in China's import to a modest figure of 0.29 percent in 2010. Conversely, China's share in New Zealand's export basket currently stands at 11.51 percent as compared to 2.62 percent in 1996, while its share in New Zealand's import basket has been 15.96 percent and 3.72 percent in that order. In particular, the growing importance of the Chinese market for New Zealand's exporters in the post-bloc period deserves special attention. While China's presence in New Zealand's export basket was 5.52 percent in 2007, the same increased to 6.11 percent in 2008, 9.57 percent in 2009 and finally to 11.51 percent in 2010. Clearly, the degree of dependence of New Zealand on China has deepened after formation of the FTA. However, the converse is not true.

Diagram 1: Relevance of China and New Zealand in each other's market

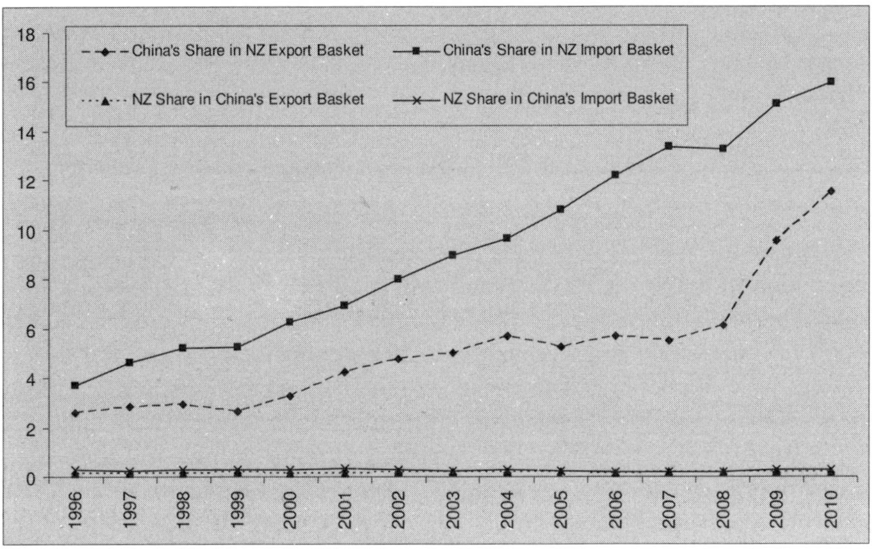

Source: Constructed by the Author from WITS data.

South Pacific Islands

In addition to the geographical proximity, a large number of New Zealand population shares ethnic ties with the Pacific people. New Zealand Maoris are Polynesian people and therefore there is deep political linkage and cultural affinity between them and the Oceanic Island countries. People from the Pacific Islands have been in New Zealand for over a hundred years. In 1991, there were 167,000 (4.9 percent) Pacific people in New Zealand and in 2001 more than 231,802 (6.5 percent) were living in the country. In 2006, it had risen to just under 266,000 people, and increase of 15 per cent since 2001.[22]

Accordingly, New Zealand shares a special relation with the Polynesian Island countries and takes primary responsibility towards the oceanic region. It includes Kiribati, Tuvalu, Samoa (part of which is an American flag territory), Tonga, Cook Islands, Niue and Tokelau, which tend to be oriented to New Zealand through treaties, diplomacy, migration, and aid links.[23] The New Zealand Government allocated $586 million to official development assistance (ODA) in 2010/11 for the region. New Zealand's international development assistance is scheduled to increase over time to $620 million in 2014/15.[24]

Table 4: New Zealand's Aid Flows to Select Pacific Island Countries (2010)

Country	Amount Spent $ NZ	% of Total Expenditure
Cook Islands	18,947,308	4
Kiribati	8,7811,321	2
Niue	23,747,706	5
Pacific Regional	60,273,938	12
Papua New Guinea	31,415,435	6
Samoa	18,465,556	4
Solomon Islands	33,350,815	7
Tokelau	20,496,211	4
Tonga	14,608,991	3
Vanuatu	16,658,886	3

Source: New Zealand MFAT website.[25]

During the Cold War period, New Zealand's primary concern was Soviet penetration in the South Pacific Island countries. The 1970s and 1980s saw the Soviet Union offering aid and other economic benefits to island governments in return for port access and diplomatic ties. Consequently, New Zealand and its Western allies were obliged to make economic counter-offers and pay more attention to local political demands in order to maintain their collective influence in the Pacific region.[26] During this period, in order to counter Soviet presence in the South Pacific region, New Zealand government invited China to the region and was keen to collaborate with Beijing in the development and stability of the Island countries. In fact, New Zealand considered the involvement of external actors as a welcome supplement to the region's prospects.[27]

The end of the Cold War faded the interest generated among the western players towards this region. In fact, there was complete withdrawal in the early 1990s of British diplomats and the ending of United States aid for all but US dependencies.[28] With the end of the Cold War rivalry and beginning of the New World Order and subsequent change in the strategic architecture with the emergence of China, another phase of rivalry for influence in the Pacific island region began. This brought in new source of aid, diplomatic support and other assistance in the region. China became the main player surrounding whom the region received increasing focus in the international diplomatic efforts.

The Pacific Island countries have in the last two decades become small yet significant for the Chinese foreign policy. The natural resources of some of these islands have been the driver in view of latter's economic growth, for instance, the natural gas and minerals in Papua New Guinea. But the primary motivation has been to gain support of the island states on a range of political issues, most notably its ongoing efforts to isolate Taiwan. Taiwan is relatively successful in Oceania, claiming the support of six island states, but is unlikely to able to sustain its aid-based efforts in the face of China's superior resources.[29]

China's increasing presence in the Pacific island region has raised concern among other regional players. The US and other western allies are particularly skeptical despite little sign of instability with the Chinese presence. The US officials talk about keeping the island states "firmly on our side."[30] Japan, in its' effort to counter the Chinese presence, is taking renewed interest. The Malaysia and Singapore remain modest aid donors. However, New Zealand has been reluctant to criticize China's growing profile in the region. In the Annual Report of 2005-06, the MFAT mentioned New Zealand's increased levels of engagement on Pacific issues with other external partners particularly, the European Union and China.[31] New Zealand's Minister of Defence and Pacific Islands Affairs, Phil Goff described China's presence as a "growing reality," but urged Beijing to work in partnership with other donors and "pay proper heed to the interests of the Pacific."[32]

Perspective on Rising China

Although New Zealand has not been vocal as compared to its western allies in advocating threat from rising China, nevertheless, it has been prudent to realize the implications of China's rise. The Defence White Paper 2010 published by the New Zealand government provides a view of its' strategic thinking towards China's rise. The document mentions, "The strategic balance in North Asia is shifting. China both benefits from and contributes to regional stability and prosperity, but there will be a natural tendency for it to define and pursue its interests in a more forthright way on the back of growing wealth and power. The pace of China's military modernization and force projection programme, and the response this could prompt from neighbouring states, may test the relationships of the major regional powers".[33] The White Paper considers a range of objectives while submitting that the New Zealand Defense Force intend to "support strategic stability and promote New Zealand's interests in the Asia-Pacific region with military assets". One of the objectives highlighted in the Paper underlines, "China's increasing power managed constructively".[34] This hints at common ground reached between Wellington's strategic position and other major players in the Asia Pacific region.

New Zealand's perception on China's unprecedented rise as a major power, can be understood from its outlook on India as well. Despite limited interaction with India so far, in the Defence White Paper 2010, New Zealand government assesses India's growing power as "more an opportunity for New Zealand than a threat". The Paper sanguinely mentions that "this is likely to be reflected in greater military engagement". However, similar optimism is absent while assessing

Wellington's "special relationship" with China. Moreover, the Defence White Paper highlights that New Zealand, like Australia, seeks a continued strong US presence in the Asia Pacific region. This is primarily because the balance of power in the Asia Pacific is shifting with the rise of China and the US as a formidable player in the region will ensure sustainable balance in the future.

New Zealand's involvement in the Southeast Asian regional institutions also underlines its willingness to help sustain positive major power relations, particularly involving the rising China. Since 1994, New Zealand has been an active participant of ASEAN Regional Forum. The MFAT Annual Report 2002 -2003 mentions that New Zealand made consistent effort to influence the path underway to adapt or add to existing regional bodies linking South East and North Asia, and to develop new links between South and Southeast Asia, as the region continues to position itself to address the growing influence of China as a major economic and political power.[35] As a result, New Zealand is forthcoming on the US and Russian membership in the EAS.[36] Therefore, New Zealand's perspective on the rising China adopts a middle ground, wherein on the one hand, it is seeking peaceful relationship with the rising China, while cautiously not bandwagoning in order to look for its approval.

The importance of the Asia Pacific stability and security can be underlined from New Zealand's commitment to the Five Power Defence Arrangements (FPDA) set up more than forty years ago for the external defence of Malaysia and Singapore. The Defence White Paper 2010 states, "As New Zealand's most significant operational security link to Southeast Asia, the FPDA will continue to provide a valuable anchor for the presence of our defence assets in the region". In fact, the White Paper brings to the light that the New Zealand government seeks a defence force which is able to deploy beyond their immediate region – that is, it wants to send a message that Asia matters.[37]

It is significant to note that New Zealand maintains prudence as compared to its closest ally Australia while assessing China's rise. This is primarily because of the geographical remoteness as well as the protection it gets from the Australian continent.[38] In addition, New Zealand's sense of itself as a small player, its limited resources and hard power and its' disinclination to take strategic risk in terms of posting military assets beyond the South Pacific region, makes it watchful while talking about China and its increasing military prowess as compared to its Tasman neighbour—Australia. As a result, Wellington is vigilant not to antagonize China and increasingly makes efforts to create an environment which would draw maximum benefit from China's rise. Accordingly, New Zealand's official line emphasizes on constructively engaging China in the international institutions. In 2003, New Zealand Prime Minister Helen Clark stated in an interview with *The Guardian* that (among other reasons) she opposed the Iraq War because it set a precedent of large powers ignoring the United Nations and international law. She used China as an example of exactly to whom this might set a bad example.[39] Therefore, while Wellington is in no denial that China's rise is the leading feature in shaping the Asian security landscape, nevertheless, New Zealand's defence capabilities in terms of its' respective relevance for advanced combat operations in maritime East Asia as compared to Canberra does not make it a serious potential contributor in shaping the strategic space at the helm of major power competition in the Asia Pacific. Therefore, Wellington's stand on China appears less assertive as compared to Canberra.

Conclusion

The most conspicuous aspect of New Zealand-PRC relations has been the independent path Wellington has followed despite its commitment towards the traditional western allies. From the 19th century, New Zealanders have had extended their warmth and support to China, irrespective of their governments' efforts. This warmth was transformed to deeper appreciation and understanding between the two governments when the Cold War dynamics provided them the opportunity to formally establish contacts. Gradually, New Zealand became first among the western countries in facilitating several opportunities for China to engage in the international podium. In the 21st century, aware of the changing global strategic landscape, New Zealand recognizes China as the major power, next only to the US.

In the last two decades, New Zealand government has taken steps to seek China's close proximity. One of the motivations has been "intensified engagement at leaders' level and below, especially with China, allows New Zealand to register and advance its interests in the future stability and prosperity of the (Asia Pacific) region".[40] Nonetheless, New Zealand is aware of challenges ahead of China's rise. As a result, it is currently engaging other Asia Pacific players such as Japan and India. Therefore, despite New Zealand's limited strategic role in the Asia Pacific regional architecture and scarce resources at hand as compared to other EAS players, its special relationship with China encourages the latter to engage constructively in international affairs.

End Notes

1. Nicholas J. Spykman, "Geography and Foreign Policy, II", *The American Political Science Review*, 32 (2) April, 1938, p. 216.
2. Annual Report 2009-10, Ministry of Foreign Affairs and Trade, New Zealand Government website, URL: http://www.mfat.govt.nz/downloads/media-and-publications/annual-report/annualreport09-10.pdf, p.18.
3. New Zealand GDP Growth Rate, URL: http://www.tradingeconomics.com/new-zealand/gdp-growth (Accessed on 2 November 2011).
4. Ibid. n. 1.
5. Annual Report of 2003-04, Ministry of Foreign Affairs and Trade, New Zealand Government website, URL: http://www.mfat.govt.nz/downloads/media-and-publications/annual-report/mfatannualreport2003-2004.pdf, p.12.

6. James Ng, "Chinese settlement in New Zealand, past and present", October 2001, URL: http://www.stevenyoung.co.nz/The-Chinese-in-New-Zealand/History-of-Chinese-in-NewZealand/Chinese-settlement-in-NZ-past-and-present.html, (Accessed on 11 November 2011).
7. Anne-Marie Brady, "New Zealand-China Relations: Common Points and Differences", *New Zealand Journal of Asian Studies,* 10 (2) December 2008, p. 3.
8. Ibid. p. 4.
9. Ibid. p. 5.
10. Ibid.
11. "New Zealand Aims to Conclude FTA Talks with China First," URL: http://english.peopledaily.com.cn/200505/31/eng20050531_187594.html (Accessed on 19 November 2011).
12. New Zealand Embassy Beijing website, "New Zealand and China", URL: http://www.nzembassy.com/china/relationship-between-new-zealand-and-china/new-zealand-and-china, (Accessed on 20 October 2011).
13. Huiping Tan and Li Cai, "Quantitative Analysis on the Impact of China-New Zealand FTA on Both Sides' Economies", *International Review of Business Research Papers,* 6 (6): December 2010, p. 133.
14. n. 5 Ibid., p. 11.
15. Annual Report 2008-09, Ministry of Foreign Affairs and Trade, New Zealand Government website, URL: http://www.mfat.govt.nz/downloads/media-and-publications/annual-report/ar-mfat-2008-09.pdf p. 19.
16. Attacking Iraq-International Reaction, URL: http://www.globalsecurity.org/military/ops/iraq-view.htm (Accessed on 5 December 2011).
17. Deborah Coddington, "Asian Angst: Is it Time to Send Some Back?" *North and South,* November 2006 quoted in Anne-Marie Brady (2008), p. 18.
18. Annual Report 2002-03, Ministry of Foreign Affairs and Trade, New Zealand Government website, URL: http://www.mfat.govt.nz/downloads/media-and-publications/annual-report/mfatannualreport02to03.pdf, p. 57.
19. n. 5 Ibid., p. 18.
20. Background Note: New Zealand, U.S. Department of State, URL: http://www.state.gov/r/pa/ei/bgn/35852.htm (Accessed on 6 December 2011).
21. Annual Report 2003-04, Ministry of Foreign Affairs and Trade, New Zealand Government website, URL: http://www.mfat.govt.nz/downloads/media-and-publications/annual-report/mfatannualreport2003-2004.pdf, p. 43.
22. Colin Tukuitonga, "Pacific Peoples in New Zealand", URL: http://www.mcnz.org.nz/portals/0/publications/coles/006%20-%20george.pdf, (Accessed on 29 October 2011).
23. Stephen Hoadley, "Pacific Island Security Management by New Zealand and Australia: Towards a New Paradigm", Working Paper no. 20/05, Centre for Strategic Studies, Victoria University of Wellington, URL: http://www.victoria.ac.nz/css/docs/Working_Papers/WP20.pdf (Accessed on 28 November 2011).
24. New Zealand MFAT website, NZAID Programme, URL: http://www.aid.govt.nz/about-aid-programme/aid-statistics/20102011-annual-statistics (Accessed on 2 December 2011).
25. Ibid.
26. Ibid., n. 23, p. 5.
27. Interview of Rt Hon Mike Moore, New Zealand's Ambassador to the United States, *The Diplomat,* URL: http://the-diplomat.com/new-leaders-forum/2011/09/27/new-zealand-in-asia/ (Accessed on 2 November 2011).
28. Ibid., n. 18, p. 8.

29. Terence Wesley-Smith, "China in Oceania: New Forces in Pacific Politics," East-West Center, URL: http://www.eastwestcenter.org/fileadmin/stored/pdfs/pip002_1.pdf (Accessed on 2 December 2011).
30. Ibid., p. 5.
31. Annual Report 2005-06, Ministry of Foreign Affairs and Trade, New Zealand Government website, URL: http://www.mfat.govt.nz/downloads/media-and-publications/annual-report/annualreport0506.pdf p. 10.
32. Ibid., n. 23.
33. The New Zealand Ministry of Defence website, Defence White Paper 2010, URL: http://www.defence.govt.nz/reports-publications/defence-white-paper-2010/contents.html (Accessed on 11 October 2011), p. 30.
34. For details, see Robert Ayson, "Force and Statecraft: Strategic Objectives and Relationships in New Zealand's 2010 Defence White Paper", *Security Challenges*, Vol. 7, No. 1 (Autumn 2011), pp. 11-29.
35. Annual Report 2002-03, Ministry of Foreign Affairs and Trade, New Zealand Government website, URL: http://www.mfat.govt.nz/downloads/media-and-publications/annual-report/mfatannualreport02to03.pdf, p. 9.
36. New Zealand Foreign Minister, Murray McCully Speech on "Future of Asia" Conference, Tokyo, Japan, 27 May 2011, URL: http://www.beehive.govt.nz/speech/nikkei-shimbun-%E2%80%9Cfuture-asia%E2%80%9D-conference-tokyo-japan, (Accessed on 28 November 2011).
37. Robert Ayson, "China's Rise: South Pacific Perspectives—New Zealand and Australian Security Perceptions of China", Associate Paper, Future Directions International, 12 September 2011, URL: http://futuredirections.org.au/publications/associate-papers/218-chinas-rise-south-pacific-perspectives-new-zealand-and-australian-security-perceptions-of-china.html (Accessed on 6 December 2011).
38. Robert Ayson raises the point that Australia's closer proximity to East Asia, and its more intense historical experience of Japan's rise in power in the Second World War period versus New Zealand's sense of relative isolation adds to the trans-Tasman difference of relative position on implications of China's rise. For details, see Ayson 2011, n. 22.
39. Ibid., n. 7, p. 13.
40. Annual Report of 2006-07, Ministry of Foreign Affairs and Trade, New Zealand Government website, URL: http://www.mfat.govt.nz/downloads/media-and-publications/annual-report/annualreport0607.pdf, p. 35.

9

India and New Zealand: the Evolving Domain in East Asian Community Building

Tridib Chakraborti and Mohor Chakraborty

In the chronology of Asian history, this region experienced a history of colonial domination. This colonial domination and the exploitation by the colonial powers and their legacies still have a lingering effect on the soil of these countries. Asia as an emerging force since the end of the Second World War never came into prominence, and their development was further retarded on account of Cold War politics. As against such background, regionalism and the development of multilateral institutions never came into limelight as an identity of the Asian countries, except the formation of ASEAN in 1967 and SAARC in 1985. What happened in Asia and Africa was a resurgence of the existing mindset for the survival of the weak and less developed economies of the region, which ultimately led to a movement under the leadership of Jawaharlal Nehru, Nasser and Tito, known as non-alignment. In fact, the countries of the Third World, in spite of their internal differences were oxygenated through this movement and they used the UN General Assembly as a vehicle for expressing their protest and thereby voicing their demands against the developed countries of the world. In 1974, on account of their growing strength, the Third World countries raised the issue of a New International Economic Order (NIEO), which ultimately became a futile exercise and failed to obtain the demands made by the developing countries of their developed counterparts. They initiated an alternative movement for their economic development, which was known as South-South Cooperation. In spite of severe differences among the developing countries on several issues, the South-South experience in the cold war years, flavoured with NAM made many countries of the South gather an experience of how to deal with the developed world in the then global milieu.

The situation was drastically altered with the sudden fall of the Soviet Union and emergence of the New Global Order, pinpointed with the globalization and liberalization processes. Initially, the paradigms of globalization and liberalization put many countries of the South in hardship, due to their asymmetrical political and economic structures. However, today, because of the past experience against the developed world, many of these Asia-Pacific countries are strengthening their economic clout and, thereby, emerging as economic hubs in their respective sub-regions, such that even the Western world now describes the 21st Century as the Asian Century and that feeling has been percolated within the psyche of the Asian countries themselves. The most important component of the 21st Century is that the economic growth, coincident with the strategic importance of countries like India, China, Japan, South Korea, Australia, Singapore, Malaysia, etc, has placed them as frontal powers. Moreover, since the end of the Cold War era, the issue of multilateralism, with the performance of regional blocks established earlier, as well as the formation of new sub-regional organizations, has made it imperative that their development would depend on regional cooperation, which will be the backbone of regional community building. From this perspective, the emergence of the East Asian community in the present juncture is visualized to be the most viable ground to develop cooperation among the regional countries.

The rising hotspot of East Asia brought India and New Zealand under one umbrella, against the backdrop of their convergence of national and economic interests due to their changing mindset in the post-Cold War global milieu. Both New Delhi and Wellington are full dialogue partners of ASEAN and signatories of TAC, where ASEAN acts as a linking bridge between them. The dividend of this linking was clearly evident when India and New Zealand participated in the ASEAN-initiated First East Asia Summit (EAS) held in 2005 at Kuala Lumpur, and thereby gave a better space to interact with each other. The purpose of this article is to highlight the rationale behind the proximity between India and New Zealand in the context of the evolving community-building space, within the framework of the East Asia Summit.

The Evolving New Global Order and Multilateralism in the Asia-Pacific

Regionalism is a challenge in Asia, given the diverse political and economic systems and differences based on historical legacy and sovereignty issues between and among member states. The notion of community-building in the Asia Pacific region can be traced back to the theory of social constructivism, developed and theorized by Alexander Wendt in the early 1990s. The theory of social constructivism emphasizes the essence of ideational factors in the constitution of individual national interests of states, thereby demonstrating it as a process of inter-activity with other agents in a social system that determines the understanding of the structure of that particular system. Moreover, constructivism's appeal lies in the possibility of a transformative international political system, by which "egoists learn to cooperate in, at the same time, the process of reconstructing their interests in terms of shared commitments to social norms. Over time, this will tend to transform a positive interdependence of 'outcomes' into a positive interdependence of 'utilities' or collective interest organized around the norms question. The 'process of cooperating' will assist in reconstituting identities and interests in terms of new inter-subjective understandings and commitments."[1] Broadly speaking, regionalism may be defined as 'structures, processes and arrangements that are working towards greater coherence within a specific international region in terms of economic, political, security, socio-cultural and other kinds of linkages.[2] In keeping with the central premise of the theory of social constructivism, the nation-states of the Asia Pacific, under the framework of ASEAN, established a phenomenon of interactive communication and exchange on a plethora of social, political, economic and strategic issues, thus transcending the debilitating burden of self-interested, competitive state relations. This initiative merged with the period in international relations, when Asia was undergoing a transformation, not only in terms of the perceptions of being an integral part of 'broader Asia', but also of including countries like China, Japan, South Korea, India, Australia and New Zealand, within its scheme of things. Since ASEAN played a crucial role in the process of regional community building through different mechanisms, this socialization process demonstrated that the "East Asian region is so closely connected in political, economic, social and ecological terms that it is impossible to consider one state's fate independently from another."[3] Logically then, in the context of enhanced multillateralism and economic interdependence in the wake of the onset of globalization, the Asia Pacific region has traversed the path of greater interdependence and institutionalization, accompanied by the three northeast Asian states—China, Japan and South Korea on the one hand—and India, Australia and New Zealand on the other, within the EAS framework.

However, the trajectory of community-building in the Asia Pacific region had its fair share of ups and downs. The first hope for multilateralism in this region emerged from the formation of APEC, in the immediate aftermath of the demise of the cold war, as a vehicle for the promotion and facilitation of free trade and greater economic integration in the region. Shortly after the establishment of APEC in November 1989, its utility and relevance appeared to some countries of Southeast Asia as a manifestation of the identity crisis of their own regional organization, that is ASEAN. Some ASEAN members expressed deep concerns about a new body that they apprehended would usurp its role in regional economic cooperation or felt that ASEAN would be eclipsed with the establishment of APEC. Besides, it was also apprehensive of an APEC dominated by Tokyo and Washington. As a result, in 1991, Malaysia's Prime Minister, Mahathir Bin Mohammad proposed the East Asian Economic Caucus (EAEC) which would function as an 'informal forum' within APEC involving all its Asian members only. Mahathir's brainchild was engineered to be as much a group of East Asian nations to discuss issues informally as it would be a forum for sharing a common culture, to talk and arrive at conclusions by consensus, that was identified as the "Asian Way". Unfortunately, devoid of support from either US or Japan, EAEC died its natural death before it could take off the ground.[4]

The situation in the Asia Pacific region changed drastically when the Economic Crisis befell the region in 1997-98. The Crisis pushed the regional countries to a precipice and stimulated greater cooperation between the ASEAN members and East Asian countries (particularly China, Japan and South Korea), to tide over the problem. The situation was compounded by measures dictated by International Monetary Fund (IMF), with the US Treasury and the Federal Reserve exerting influence behind the scenes. Although the IMF programmes were meant to restore confidence and generate growth in foreign exchange reserves to enable countries under its programmes to eventually recover from their conditions of liquidation, yet the nature of the conditions imposed by the Fund was rather controversial and unsuitable for the Asia Pacific victims of the Crisis. As an immediate logical conclusion of these trepidations, the members of ASEAN took a coordinated stance, and thereby formed the ASEAN Plus Three Framework (constituting ASEAN states plus China, Japan and South Korea) the first meeting of which took place in December 1997 on the sidelines of the Second Informal ASEAN Summit in Kuala Lumpur. It may be mentioned in this context that, the first proposal for post-Crisis regional financial cooperation was actually put forward by Japan at the IMF Meeting in Hong Kong, held in September 1997 for establishing an Asian Monetary Fund (AMF). Unfortunately, this idea not did not receive much support within the region and was strongly opposed by the IMF and the US. Consequently, the AMF proposal was put on the backburner. However, it was at a meeting of Asian Finance and Central Bank Deputies in Manila, held on 18-19 November 1997, that the "Manila Framework", also christened as "A New Framework for Enhanced Asian Regional Cooperation to Promote Financial Stability" was developed. This framework recognized the central role of the IMF in the international monetary system and included initiatives for setting up a mechanism for regional surveillance to complement global surveillance by the IMF as well as a cooperative financing arrangement that would supplement IMF resources. The "Manila Framework" was endorsed at a meeting of Finance Ministers from ASEAN, US, Australia, China, Japan, South Korea and Hong Kong, that is, a majority of APEC members, on 2 December 1997 at Kuala Lumpur. Furthermore, as a means of strengthening regional cooperative financing arrangements within the "Manila Framework", the ASEAN+3 Finance Ministers' Meeting in Chiang Mai, held in May 2000,[13] expressed "a need to establish a regional financing arrangement to supplement the existing international facilities", thereby forming the Chiang Mai Initiative (CMI), in addition to including a plethora of agreements on economic scrutiny and bond market development (Asian Bond Market Initiatives, ABMI, together with the Asian Bond Funds)—aimed at bailing the region out of the financial doldrums. As a matter of fact, taking stock of the volatile situation in the region, the Japanese Premier, Junichiro Koizumi's call for an East Asian Community envisaged the ASEAN+3 framework broadening to embrace economically viable countries like Australia and New Zealand for widening the matrix of a free trade area and greater economic integration.[5]

Thus, the outbreak of the Asian Financial Crisis in 1997, gave birth to an "East Asian Consciousness", in the context of which, geographic configuration played an important part and boosted cooperation among the countries of Southeast and Northeast Asia, particularly China, Japan and South Korea.[6] In keeping with the actions and rhetorical position of its proponents, East Asian regionalism had taken a concrete shape in the aftermath of the East Asian Economic Crisis. Consequently, when the Third Summit of ASEAN Plus Three was held in November 1999 in Manila, the then ASEAN Secretary General, Rudolfo Severino described it as "part of a general convergence of purpose in East Asia, a process that has been building up."[7] Moreover, at the ASEAN-China Summit meeting held in November 2004 in Vientiane, Beijing observed that as a follow-up of the signing of the CAFTA (China-ASEAN Free Trade Agreement) in goods, time was ripe for considering the conclusion of an East Asian FTA (comprising APT members), as a further measure of consolidating regional economic integration. Thus, the APT process acted as a positive catalyst in signaling a novel era of broader and incisive East Asian collaboration in economic, political, security and social issues, and in the backdrop of an agreement signed during the 2004 meeting of the APT countries, it was decided that the First EAS would be convened in 2005. In addition to this decision, two other developments —the establishment of the East Asia Vision Group (EAVG) in 1999 as a Track-II group and the East Asia Study Group (EASG) in 2000—facilitated the formation of EAS further. While the EAVG, formed on the basis of the proposal by the then President of South Korea, Kim Dae-jung to outline a vision towards enhancing regional cooperation, submitted its report entitled "Towards an East Asian Community: Region of Peace, Prosperity and Progress"[8] in 2001, the EASG, recommended the 'evolution of the annual Summit meetings of ASEAN+3 into the East Asia Summit' in a set of reports in 2001 and 2002. The 2001 report of the EAVG, which formed the cornerstone of the EAC, summed up the following rationale guiding its formation: prevention of conflict and maintenance of peace among East Asian nations; closer economic cooperation in trade, investment, finance and overall development; insurance of human security through environmental protection and good governance; fostering common prosperity through cooperation in education and human resource development; and promoting the identity of an EAC, culminating in inclusive regional thinking and progressive institutionalization.[9] Furthermore, the creation of an East Asian FTA (EAFTA) to foster the holistic identity of an EAC, underscoring a list of short, medium and long-term measures remained a salient initiative of this process of community-building, given the "irreversible and accelerating tendency of interdependence" among the countries of the region.[10] In conjunction with the promotion of trade and commercial collaboration among the member countries as envisaged in the EAVG Report, another policy report, christened "The State of the Concept of East Asian Community and Japan's Strategic Response Thereto", published by Japan's "Council on East Asian Community" in May 2004 prescribed that, "...other areas like politics, security, environmental[11] protection, social, and cultural issues are also firmed up as a solid foundation to the community."

Meanwhile, there were two conflicting views on the question of whether the EAS would simply be an expanded version supplanting APT, or be an independent entity. While some ASEAN countries favoured the replacement of APT by the EAS, the other counterparts apprehended that this would mellow the ASEAN's weight in the proposed structure. Finally, it was decided that the EAS would exist as an independent entity, making way for politics to dominate the economic calculus of regional integration. The EAS held its inaugural summit in Kuala Lumpur in December 2005, comprising 16 nations—ASEAN-10, China, Japan, South Korea, India, New Zealand and Australia. This Kuala Lumpur summit was regarded as the first step towards promoting greater intra-regional economic collaboration by taking the fullest advantage of the economic growth chronicle of the region, such that a region-wide 'integration' would be reached in eventuality, as a prelude to achieving the ambitious goal of creating an 'East Asian Community'. The Summit also aimed at moving from a relatively restricted economic agenda gradually to look at "security, democracy, good government, rule of law and every aspect of human security." The rationale underpinning this endeavour for community building was premised on the following factors: Asia's rise in the global economic scenario was demonstrated in terms of its dramatic increase in trade and commercial activities within itself more than with the outside world; much of the direct investments were increasingly inward bound by the capital exporting countries and market-driven economic dynamics of the region; and finally, a number of FTAs and CECAs (already negotiated or under negotiation) between the regional countries, thereby reducing their dependence on external markets, especially the traditional markets of America and Europe added further momentum to the process of economic integration. Nevertheless, three important conditions were pinned down for participation of member countries in EAS, which included: adherence to TAC; Dialogue Partner status of ASEAN; and maintenance of "substantial" relations with ASEAN.[12]

However, the most contentious issue of EAS was regarding the inclusion of new members and under what criteria would they be included. While Malaysia and China preferred to delimit the membership of EAS to the APT countries only, other countries like Indonesia, Singapore and Japan believed that the membership should be enlarged to embrace potential and emerging economies like India, New Zealand and Australia in order to accord greater depth and outreach of the EAS, in addition to maintaining a geo-political balance in the region, because they felt that, otherwise, EAS would be ultimately dominated by China due to its growing economic and strategic clout. During the preparatory working level meeting held in Kuala Lumpur on 10-11 November 2005, Japan and China diverged on the issue of India's role and status in the EAS.[13] Furthermore, in keeping with its emphasis on the inclusion of India, Australia and New Zealand within the EAS framework, Japan's Ministry of Foreign Affairs, in an 'Issue Paper' published in 2004, stated that, "Australia and New Zealand are essential partners in various forms of regional cooperation.... India also plays an increasingly important role in regional cooperation. ASEAN+3 should continue to be mindful of the importance of providing sufficient opportunities to other partners to participate in regional cooperation."[14] Thus, Japan, in apposition with a majority of the ASEAN members, has been instrumental in expanding the scope and politico-geographical delineation of EAS, as an outward looking and ambitiously inclusive step towards East Asian community building.

This debate over the composition and membership criteria of the EAS revealed a simmering divergence in the opinion of China and Japan with respect to the constitution of the East Asian balance of power. Pragmatically enough, most of the ASEAN countries and Japan were of the view that, in the then given international order, it would be wise to constrain Beijing's regional assertions through diplomatic engagement with emerging economies, stable democracies and benign powers like India, Australia and New Zealand. Eventually, it was held unanimously that India, Australia and New Zealand would be invited to join the EAS architecture based on the following factors: first, they were full dialogue members of ASEAN; secondly, they enjoyed substantive relations with ASEAN on issues of politico-economic and security import; and finally, they agreed to accede to ASEAN's Treaty of Amity and Cooperation (TAC).[15] Therefore, the establishment of EAS in 2005 primarily as a platform "for dialogue on broad strategic, political and economic issues of common interest"[16] underscored the imperative need of focusing on the promotion of development, financial stability, energy security, economic integration, holistic regional growth and deeper cultural understanding among the member states. Summarily then, the quest for regional community building that was initiated in the aftermath of the 1997 Financial inferno in the Asia Pacific region reached its consummation in the evolving regional sculpture of the EAS. Indeed, the Chairman's Statement at the Inaugural EAS meeting proposed the eventual establishment of an East Asian Community (EAC), when it declared that, "We also agreed that the East Asian region has already advanced in its efforts to establish an East Asian Community through the ASEAN+3 process. In this context we believed that the EAS together with the ASEAN+3 and the ASEAN+1 processes could play a significant role in community-building in the region."[17] However, ASEAN has been at the centre of this process of regional community building, as reflected in an official press release preceding the First EAS, which stated, "ASEAN also believes that it should be in the driver's seat in the East Asia Summit and that the East Asia Summit will be open and outward looking."[18] It deserves mention at this juncture that, the vision for setting up an Asian economic community was originally put forward by the Prime Minister of India, Atal Behari Vajpayee at the ASEAN-India Summit in Bali in October 2003, when he expressed New Delhi's keenness in constructing an inclusive phenomenon of East Asian economic integration, in which India would play a vital part as well, within the scaffold of its extended 'Look East' (Phase II) Policy. The fact that India had become a principal regional player particularly on account of its integration within the orbit of ASEAN as a Summit-level partner was clearly exemplified by the then Indian Prime Minister, Atal Behari Vajpayee in the 21st Singapore Lecture on "India's Perspectives on ASEAN and the Asia-Pacific Region", which he delivered in April 2002. In this momentous Lecture, Vajpayee said: "India's belonging to the Asia-Pacific community was a geographical fact and a political reality, which did not require formal membership of any regional organization for its recognition or sustenance."[19] Thus, India believed that it was already an integral part of the evolving community structure by virtue of its historical legacy and geographical proximity and its inclusion as ASEAN's Summit-level partner would further consolidate its regional stature by extending its footprints into the East Asian region, as envisaged in Phase II of its 'Look East' Policy. This sentiment was reiterated by Vajpayee's successor, Manmohan Singh, when he proposed the "eventual creation of an Asian Economic Community or the arc of prosperity that I envisage to become a reality in the early part of the 21st century",[20] while addressing the ASEAN Business Advisory Council in Kuala Lumpur on 12 December 2004. The idea of an Asian Economic Community was further affirmed when Prime Minister, Manmohan Singh, in his address at the 5th ASEAN-India Summit held in Cebu, the Philippines in January 2007, said:

> In the present phase of our 'Look East' policy, we in India seek to deepen our economic integration by entering into Free Trade or Comprehensive economic Partnership agreements both with ASEAN as a whole and with individual countries of the region. Such agreements are already under different stages of discussion or implementation with Singapore, Thailand, Malaysia and Indonesia. This web of mutually beneficial partnerships can, we believe, be brought together in a Pan-Asian FTA that could light up the future of this region.[21]

Thus, the EAS was conceived as a mega-gathering of emerging Asian countries, accounting for nearly half, quarter and one-third of the global population, trade and GDP respectively,[22] attesting to the veracity of Asia's resurgence as a moving avalanche to be reckoned with.

Re-generation of India's Economic Thinking: EAS as a Platform

In the early 1990s, the global and regional politics had undergone qualitative transformations. With the crumple of the former Soviet Union and the end of the cold war, coupled with the onset of globalization, nations were beginning to perceive that the means to making wealth was by securing international trade and encouragement of foreign investments for their survival in the emerging competitive global market. Free market rules following the proven philosophy of mass capitalization dominated the international political scene over governing ideology in this period. The new world order provided scope for redefining the territorial compass of the groupings of the future. Thus, India in the new global milieu, inaugurated the New Economic Policy under the leadership of the then Prime Minister, P.V. Narashima Rao in 1991. This novel policy had embarked on a substantive and wide ranging programme of economic reforms, restructuring and liberalization, and thereby, brought the Indian economy in line with the economies of the world and the ASEAN countries at large. Simultaneously, India announced its 'Look East' policy, which was very well-calculated, well-timed and thought-out,[23] and bolstered by India's objective attempt to engage with the East Asia. This policy was also anchored on the perception that the end of the Cold War had given India an opportunity to broaden its relations with and to focus on countries, which were traditional friends and partners of long-standing and special importance, but with whom relations were compromised due to the imperatives of cold war politics. Therefore, India's 'Look East' Policy was a product of both the vigour of liberalization and the craving to replicate the East Asian growth miracle.

On the other side of the spectrum, India had emerged as a politically successful and economically rising power in the Asia Pacific region, dominated by its geographical extent, population, educated middle class, industrial base, military strength, technical capability, ancient cultural history and presence of overseas Indians in different countries of Southeast and East Asia. Moreover, ASEAN's perception of New Delhi as an emerging regional power and China as a source of perennial security threat, coupled with the grim situation in the South China Sea because of conflicting claims over the Spratly Islands, the stand off in the Taiwan Straits and the Korean Peninsula and the troubled ties among US, Japan and China, had convinced ASEAN of the need for a paradigm shift in India-ASEAN attachments. It was also felt by the ASEAN members that India's image and peaceful rise as a benign power accrued significant strategic benefits for them to play a more effective role in the region to counter China as a source of security threat. Thus, the coincidence of their mutual needs catalyzed the upgradation and enhancement of relations between India and ASEAN, and interestingly enough, New Delhi's 'Look East' Policy appeared as a shadow of ASEAN's 'Look West' line of thought. This newfound drive towards regionalization and ultimate community building led to the overall optimism in the trend of emerging ties between India and ASEAN.[24] Consequently, the ASEAN countries took full cognizance of India's steady development not only from its politico-economic perspective, but also from the standpoint of its strategic location. Resultantly, within a short span of time, India graduated from sectoral dialogue to Summit-level partner within the ASEAN orbit (in 2002) and it was promoted as a participant of the East Asia Summit in 2005. This ascendance in New Delhi's stature was an integral part of the Second Phase of India's 'Look East' Policy, which implied an expanded definition of 'East' - extending from Australia, New Zealand to China and East Asia, with ASEAN as its core - and marked a shift in focus from exclusively economic issues to economic and security issues, including joint efforts to protect sea-lanes, coordination on counter-terrorism etc. Therefore, India's promotion within the institutional framework of ASEAN was not a one-way story; rather it was a positive upshot of the definitive priority that the Indian foreign policy makers accorded to this region. Thus, with these mutually reciprocal interactions, ASEAN's closer ties with India began to take shape in world politics by displaying the decades of relative ignorance of an economically emerging, politically mature and strategically vital, dynamic India in the orbit of the Southeast Asian region.

Furthermore, another important event, which provoked New Delhi to extend its 'Look East' Policy more towards East Asia, was the inclusion of Myanmar in the ASEAN orbit. The ingress of Myanmar in the ASEAN Regional Forum (ARF) in July 1996, followed by the status of full membership of ASEAN in July 1997, gave New Delhi the opportunity to share a common land border with an ASEAN member state. India's emphasis on developing its eastward trade access to Myanmar clearly illustrated the Indian Government's resolve to mend and enhance its historic ties with Myanmar,[25] and thereby dilated New Delhi's economic, security and political opportunities with the countries of Southeast Asia. But, in spite of knowing fully well the economic weaknesses of Myanmar, New Delhi's strategy to reshape its historical links and develop its common land border with Myanmar in order to alleviate the poverty and under-development in the region was determined mainly to overcome the reduction of unremitting tensions in the Northeast region of India on the one hand, and to win the minds of the Myanmar leadership through different aid and development projects, and thereby reduce the chances of its exclusive dependence on China, on the other. Moreover, by improving the road route between India and Myanmar via Northeast, New Delhi envisaged the eventual connection of a section of the Asian highway from Singapore to Istanbul. Another symbolic event, which took place during this time, as a measure to accelerate the momentum of convergence between India and ASEAN was the establishment of sub-regional organizations, under New Delhi's tutelage, of which, the signing of Mekong-Ganga Cooperation (MGC) Initiative on 10 November 2000 in Vientiane among six neighbouring countries namely India, Myanmar, Thailand, Cambodia, Laos and Vietnam, paved the way for improved bilateral ties between India and the less developed countries of Southeast Asia. The main aim of this initiative was the broadening and intensification of joint efforts at economic cooperation between India and ASEAN countries in the Mekong Basin, with a goal of enhancing the transport links that span India, Myanmar, Thailand, Cambodia and Vietnam and thereby would facilitate cross-border movements of goods and services in order to strengthen the India-ASEAN Free Trade Area (FTA). A major vision of this programme was to establish a Delhi-Hanoi road and railway link in the near future, and also to develop transportation networks including the East-West Corridor project. Further, the linkages between India and these countries of Indochina over land might give New Delhi an opportunity to expedite economic development of its Northeast region. Therefore, though clogged, India's 'Look East' Policy towards the less developed countries of Southeast Asia, amply demonstrated an upward mobility of bilateral relations. Alike this initiative, in June 1997, under the auspices of India and Thailand, BISTEC (Bangladesh, India, Sri Lanka, Thailand—Economic Cooperation) was formally launched- later known as BIMSTEC—with the primary goal of acting as a vehicle for promoting trade and tourism in the Bay of Bengal region and offered New Delhi with an opportunity to strengthen its ties with the eastern neighbourhood, much in conformity with the core of its 'Look East' Policy. It was also felt by the Indian policy makers that in order to foster political partnerships with the countries of Southeast Asia, working out physical connectivity through road and railway links, and negotiating free trade arrangements would remain the main guiding principles, since BIMSTEC has logistically placed India closer to Southeast Asia through the Myanmar-Thailand link. Thus, BIMSTEC acts as a bridge between South and Southeast Asia through its developmental initiatives.[26]

India's pro-active mobility of its 'Look East' diplomacy generated confidence in the mindset of the ASEAN leaders and their decision to include India as a Summit-level partner at the Seventh ASEAN Summit held in Brunei in November 2001, remains a major achievement in its entirety. The decision for a separate ASEAN-India Summit clearly demonstrated that New Delhi was not treated at par with the countries of East Asia (i.e. Japan, China and Korea), but it provided an opportunity to India to prove its economic influence and dynamics in the region. This promotion of India as a new actor in the orbit of ASEAN's economic, political and strategic processes was a product of history of more than one decade. While highlighting this Summit as a major achievement of India's 'Look East' policy, the Ministry of External Affair's Annual Report: 2002-03 described this event as "a significant development in our relations with ASEAN countries, as India joined the ranks of a handful of countries with which ASEAN has Summit dialogues, namely, China, Japan and South Korea. This up-gradation is a natural culmination of ten years of progressive engagement with ASEAN…. It is also a vindication of India's 'Look East' policy which seeks to build on our historical and cultural ties with the region to create a mutually beneficial strategic and economic relationship."[27] Apart from participation in the Summit, the Indian Prime Minister, Atal Behari Vajpayee proposed to create an ASEAN-India Free Trade Area by the year 2012, which would cover about 1.5 billion consumers with a combined GNP of US$ 1.7 trillion, and would gradually eliminate the trade barriers between the member countries of ASEAN on the one hand and India, on the other.

Meanwhile, India's growing propinquity with the Southeast Asian countries received more vigour, when in October 2003, Prime Minister Atal Behari Vajpayee attended the Second India-ASEAN Summit in Bali, and sent a strong message about New Delhi's importance and vow to forge closer links with the region. In this Bali Summit, three important accords were signed on comprehensive economic cooperation, combating terrorism and facilitating India's accession to the Treaty of Amity and Cooperation (TAC) with Southeast Asia respectively. The Indian Prime Minister also went a step further by offering a unilateral "open skies" policy to specified Southeast Asian airlines, which would be allowed to operate daily flights to the four metros in India and unlimited flights to eighteen tourist destinations in India,[28] and also announced New Delhi's decision to extend special and differential treatment to ASEAN countries depending on their levels of development to improve their market access to India. Taken together, these steps clearly assured considerable improvement in economic, political and security cooperation between India and its Southeast Asian neighbours, following which, the confidence of Southeast Asian countries on India once again received a major boost when in May 2004, the United Progressive Alliance (UPA) under the Prime Ministership of Manmohan Singh, came in power by replacing the NDA government. This new government, like its precursor, renewed India's closer ties with the countries of Southeast Asia, and commenced the foreign policy, which was purposeful, result-oriented and highly pro-active in its entirety. In this context, the Minister of External Affairs, K. Natwar Singh, categorically emphasized in a meeting with top Indian diplomats from SAARC and ASEAN countries, held on 31 May 2004, on the future policy options of New Delhi and strongly reiterated the political, economic and strategic importance of Southeast Asia in India's foreign policy domain, when he said, "We will further strengthen bilateral relations with them, as well as our interaction with ASEAN since it constitutes a major dimension of our foreign policy." The same mindset was reiterated, when K. Natwar Singh in an interview to *The Jakarta Post* on 2 July 2004 stated, "India's foreign policy attaches primary importance to relations with our immediate neighbours in South Asia Association for Regional Cooperation (SAARC) as well as in ASEAN. We remain committed to strengthening India's 'Look East' policy and to constructing a long-term partnership with ASEAN. Under the Framework Agreement concluded last year, we have just commenced negotiation of a Free Trade Agreement. We are also working on an India-ASEAN Summit in November this year. Politically, we completely share ASEAN's vision and the principles of harmonious and good neighbouring relations established by the ASEAN Treaty of Amity and Cooperation, to which India acceded last year."[29] Thus, India's 'Look East' Policy had attained its multi-dimensional and multi-pronged outlook by 2004, which was accentuated by the signing of a historic partnership pact between India and ASEAN, titled "India-ASEAN Partnership for Peace, Progress and Shared Prosperity" in the 3rd India-ASEAN Summit held on 30th November 2004, in Vientiane.

The multi-dimensional approach through India's 'Look East' Policy received its dividend when the Indian Prime Minister, Manmohan Singh, was invited to be a part of the ASEAN-initiated First EAS, held in Kuala Lumpur on 14 December 2005. The Indian Prime Minister, Manmohan Singh, being the only South Asian representative, in this First East Asia Summit, clearly asserted that it was important for India to be in a group that had the "potential to play a major role in global affairs. Its composition, evolving agenda and format give it the potential to play a major role in global affairs. India's presence in this group from its very outset is an opportunity we value."[30] At the end of this meeting, Manmohan Singh described the East Asia Summit as "a historic meeting". Thus, India's presence and participation, in the First East Asian Summit, was indubitably a good beginning for the country's ultimate integration with the East Asian region. Furthermore, the network of Free Trade Agreements (FTAs) and Comprehensive Economic Cooperation Agreements (CECAs)[31] signed and negotiated with India on the one hand and the members of EAS, on the other (some are still being negotiated), is the building block of an East Asian economic community, through active contribution and closer cooperation for community building in the Asia Pacific region. Therefore, for New Delhi, the EAS can be seen as the penultimate step in its integration with Northeast Asia and Southwest Pacific, and a stepping-stone to joining the Asia Pacific Economic Cooperation (APEC) forum. Summarily then, New Delhi's participation in the East Asia Summit has provided a new politico-economic and strategic breathing space, which New Delhi has obtained through its efficient handling of its 'Look East' Policy.[32]

Tracing New Zealand's Regionalism Fervour: EAS as a Space

Since the dawn of the cold war era, New Zealand engaged itself in rebuilding the foundations of peace and prosperity in the Asia Pacific region through development assistance and deployment of its defence forces, premised essentially on its foreign policy, centred around a commitment to multilateralism, constructive participation in regional organizations, the values of a modern and multicultural democracy; an open, successful, globally competitive economy; international-standard corporate governance and business practice, and desire to contribute to peace and prosperity in the region. This region was viewed by New Zealand as an area of great diversity and increasing dynamism and economic prosperity, with which, Wellington's political, economic and strategic interests were closely interlinked. In fact, with the formation of ASEAN in 1967, New Zealand's ties with the Southeast Asian countries were institutionalized, organized and accentuated by the imperative of dialogue, negotiation and collaboration between them, both bilaterally and multilaterally. New Zealand became a dialogue partner of ASEAN in 1974; joined the *ASEAN Regional Forum in 1994*, and in 2005 acceded to ASEAN's Treaty of Amity and Cooperation (TAC). This closeness of New Zealand with the countries of Southeast Asia was never obstructed in spite of its closer alignment with the Western world and as a result, during the cold war years, New Zealand maintained very friendly ties with these countries.

With the end of the cold war and ushering in of a globalized world order, New Zealand took cognizance of the dynamics of economic and trade relations, and the need to continue developing formal trading relationships in Asia, in the backdrop of the transformed global system. Subsequently, as ASEAN blossomed its structure by introducing new pedestals like ARF, APT, and ASEAN+1 within the associational framework and embraced China, Japan, South Korea and India, New Zealand realized that its hitherto engagement with the ASEAN countries would be strengthened more and more on account of the growing economic and strategic resilience, which had emerged in the region, since it accounted for a third of New Zealand's foreign trade, a fifth of inward investment, and a third of tourism revenues. The groundwork for enhancing its relations with the ASEAN member-states was laid by a project launched by Wellington, christened "Seriously Asia",[33] in 2003, involving the Government, business, local communities, educational institutions and others in a collective effort for linking New Zealand with this region. Moreover, the Government of New Zealand, which had long recognized Asia's importance to its security and prosperity, asserted in the "Asia White Paper" that, "as a nation we have worked at many levels over the past half century to strengthen our ties with the region. The countries of Asia today are undergoing rapid and fundamental changes. We have much to learn from these changes. If we can keep pace, many new opportunities will open to us." This White Paper identified the following realms—namely, formal engagement through a network of official representation throughout the region to support work in diplomacy, trade, education, development assistance, migration etc.; leadership diplomacy; enhancing links with business and industry groups, counterpart groups and corporations; and non-official ties, including academic, "Track II", sister city, cultural and people-to-people exchanges—in the pursuit of bolstering ties with the ASEAN members. With this outlook, it amply exhibits that in the context of the new world order, as well as the evolving new situation in the Asian region, the New Zealand Government considers Asia as an important vehicle of its economic development and overall prosperity. To make this mindset an effective one, Wellington used multilateralism as a potent instrument and for that, it actively participated in different types of regional organizations to uphold its dream of Asianism.

As New Zealand was seriously engaged and endeavoured to raise the level and content of its relations with the Asia Pacific region, via ASEAN's anchorage, a reciprocal gesture was extended by the ASEAN countries as well, when it beckoned New Zealand to join the EAS in July 2005. This initiative of ASEAN to integrate New Zealand more within their process was a dividend on account of the latter's past performances in the region. Thus, the EAS became a platform for the meeting of leaders from New Zealand on the one hand and the northeast Asian countries (in addition to core ASEAN members), in conjunction with emerging powers like India and Australia, on the other. In the White Paper, the Prime Minister of New Zealand, Helen Clark asserted that:

> Its involvement in regional groupings such as the East Asia Summit, provide opportunities for us to deepen our links. The EAS is a new avenue for us to contribute to community building in this neighbourhood. We must also be cognizant in order to maintain New Zealand's place in the market. Our future with Asia acknowledges the valuable contribution that people-to-people links between New Zealand and Asia make in deepening our understanding of each other. The EAS is an important new development in the region at a time when political and economic relationships in Asia are undergoing rapid and potentially far-reaching changes. I am delighted. The summit was originally to involve leaders from the ten countries of the Association of Southeast Asian Nations (ASEAN) and its North Asian neighbours China, Japan and Korea. Now (July 2005) ASEAN has invited participation by New Zealand, Australia and India. The government recognizes that it is vital for New Zealand to engage wherever possible in the developing regional structures. Roughly are with or from Asian countries. The summit will offer further opportunities for deeper and more inclusive regional integration between New Zealand and Asia. New Zealand's participation in the EAS in December will cap a year of reinvigoration of New Zealand's ties with the region. It is particularly satisfying that these positive developments in our relations with Southeast Asia are unfolding as we celebrate the 30th anniversary of New Zealand's Dialogue Partnership with ASEAN.[34]

Therefore, New Zealand perceived its evolving tempo in the sphere of regionalism and community building as a two-way process, not only seeking to build greater understanding of Asia in New Zealand, but also underlining the relevance of New Zealand to its key partners in the region, through a long-term and sustained commitment to contributing to the development of the region as a whole. The Asia Pacific region's relevance to New Zealand's policy outlook impinged upon the rapidly growing economic links with the region, especially in services, tourism and education sectors, which are supported by an expanding network of trade agreements and other forms of economic cooperation, culminating in the financial integration of the region. The pressures of economic competition in the Asian region, fostered by the steady economic advancement of countries like India and China, opened up newer avenues of forging cooperation in skills development, manufacturing, sharing of technological know-how and information, thereby creating new flows of business. Besides, the comprehensive development of Preferential Trading Arrangements (PTAs), FTAs and other regional trading arrangements with its Asian partners provided New Zealand with a space of connecting and competing with them. In fact, New Zealand's growing web of economic linkages with the regional countries added a multi-dimensional focus to its trade and commercial outlook through the improvement of support for business connections between Asian countries and New Zealand; enhancing access to markets through trade agreements; and building the skills and capacity of New Zealand's businesses, entrepreneurs, chambers of commerce and industry associations to engage in Asia. In this context, the most significant cooperative endeavour between ASEAN and New Zealand, along with Australia, has been the conclusion of the *ASEAN-Australia-New Zealand Free Trade Area*[35] (AANZFTA) on 27 February 2009 at the ASEAN Summit in Hua Hin, Thailand, following four years of economic and technical cooperation under the AFTA-CER Closer Economic Partnership in October 2004 at Vientiane. The AANZFTA (The Agreement entered into force for and between Australia, Brunei, Malaysia, Myanmar, New Zealand, Singapore, the Philippines and Vietnam on 1 January 2010 and for Indonesia, Laos and Cambodia two months after ratification by the eight other countries) is designed to remove barriers to trade between New Zealand and its trading partners, such that trade and commercial ties between New Zealand and ASEAN are expanded for further progress in regional integration. For New Zealand there are three key inter-related reasons beyond these shared objectives for having negotiated this Agreement and they are as follows: first, the Agreement offers the potential to deliver significant commercial commitments in a growing and important market, particularly since the ASEAN economies are an increasingly important destination for New Zealand's service suppliers (including education, engineering and environmental services) and outward investment. Secondly, this FTA allows New Zealand entrepreneurs to maintain a competitive presence in this burgeoning region; and finally, the Agreement would broaden Wellington's long-term interests in engagement and interaction with the region as a whole.[36]

Apart from economic collaboration, the EAS opened up new vistas of Wellington's deeper engagement with the Asia Pacific region, by integrating itself into "an already integrating region", by focusing on steps towards new mechanisms for political cooperation. The EAS has enabled New Zealand to express its constructive willingness in becoming a "good neighbour" for developing shared regional interests like the maintenance of regional security and stability, based on the emergence of non-state actors; addressing trans-national issues of concern; building up scientific knowledge and expertise in environmental protection; protecting and promoting human rights, etc. Furthermore, New Zealand's participation in EAS has endorsed its military engagement with the Asia Pacific region as well, premised on the Five Power Defence Arrangements (FDPA), and thereby enabling substantial military modernization programmes in Southeast Asia, including naval and submarine fleets, targeted at establishing an inclusive and comprehensive regional community. Significantly enough, New Zealand's Defence White Paper: 2010[37] envisions that the country would derive significant "benefits from a stable and prosperous Asia and it is in our national interest to uphold and contribute to that favourable environment by supporting regional peace and security",[38] through a variety of defence, diplomatic and confidence-building activities, like supporting open and inclusive regional security and defence structures; maintaining contribution to defence arrangements in Malaysia and Singapore through the FPDA; developing substantive bilateral defence and strategic relations with other EAS member-states; contributing to efforts to prevent the proliferation of WMD and related delivery systems, and to achieve nuclear disarmament in the region; supporting regional efforts to deal with terrorism and other transnational security threats; and being willing and able to assist in times of natural or humanitarian disasters. Finally, New Zealand perceives its membership of EAS as an optimistic outfit in fostering its cultural ties with the Asia Pacific, on the path of becoming more "Asia literate". This can be fulfiled by the further development of Asian languages, heritage and cultural skills among its people through universities and other education providers by facilitating research collaboration, joint degrees and alumni networks as well as through people-to-people contacts, catalyzed by both government and non-governmental agencies.

It has become conventional wisdom that notwithstanding New Zealand's genuine global interests, its future will be shaped by economic and social progress in East Asia, where the transformation since the demise of the cold war has radically changed political and economic order in the region, with its spillover effects on the entire global order. For New Zealand there is a political dimension to the economic opportunities offered by East Asia that requires sound government-to-government relationships and foreign policy convergence on issues where shared interests offer the potential for such convergence - such as resource security, climate change, reform of international institutions (to permit Asian governments a rightful place in their operations and management), disarmament and non-proliferation etc. New Zealand believes that the essence of comprehensive and collective or cooperative security demands a multilateral approach. In fact, the building up of a multilateral regime on the basis of economic and strategic cooperation between the concerned states facilitates the establishment of an inclusive system, aimed at holistic and integral development and prosperity of the participating units. Insofar as New Zealand is concerned, "the absence of critical mass diminishes New Zealand's negotiating leverage in bilateral dealings. It is active therefore in multilateral diplomacy, seeking coalitions of like-minded interest and supporting even-handed negotiation where agendas and outcomes are fair to all involved."[39] Therefore, New Zealand's constant emphasis on regionalism and community building, based on its stance of political openness, a non-threatening and benign profile, a problem solving mentality, and a capacity for adopting an impartial outlook on international and regional issues has culminated in the wide convergence of Wellington's policies with most of the EAS members.[40] As against such a backdrop, New Zealand's membership in the East Asia Summit (EAS) projects an unwavering stance for enhancing constructive, interdependent and rewarding relations with the Asia Pacific region.

India and New Zealand in EAS Platform: Rationale of ASEAN's Willingness

The inclusion of India and New Zealand within the EAS orbit was conditioned by historical, geographical, socio-economic and strategic exigencies of the globalised world order. While scrutinizing the rationale of ASEAN's beckoning to New Delhi and Wellington within the exclusive realm of EAS, the following determinants remain the moot factors: **first,** a majority of the ASEAN countries harboured a Western flavour in their foreign policy domain during the cold war era. Naturally, New Zealand, which was historically an ally of US and even a member of the cold war military alliance, ANZUS, became a dialogue partner of ASEAN in 1974, fostered by the confidence of the ASEAN members reposed in New Zealand, not only because of its Western patronage, but also augmented by convergence of economic interests spearheaded by their open and liberalized economic stance, thus offering itself as a dynamic and potential market for ASEAN entrepreneurs. Thus, New Zealand remained an automatic choice for ASEAN in the cold war years, on account of their historical experiences. India, on the other hand, in the cold war era, due to great power politics, based on its own national interest, looked favourably towards the Soviet Union rather than US and China. This favourable inclination, coupled with Nehruvian thinking of socialistic orientation of economy made it a natural choice for New Delhi to follow a socialistic pattern of society, rather than to open its economy to the global market during the cold war years. This socialistic flavour of India made the countries of Southeast Asia turn a blind eye towards the former. Such an ASEAN mindset towards India moved in the opposite direction since the fall of former Soviet Union, when India, for the first time, liberalized its economy within the framework of its New Economic Policy, coincident with a new visioning of the Southeast Asian region through the prism of its 'Look East' Policy and thereby, minimized the space which had hitherto developed between them. **Secondly**, the ASEAN countries, while acknowledging the burgeoning strategico-economic rise of India and New Zealand in the Asia Pacific region, particularly in the backdrop of the post-cold war scenario, felt it imperative to embrace these countries within the EAS, as a counterweight to the emerging prowess and political clout, mainly China and some other regional countries. **Thirdly**, in the case of India, the growing economic clout as well as its strategic position, mainly in the Indian Ocean region, in conjunction with its day-to-day increasing military prowess, assorted with nuclear capability, made it felt by many countries of Southeast Asia that New Delhi could act as a balancer, if China emerged as a threat to them, which in other words meant that, ASEAN members deciphered in India the much-needed countervailing potential to checkmate China's ambitious rise in the region. **Finally**, the impact of India culture, which was imprinted in the pages of Southeast Asian history and its historical role in the Non-aligned movement gave New Delhi a natural advantage of space among the ASEAN countries. This space was further deep-rooted on account of its rapid technological acumen, followed by enhanced naval presence stretching from the Indian Ocean to the South China Sea, and its benign, collaborative and humanitarian image largely contributed a sense of security relief in the mindset of these countries and demonstrated the strength of New Delhi to engage in competition with prominent regional naval powers in the Asia Pacific region, if circumstances so demanded. Summarily then, based on the above factors, the ASEAN members inducted India and New Zealand within the EAS regional community building endeavour, which was reciprocated pragmatically and enthusiastically by both New Delhi and Wellington, as they participated in the First EAS meeting held in Kuala Lumpur on 14 December 2005. It is to be noted in this connection that, US failed to participate in this Summit as it refused to sign the TAC, which remains an essential precondition to be a part of the EAS framework.

Linking India and New Zealand: EAS Summits as a Bridging Platform

The First EAS Summit held in Kuala Lumpur on 14 December 2005 brought together for the first time the leaders of India and New Zealand at a multilateral forum for increasing linkages and interdependence, thereby making the region an engine of growth for the international economy. This Summit manifested itself as a historic event in the emerging global scenario, by fostering the convergence of member-countries like India and New Zealand on "broad strategic, political and economic issues" of common interest and concern to promote peace, stability and economic prosperity in East Asia", through their dialogue focusing on development, financial stability, economic integration and growth, eradicating poverty and narrowing the development gap through technology transfer and infrastructure development, capacity building, good governance, humanitarian assistance and promotion of financial links, trade as well as investment, expansion and liberalization, as envisaged in the Kuala Lumpur Declaration. Besides, the East Asia Summit Declaration on Avian Influenza Prevention, Control and Response, and planned collaboration in environmental protection and natural disaster mitigation,[41] particularly in the aftermath of the disastrous Tsunami of December 2004, boosted New Zealand's engagement with India within the wide spectrum of EAS.[42] While describing this meeting as "historic", the Indian Prime Minister, Manmohan Singh highlighted that India had the "potential to play a major role in global affairs", thus signaling the ambitious beginning of New Delhi's ultimate integration with the East Asian region. In his address, Manmohan Singh urged the member-countries of EAS, including New Zealand to strive for harmonious relationships and seamless trade and investment ties among themselves, through a long-term vision, aimed at the development of a prosperous community of Asia Pacific nations. As a matter of fact, the Indian Prime Minister proposed the establishment of a robust and institutional architecture—the pan-Asian Free Trade Agreement (FTA)—that would form the basis for regional cooperation and concerted action for the East Asian counterparts, when he said, "We are on the cusp of a new opportunity. India's presence in this group from its very outset is an opportunity we value."[43] The Chairman of the First EAS, the Prime Minister of Malaysia, Abdul Ahmad Badawi, also voiced this spirit of integration and greater collaboration within the EAS structure, when he said:

> We recognized the increasing inter-linkages and growing inter-dependence among our countries and agreed to deepen integration and cooperation in order to promote the creation of a harmonious and prosperous community of nations.... We also had an exchange of views on the effort at community building being undertaken in the East Asian region. In this regard we expressed our full support for ASEAN's efforts to realize the ASEAN Community. We also recognized that the East Asian community is a long-term goal that would contribute to the maintenance of peace, security, prosperity and progress in the region and beyond.[44]

In this backdrop, the meeting of the leaders from India and New Zealand at the EAS pedestal opened the sluice gates of deeper and more substantive collaboration, as borne out by a flurry of diplomatic high-level exchanges, not only at the political level, but also in the defence spectrum between New Delhi and Wellington. To start with, cooperation in the field of maritime defence carved its ascending trajectory with the visit of Rear Admiral David Ledson, Chief of the Royal Navy of New Zealand to oversee joint exercises held between "Te Mana" – New Zealand's naval frigate with Indian Navy ships at the ports of Kochi and Mumbai in June 2006. In a reciprocal gesture of cordiality, the Indian naval ship, INS 'Tabar', led by Vice Admiral Sureesh Mehta, Flag Officer Commanding-in-Chief, Eastern Naval Command, Indian Navy, made a port call to Auckland in July 2006. In addition to naval exchanges between India and New Zealand, economic coordination between the two countries was emphasized when the Indian Minister of Finance, P. Chidambaram visited New Zealand on 19-23 November 2006, within the course of which, he held discussions with his counterpart, Michael Kullen on the prospects of encouraging trade and investment at the mutual sphere.[45] Thus, the EAS promenade provided both India and New Zealand a better coordinating and linking space in catalyzing the surge in the horizon of their bilateral relations as well.

The space that was developed between India and New Zealand was further expanded when the two countries met for the second consecutive time in Cebu, the Philippines to participate in the second EAS, held on 15-19 January 2007, at which, the leaders voiced their concerted opinion on issues of politico-economic importance like poverty eradication, energy, education, mitigation of natural disaster, economic development and regional integration. One of the significant highlights of this Summit was the signing of the Cebu Declaration on East Asian Energy Security by India and New Zealand, in consort with their fellow EAS counterparts, with the avowed objectives of "improving the efficiency and environmental performance of fossil fuel use; reducing dependence on conventional fuels through intensified energy efficiency and conservation programmes, hydropower, expansion of renewable energy systems and bio-fuel production/utilization, and for interested parties, civilian nuclear power; encouraging the development of open and competitive regional and international markets geared towards providing affordable energy at all economic levels; mitigating greenhouse gas emission through effective policies and measures, thus contributing to global climate change abatement; and pursuing and encouraging investment in energy resource and infrastructure development through greater private sector involvement."[46] Furthermore, as a booster to the spirit of economic collaboration and greater integration among the EAS participants, the Summit agreed to launch a study on a "Comprehensive Economic Partnership in East Asia" (CEPEA)[47] among the EAS members, focusing on the need for narrowing development gaps, as well as facilitating and liberalizing trade and investment for expediting regional economic integration and East Asian community building. Besides, while appreciating the Indian Prime Minister, Manmohan Singh's proposal of reviving India's ancient seat of learning—Nalanda University - in unanimity with the other EAS members, the ASEAN Secretary General, Ong Keng Yong attested to the positive role that countries like India, New Zealand and Australia could play in treading the path of ultimate regional integration. In validation of this vision, Ong Keng Yong applied his 'aircraft analogy', which portrayed China and India as the engines, Japan as the fuselage with the wings, New Zealand and Australia as the provider of specific fuel of the East Asian "aeroplane", piloted and controlled by ASEAN.[48] The outcome of the Summit manifested a forward mobility and enhanced enthusiasm in the successive development of ties between India and New Zealand at the bilateral level, when the New Zealand Trade Minister, Phil Goff paid an official visit to India on 19-23 April 2007, and laid down the blueprint for commencing a study into the implications of a free trade agreement between the two countries.[49]

While sustaining the momentum of the EAS members towards incisive economic integration as a key element in promoting regional community building, the Third EAS Summit, which was held in Singapore on 21 November 2007, offered yet another pedestal for the confluence of India and New Zealand on a bouquet of politico-economic and strategic issues. The most significant outfit of this Summit was the signing of the 'Declaration on Climate Change, Energy, and the Environment'[50] by the EAS members "to address the adverse impact of climate change on socio-economic development, health and the environment, particularly in developing countries and thus emphasized the need to enhance their adaptive capacities to urgently act to cap the growth of global greenhouse gas emissions". The Chairman of the Summit, Singapore Prime Minister, Lee Hsien Loong, described the document as "a declaration of intent, not a negotiated treaty", as it contained no numerical targets for reducing emissions of greenhouse gases. He however, underscored the salience of seriously tackling global environmental issues in accordance with the principle of common but differentiated responsibilities, as well as the respective capabilities of the EAS member-states, for which the Declaration was a prominent forward step. Furthermore, while reiterating the common concern of the EAS countries over the spiraling oil price increases, India, New Zealand and the other EAS counterparts converged on intensifying efforts to improve energy efficiency, conservation, use of renewable energy sources, and exploration of alternative energy sources, including civilian-nuclear energy, and thereby ensuring nuclear safety, security and non-proliferation within the framework of the International Atomic Energy Agency (IAEA). Moreover, in a step to "set up an international University through an international treaty", the first meeting of the Nalanda Mentor Group chaired by the Indian Nobel Laureate, Prof. Amartya Sen, was also held in the aegis of this Summit. In this meeting, the Nalanda Mentor Group provided a roadmap to re-establish this University, and rejuvenate it as a "Centre for Excellence for Research and Teaching". New Delhi's proposal to refurbish the Nalanda University as a seat of learning for philosophy, Buddhist studies, regional history, business and management studies, international relations, peace studies and languages was highly appreciated and welcomed by New Zealand, which described it as a trail blazer in fostering inter-cultural, inter-societal and interfaith dialogue and exchange. Furthermore, the EAS Chairman, Lee Hsien Loong heralded this initiative paving the way for re-creating the exoticism of Nalanda University "as an icon of Asian renaissance".[51]

The momentum of regional cooperation and the successful ascending movement of India and New Zealand within the EAS platform was demonstrated once again, when the 4th EAS meeting, held in Cha-am Hua Hin, Thailand, on

25 October 2009, laid the groundwork for further interaction of New Delhi and Wellington within a multilateral regional scaffold. This meeting amply attested to the growing stature of India and New Zealand in the Asia Pacific region, and reiterated the impact of their socio-economic transformation in reshaping the regional economic order, and the opportunities associated with it for accelerating Asia's holistic growth and development. While expressing his optimism pertaining to the evolution of EAS as an "open, inclusive, transparent and outward looking" process, the Prime Minister of India, Manmohan Singh not only described it as "an act of foresight" because the world's eyes were now focused on Asia as the region which can lead the global economic revival from the front, but also harped on the "tremendous goodwill for India in South East and East Asia, and therefore the sky is the limit for our engagement with this region".[52] Since the Summit was conducted in the backdrop of the worldwide economic recession of 2008-2009, the leaders of India and New Zealand held a broad consensus, obviously in consonance with the other EAS counterparts that the regional countries should take cognizance of the realities unfolded by the global Crisis, with particular emphasis on three key factors: **first,** economic growth policies of the regional countries should be coordinated; **secondly,** the real economy should be kept strong on the basis of domestic demand; and finally, the flows of trade, technology and investment should be kept open, orderly and predictable. While vindicating New Delhi's eagerness on an early realization of the CECA roadmap for economic and financial integration with East Asia, Manmohan Singh called for an Asian Regional Trade Agreement as a pivotal step towards the integration of the region into a broader "Asian Economic Community" and asserted that the conclusion of the India-ASEAN Trade-in-Goods Agreement in August 2009 "is a major first step in our objective of creating an India-ASEAN Regional Trade and Investment Area."[53] In addition to the focus on accentuating the pace of regional economic integration, India and New Zealand also welcomed and appreciated Japan's idea of an East Asian Community "based on the principles of openness, transparency, inclusiveness and functional cooperation," amalgamated with Australia's proposal on an Asia Pacific Community, with ASEAN at the core and combining Philippines' suggestion for an eventual "economic community of Asia", aimed at advancing the stability and prosperity of the Asia Pacific region. Besides, India and New Zealand also recognized the imperative of boosting regional cooperation for responding effectively and spontaneously to natural disasters, towards which, the EAS members adopted the 'Cha-am Hua Hin Statement on EAS Disaster Management.'[54] This Statement emphasized the necessity of implementing measures including the preparedness and disaster risk reduction capacities in the region, in addition to exploring the possibility of establishing a network of disaster response contact points. However, the most successful initiative of New Delhi in taking the process of cultural coordination further with the countries of Southeast and East Asia was manifested when the 'Joint Press Statement of the

4th EAS on the Revival of the Nalanda University' was issued during the Summit, thus appreciating the endeavour of "strengthening regional educational cooperation by tapping the region's centers of excellence in education." The Joint Statement supported the establishment of the Nalanda University as a non-state, non-profit, secular, and self governing international institution with a continental focus that "will bring together the brightest and the most dedicated students from all countries of Asia", in a measure to enable them to acquire liberal and human education, through the pursuit of "intellectual, philosophical, historical and spiritual studies."[55] As a matter of fact, New Zealand acknowledged India's dedication in reviving the Nalanda University as an important watershed in moving towards the phenomenon of 'Asia Literacy', as envisaged in Wellington's White Paper[56] Finally, while resonating the optimistic spirit of Asia Pacific community building as members of the EAS, Manmohon Singh said:

> I am extremely satisfied with the outcome of the India-ASEAN Summit. I found a strong desire among the ASEAN countries to substantially strengthen their links with India in all areas. This includes not only economic cooperation and trade but also science and technology, human resource development, protection of the environment and deeper political and security cooperation.... and therefore the sky is the limit for our engagement with this region.[57]

As an outfit of the 4th EAS meeting, India and New Zealand, while acknowledging the imperative of bolstering trade and investment relations at the bilateral realm, especially in the context of the global recessionary trends, embarked on a process of negotiations for a India-New Zealand Free Trade Agreement (FTA), when the Indian Minister of Commerce and Industry, Anand Sharma met his counterpart, Tim Groser at the Annual Meeting of the World Economic Forum in Davos in January 2010.[58] This effort was noteworthy in the context of the increased volume of bilateral trade, as vindicated by an increase of 16% (worth US$ 442 million) in New Zealand's exports to India in 2008-2009,[59] notwithstanding the dismal portrait of the worldwide meltdown. In the aftermath of the meeting at Davos between the Trade Ministers of India and New Zealand, the first, second and third rounds of FTA negotiations were held in April, August and October 2010 respectively[60] between the two sides. Therefore, with the gradual, but steady emergence of India in the Asia Pacific milieu, and enhanced association with New Zealand within the EAS forum, the Indian Prime Minister, Manmohan Singh, while underscoring the paradigm shift of the global engine of economics and politics to Asia, asserted the importance of attaching unstinted attention to the region, especially in the aftermath of the worldwide economic meltdown, which demonstrated the non-invincibility of Western economies and said:

> The Asia-Pacific region, including South-East Asia, needs much more

> attention by us, and this must seep into our defence and foreign policy planning as never before. There is a palpable desire on the part of the countries of this region to enhance cooperation with us, which we must reciprocate.[61]

The convergence of politico-economic and strategic interests between India and New Zealand was evinced once again, when the leaders of the two countries met at the 5th EAS held in Hanoi on 30 October 2010. While reiterating the salience of the EAS as a forum for political and security collaboration as well as a framework for economic integration and ultimate community building among the countries of the Asia Pacific region, the Prime Minister of New Zealand, John Key affirmed that EAS "has a central role in shaping the region and in promoting closer regional integration"[62] in general and in stepping up the tempo of relations between ASEAN on the one hand, and other EAS partners like India, on the other. The striking point of this Summit was the invitation extended to US and the Russian Federation to join the EAS, given their expressed interest in and commitment to this process. The proposed inclusion of US (viewed as ASEAN as "a resident power" in geopolitical East Asia) and Russia as Observer members was based on the decision of the ASEAN Foreign Ministers' Meeting, held in Hanoi in July 2010, and US' response, flavoured with security activism, was conveyed by Secretary of State, Hillary Clinton, when she attended the Hanoi Summit of EAS and said:

> The East Asia Summit, where you bring other countries in addition to the core ASEAN countries together to discuss political and security matters, is a very important forum for the US to be part of. Where issues of a political, economic, and security consequence are being discussed in the region, the US wants to be there.[63]

The inclusion of US within the circuit of EAS was welcomed by the 16 existing members, including India and New Zealand, as they perceived the involvement of all major powers in the region for fostering a prosperous and secure Asia Pacific, in addition to providing the necessary dialogue forum for negotiated solutions to regional problems and incipient tensions in the region, as a whole. The space which was provided through the EAS between India and New Zealand once again accelerated its momentum when both countries had intensive and in-depth discussions on future directions of the EAS in the backdrop of the transformed regional landscape in the 5th EAS Summit meeting. In their dialogue, the two countries highlighted on the importance of expressing a coordinated stance for maintaining regional peace and stability, maritime security and safety, and peaceful settlement of disputes in accordance with universally agreed principles of international law. Moreover, New Delhi and Wellington, in apposition with their fellow counterparts reaffirmed the stature of EAS as "an important component of the evolving regional architecture, which includes other existing and mutually-reinforcing processes such as the ASEAN+1, ASEAN+3, ASEAN Regional Forum

(ARF), ASEAN Defense Ministers' Meeting Plus (ADMM+)", towards the promotion of community building efforts in East Asia.[64] Axiomatically, India and New Zealand harped on the tangible progress in cooperation within the EAS framework, especially in **six** identified priority areas, namely, **finance**, through achieving sustained economic recovery and development by trade and investment liberalization and facilitation; effective policies and measures to address **climate change**, based on the principles of "Common but Differentiated Responsibilities" and United Nations Framework of Convention on Climate Change (UNFCCC), with the financial support and technology transfer committed by developed countries; **education**, recognized as a key factor in promoting human resources development, bridging the development gap and enhancing regional competitiveness; **energy conservation**, through efforts to address market barriers and promote more transparent energy trade and investment; cooperation in **disaster management**, by welcoming New Zealand's provision of NZ$8 million towards the implementation of the Australia-initiated Work Plan of the ASEAN Agreement on Disaster Management and Emergency Response (AADMER); and **prevention of pandemic diseases**, through information sharing and strengthening of environmental and ecological conservation in the region.[65]

In a positive bid to take further the overall corpus of relations between India and New Zealand in general and the economic rhythm in particular, given the backdrop of the enhanced mutual interaction at the EAS promenade, the two countries agreed to conclude a New Comprehensive Economic Cooperation Agreement, popularly known as FTA by March 2012, covering trade in goods, services and investment, with the vision of increasing the total volume of trade from US$ 1 billion in 2010-2011, (an increase by 7.83% in 2010-2011) to US $3 billion in 2012-2013.[66] The negotiations commenced in April 2010 and up to May 2011, India and New Zealand have already completed 5 rounds of bilateral deliberations. This optimistic fervour in the trajectory of Indo-New Zealand relations was announced by the Indian Minister of Commerce, Anand Sharma, at the India-New Zealand Joint Business Council meeting, held in Auckland on 9-10 May 2011.[67] In this meeting, while welcoming New Delhi's economic vision, New Zealand's Trade Minister, Tim Groser asserted, "The FTA will not only increase the economic opportunities for both sides but will also open up big segments of investment and services, including food supply chain, green technologies, IT innovation, tourism and films", thereby encouraging India's potential for investments in New Zealand, particularly in dairy, phyto-sanitary issues relating to trade in plants and animal products, renewable energy (including civil-nuclear), agro-processing and cold chain sectors, in which New Zealand's assistance would help the Indian farmers get a better deal by reduction in the wastage incurred from transporting fruits and vegetables from farms to the markets. Thus, while heralding the prospect of an India-New Zealand FTA, as a booster for trade diversification, not only by tariff elimination, but also by addressing a spectrum of non-tariff barriers, Tim Groser reiterated that the FTA would "provide a framework for our trade and economic links to reach that potential. The more open access and investment flows that can come from the FTA will be of benefit to businesses in both countries."[68] As a matter of fact, the FTA negotiations were expedited in the context of the proposal put forward by the Indian Minister of Agriculture, Sharad Pawar to institutionalize an 'umbrella agreement' between the Ministries of Agriculture of India and New Zealand, in March 2008,[69] covering agriculture and allied activities including food processing, agricultural research, bio-security, engagement of private sector of both the countries and exchange of information in the areas of mutual interest. On this issue of agricultural cooperation between India and New Zealand, both of which are agriculture-intensive countries, the Governor General of New Zealand, Anand Satyanand, during his visit to New Delhi in September 2008, said:

> India looks to embark on a 'Second Green Revolution' to enhance India's agricultural productivity. There could be possibilities for enhanced cooperation given New Zealand's world recognized expertise in agribusiness/agri-technology whether that related to storage, transport, research and development or marketing. We agreed that the two countries could cooperate more closely in the area of climate change given that we both have large agricultural sectors and New Zealand has an objective to be the world leader in research relating to methane gas abatement from agriculture.[70]

As against this backdrop of evolving conviviality, the Prime Minister of New Zealand, John Key visited India in June 2011, thus crossing another threshold of FTA negotiations, and signed protocols with his Indian counterpart, Manmohan Singh, in film production, higher education and research to strengthen people-to-people interaction. Moreover, while acknowledging the need to diversify intra-mural ties in both traditional and non-traditional areas, such as cooperation in defence, anti-terrorism, non-conventional sources of energy, Prime Minister Key expressed his willingness to jointly work towards ensuring maritime security in general and navigable sea lanes in the Asia Pacific region, in particular, as expressed in a Defence Press Note issued by New Delhi which said, "The visit of the Prime Minister will further strengthen India-New Zealand maritime cooperation."[71] While highlighting the perils posed by international terrorism, the visiting dignitary agreed to put in all efforts to tackle terrorism as a whole, in collaboration with India, on many fronts, including "sharing information" on the global scourge of terrorism, thereby resolving to do "everything we can to make the world a safer place."[72] In addition to this outlook, New Delhi and Wellington have agreed to cooperate in the development of education, tourism[73] and motivating the Indian Diaspora in New Zealand, mostly engaged in domestic retail trade, services sector, IT, medicine, engineering, etc. Thus, as the portrait of bilateral relations between India and New Zealand, anchored on common historical linkages, a Westminster constitutional heritage, language, sports and cultural links, is acquiring a multi-dimensional and multilateral hue, the EAS provides a resilient groundwork for both countries to play a proactive role for the sustenance of peace, stability and holistic development of the Asia Pacific region.

India and New Zealand: The Differences Within

Having discussed the various Summits, which have taken place since the formation of EAS in 2005, it is amply clear that the EAS remains quite innovative in the context of the evolving global order, where coordination and better understanding are the best ways to establish tranquility and thereby reduce tensions in the Asia Pacific region. The idea of East Asian community building has been, no doubt, a long-drawn process but the EAS initiative, whatever it has achieved so far, clearly signals a line in tune with the dream of East Asian regionalism. There are still a number of important issues, where differences exist among the East Asian partners, in which they are directly involved. On the other hand, there are certain issues, which have originated outside the purview of this region, but have time and again, created a spillover effect on the psyche of these member-states. Issues like South China Sea, nuclear disarmament, membership of UN-Security Council, US policies in West Asia, the growing assertiveness of China in the Straits of Malacca, US' re-entry in the Southeast Asian region and its initiative to establish the Quadrilateral Alliance (including India, Australia, Japan, US), terrorism, piracy, etc. have occasionally created hinges among the EAS members. Naturally, these divergences, on many occasions, have demonstrated differences in outlook between India and New Zealand and resulted in situational differences in the development of bilateral coordination. The major factors, which have impeded the smooth flow of better understanding between New Delhi and Wellington, are the nuclear issue, negotiation process in WTO, and occasional differences with reference to the Kashmir issue.

With reference to the nuclear stance, India is a nuclear power and New Zealand is not so, and this difference in status as well as India's stand on NNPT as a discriminatory regime, have clearly displayed severe difference of opinion between New Delhi and Wellington. In 1974 and 1998, India blasted nuclear bombs for peaceful purposes, through which, it proved its ability to manufacture a nuclear device. India's argument behind these two blasts was solely based on its national interest against the ground reality of China's covert supplies of nuclear stockpiles to Pakistan to challenge India's position in the South Asian region. This mindset of the Indian policy makers, however, cannot be interpreted as the ultimate outlook of New Delhi regarding the policy of nuclear armaments. In fact, Morarji Desai's idea of Total Disarmament (1978) and Rajiv Gandhi's initiated Plan of Action for Nuclear Disarmament (1988) remain enough evidences of India's positive outlook towards complete and universal nuclear disarmament. Unfortunately, the traditionally nuclear and non-nuclear countries of the world, including New Zealand, did not accept this rationale of New Delhi. The anti-nuclear stand of New Zealand was clearly reflected when it, along with other countries of the world, under the banner of US, sanctioned India in the aftermath of New Delhi's nuclear blasts of 1974 and 1998. The Government of New Zealand never agreed to the rationale as mentioned by New Delhi behind its nuclear blasts and this outlook was a corollary to taken by US and other Western countries. In fact, the relationship between India and New Zealand had nose-dived following the 1998 Pokhran II experiment, as a consequence of which, New Zealand recalled its Ambassador to India, in addition to giving a dressing down to the then Indian Envoy in Wellington, even before he had presented his credentials. However, the situation was reversed following India's Nuclear Deal with US, signed in March 2006. This new evolving situation put Wellington in a dilemma, premised on the reconciliation of its earlier anti-nuclear policy and later shift for accommodating India's outlook on the nuclear issue. While New Zealand's hard-line anti-nuclear policy was manifested in the Nuclear Suppliers Group (NSG) meetings vis-à-vis India-specific exemptions, the gradual transformation in Wellington's perception with respect to New Delhi's benign role in the Asia Pacific region was borne out when New Zealand's Disarmament Minister, Phil Goff asserted at the India-New Zealand Business Council meeting in October 2007, "India has a good non-proliferation track record, it has developed, tested and possesses nuclear weapons.... New Zealand would welcome India's accession to these treaties (NPT and CTBT)".[74] Ultimately, on 6 September 2008, in an unprecedented step, New Zealand granted India the waiver at the Nuclear Suppliers Group (NSG) meeting held in Vienna, overcoming misgivings expressed by other NSG counterparts like Austria and Ireland, to a country (India), which had neither signed the Nuclear Non Proliferation Treaty (NNPT) - the cornerstone of international nuclear weapons control - nor the Comprehensive Test Ban Treaty (CTBT). However, New Zealand, which is a member of the NSG but not of the International Atomic Energy Agency's (IAEA) Board of Governors, attached a few conditions to the waiver granted to India, which included the following scenarios: New Delhi conducting nuclear tests and its signing of the IAEA Additional Protocol.[75] The Protocol—a legal document, complementing comprehensive safeguards agreements—embraces measures to strengthen the IAEA's inspection capabilities, thus enabling the IAEA not only to verify the non-diversion of declared nuclear material but also to provide assurances as to the absence of undeclared nuclear material and activities in a State.[76] Thus, slowly but steadily, New Zealand's pragmatism has evolved, based on the raison-de-etre that India mentioned time and again.

Another major bone of contention between India and New Zealand is the issue of Kashmir, which is officially viewed by Wellington "as a nuclear flash point", since the Kashmir dispute forced India and Pakistan to go nuclear, thus bringing South Asia to the brink of a nuclear standoff in 1998. According to the New Zealand Government, since the Kashmir imbroglio is directly related to the historical conflict between India and Pakistan, "the resolution of the nuclear issue also lies in the resolution of the Kashmir issue."[77] Such an outlook vis-à-vis the sensitive thorn of Kashmir evoked an acidic retort from New Delhi, stemming not only from its emotional susceptibility about the sovereignty of Jammu and Kashmir, but also its vehement rejection of identifying the nuclear issue with the contention about Kashmir. In spite of the cleft between New Delhi and Wellington regarding the Kashmir conundrum, New Zealand has welcomed the mutual efforts of India and Pakistan to re-engage with each other, in the context of the interdependent global order. Optimistically enough, New Zealand hopes that the evolving spirit of dialogue and coordination between New Delhi and Islamabad will foster an ambience of confidence and peaceful negotiations, with respect to issues of bilateral discord, including Kashmir and nuclear proliferation.[78] In fact, the recent thaw in bilateral ties between India and Pakistan which started from the 16th SAARC Summit at Thimphu in April 2010 and culminated in the visit of the Pakistani Foreign Minister, Hina Rabbani to India in July 2011 has been wholeheartedly welcomed by the Government of New Zealand since the stagnant "trust deficit" between New Delhi and Islamabad has changed its direction.

Finally, another area of divergence between India and New Zealand, which has time and again hitched the evolution of their ties, is India's economic policy, with special reference to import restrictions in agriculture. For a number of years, India had maintained quantitative import restrictions on over 2700 types of agricultural, textile and industrial products, by claiming its entitlement to maintain these restrictions, based on the rationale of balance of payments. However, after India joined the WTO in 1995, New Zealand strongly objected to India's quantitative restrictions on agricultural products and brought the issue to the WTO Dispute Settlement Understanding[79] in July 1997. In this context, New Zealand's Minister of Trade, Phil Goff, while addressing the concerns of the developing countries, which had long suffered from the farm subsidies imposed by developed countries, mainly US and EU, stated that India and other major developing countries needed to improve their market opening offers and seek parity in tariff reduction vis à vis the developed world.[80] Although such a stance held by New Zealand appeared to echo the unheard and trampled voices of the developing members of WTO, New Delhi perceived it as Wellington's ploy to persuade agriculture-intensive countries like India and Brazil to liberalize their markets, and thus provide greater access to major agricultural exporters of the ilk of New Zealand, ultimately leading to the emaciation of India's domestic agricultural base. From the viewpoint of India, its reservation and restrictions of the flow of agricultural goods from the developed world is based on its own national economic interest. The economies of India, China and Brazil maintain their sustenance through their strong base of agricultural production and have balanced the internal economic system. If India allows external agricultural products in its domestic market, it would naturally disturb the internal balance on the one hand and make the agricultural products less competitive, on the other. Thus, India has not welcomed New Zealand's prescription of reducing quantitative restrictions on agricultural goods, as a result of which, occasional simmering tensions exist between the two countries at the WTO platform.

The Road to Future

In spite of these minor differences, the overall relations between India and New Zealand, especially in the post-cold war years, exhibit a progressive trend. This improved trend has evolved due to a number of factors and among them, the emerging global order, which led to the inevitable reality to survive; the drastic improvement in Indo-US relations and its spillover effects on the overall corpus of India's foreign policy outlook; the emergence of India as a potential economic power in the Asian region; New Delhi's 'Look East' Policy and its extension to 'Move East' which brought India into the orbit of East Asian regionalism; and India's growing strength in naval power, ranging from the Indian Ocean to South China Sea, which can balance China's growing assertiveness in that region on the one hand, and act as a balancer, on the other, gave many regional powers located in Southeast and Asia Pacific regions a sort of security relief. Naturally, India's growing ties with New Zealand cannot be treated as an isolated event, but the factors mentioned above should be reckoned with in its entirety. Therefore, the East Asia platform, which brought India and New Zealand closer to each other, has generated a feeling in the diplomacy of world politics that distance is not at all a factor in the emerging global order, but it is the mindset, which is essential for better coordination. While summing up, the evolving ties between India and New Zealand, mainly through the EAS promenade remain quite prominent in the context of budding Asian regionalism, since multilateral institutions is one of the important vehicles to develop better understanding in the present juncture for a just, equitable world order and proper global governance. India and New Zealand must continue the development spree, which they have gathered through the EAS platform and sustain it in an irreversible manner, so that the strings of relations are not disconnected between them. They must take lessons from the pragmatic nature of the globe, experienced through the past and EAS and thus, resolve differences, whatever they may be, amicably. The kaleidoscopic political complexion of the EAS may compel these countries to set common but differential goals in such areas as climate change, energy efficiency, maritime security, agriculture and nuclear non-proliferation. They must play a more effective role in minimizing the economic gap, which existed among the ASEAN members and should also employ diplomatic means in order to reduce the present state of political and security threats emanated with reference to South China Sea in the ARF platform and other issues have to be dealt with not in an assertive manner, but through mutual acceptance, with a sober flavour. The peaceful mindset, which both countries have displayed over the years, must be used as a vehicle for implementing the dream, which was envisioned in the First EAS Summit in Kuala Lumpur in 2005 and this could also be a major lesson for other countries of EAS, since it is not dispute, but peace which can sustain the initiative of regionalism, not only for the region, but also for other regions to adhere.

End Notes

1. Alexander Wendt, "Anarchy is What States Make of It: The Social Construction of Power Politics", *International Organization*, Vol. 46, 1992, p. 417.
2. Christopher Dent, *East Asian Regionalism*, Routledge, London and New York, 2008, pp. 6-7.
3. David Martin Jones and Michael L.R. Smith, "Constructing Communities: The Curious Case of East Asian Regionalism", *Review of International Studies,* Vol. 33, British International Studies Association, 2007, p. 173.
4. Tridib Chakraborti and Mohor Chakraborty, "India and the Asia Pacific Region: Dilemma of a Changing APEC Mindset", *Asia Pacific Journal of Social Sciences*, Special Issue No. 1, December 2010, International Society for Asia Pacific Society, p. 6.
5. Ignatius Low, "Wanted: An E. Asian 'Community'", *Straits Times*, 16 January 2002.
6. Tridib Chakraborti and Mohor Chakraborty, "India and the Asia Pacific Region: Dilemma of a Changing APEC Mindset", n. 4, pp. 6-7.
7. *Far Eastern Economic Review*, 23 December 1999, p. 27.
8. *Final Report of the East Asia Vision Group*, 4 November 2002, Phnom Penh, http://www.aseansec.org/viewpdf.asp?file, accessed on 14 January 2003, *The phrase 'community' was used for the first time in this report.*
9. *Final Report of the East Asia Vision Group*, 4 November 2002, Phnom Penh, see also http://www.mofa.go.jp/region/asia-paci/report2001.pdf , accessed on 14 January 2003
10. G.V.C. Naidu, "East Asian Regionalism and Multilateralism: An Indian Perspective", *IDSA-JIIA Bilateral Round Table Papers*, New Delhi, 2007, p. 60.
11. Arpita Mathur, "Japan's Approach to Regionalism: Outlook Towards the EAS and EAC", *Strategic Analysis*, IDSA, New Delhi, Vol. 33, No. 5, September 2009, p. 681.
12. David Shambaugh and Michael Yahuda (eds.), *International Relations in Asia*, Rowman and Little Field Publishers, United States, 2010, p. 209.
13. *The Japan Times*, 13 December 2005 (http://www.japantimes.co.jp)
14. Arpita Mathur, "Japan's Approach to Regionalism: Outlook Towards the EAS and EAC", *Strategic Analysis*, n. 13, p. 681.
15. See Chak Mun, *India's Strategic Interests in Southeast Asia and Singapore*, Institute of South Asian Studies (Singapore) and Macmillan Publishers India Ltd., 2009, p. 90.
16. *Kuala Lumpur Declaration on the First East Asia Summit*, Kuala Lumpur, 14 December 2005, http://www.aseansec.org/18098.htm, accessed on 30 December 2005.
17. Chairman's Statement, First East Asia Summit, Kuala Lumpur, 14 December 2005, http://www.aseansec.org, accessed on 18 December 2005.
18. Man Mohini Kaul, "India's Look East Policy: New Era of India-ASEAN Relations", *World Focus,* Special Issue, New Delhi, October 2010, p. 433.

19. *The Hindu*, 9 April 2002.
20. For details, see http://www.aseansec.org, See also, http://www.mea.gov.in/staticfile/meapublication/sec047
21. *Manmohan Singh's Address at the 5th India-ASEAN Summit*, 14 January 2007, Cebu, the Philippines, Visit of Prime Minister, Dr. Manmohan Singh to the Philippines, 13-15 January 2007, Public Diplomacy Division, Ministry of External Affairs, New Delhi, March 2007, pp. 15-17.
22. Ibid. p. 64.
23. Tridib Chakraborti, "Disparate Priorities: Explaining the Penumbra of India's Look East Policy", in K. Raja Reddy (ed.), *India and ASEAN: Foreign Policy Dimensions for the 21st Century*, New Century Publications, New Delhi, 2005, p. 53.
24. Ibid., pp. 53-54.
25. Faizal Yahya, "India and Southeast Asia: Revisited", *Contemporary Southeast Asia*, Vol. 25, No. 1, April 2003, p. 93.
26. Tridib Chakraborti, "BIMSTEC: Origin, Growth and Progress", *World Focus*, New Delhi, January 2008, p. 14.
27. *Annual Report: 2002-2003*, Ministry of External Affairs, Government of India, New Delhi, 2003, p. 24.
28. *Annual Report: 2003-2004*, Ministry of External Affairs, Government of India, New Delhi, 2004, p. 38.
29. *The Jakarta Post*, 2 July 2004.
30. For details, see http://www.aseansec.org/speech.
31. *India-ASEAN FTA in goods has been signed in 2010; CECAs have been signed between India and other EAS members like Thailand, Singapore, Indonesia, Japan and South Korea, while FTA negotiations with New Zealand in under way.*
32. Tridib Chakraborti, "India's Conviviality with Southeast Asia: Traversing the Saga of 'Look East' Achievements-Hindrances Dichotomy", Unpublished Paper Presented at the International Conference on "India and ASEAN in the Asia-Pacific: Challenges and Strategies", School of International Studies, Jawaharlal Nehru University, New Delhi, India, 25-26 March 2010.
33. "Our Future With Asia: Seriously Asia", *Asia White Paper*, New Zealand Ministry of Foreign Affairs and Trade, Wellington, 2003, http://www.mfat.govt.nz/Media-and-publications/Publications/Asia-White-Paper/0-seriously-asia.phpauck, accessed on 23 June 2010.
34. Foreword by Rt. Hon. Helen Clark, Prime Minister of New Zealand, "Our Future With Asia: Seriously Asia", *Asia White Paper*, n. 35.
35. For details, see, "ASEAN-Australia-New Zealand Free Trade Area Agreement", Department of Foreign Affairs and Trade, Government of Australia, Canberra, http://www.dfat.gov.au/trade/fta/asean
36. "ASEAN and New Zealand: Trusted Friends, Dynamic Partners", New Zealand Ministry of Foreign Affairs and Trade, http://www.mfat.govt.nz/Foreign-Relations/Asia/0-trusted-friends.php, accessed on 5 June 2011.
37. *Defence White Paper: 2010*, Ministry of Defence, Government of New Zealand, Wellington, November 2010, See also *Defence Assessment,* Ministry of Defence, Government of New Zealand, Ministry of Defence, Wellington, July 2010, http://www.defence.govt.nz/pdfs/defence-review-2009-released-defence-assessment-july-2010.pdf, accessed on 4 June 2011.
38. "New Zealand's Strategic Outlook to 2035", *Defence White Paper: 2010,* Chapter 3, Ministry of Defence, Government of New Zealand, Wellington, 2010, http://

www.defence.govt.nz/reports-publications/defence-white-paper-2010/chapter3-nz-strategic-outlook-to-2035.html, accessed on 14 May 2011.

39. Terrence O' Brien, "Facing the World the New Zealand Way", *New Zealand International Review*, Vol. 30, No. 1, Wellington, January-February 2005, pp. 25-27.
40. Terrence O'Brien, "Strengthening New Zealand Relationships in East Asia", http://www.eastasiaforum.org/2008/12/31/new-zealand-in-2008-and-2009/, accessed on 15 January 2009.
41. *Kuala Lumpur Declaration on the First East Asia Summit*, Kuala Lumpur, n. 18.
42. "New Zealand's Strategic Outlook to 2035", *Defence White Paper: 2010,* Chapter 3, Ministry of Defence, n. 39.
43. Tridib Chakraborti, "India's Southeast Asia Policy in the 21st Century: Perambulating the Horizon", in Y. Yagama Reddy (ed.), *Emerging India in Asia-Pacific*, New Century Publications, New Delhi, 2007, p. 154.
44. Chariman Dato' Seri Abdullah Ahmad Badawi, Prime Minister of Malaysia's Statement of the First East Asia Summit Kuala Lumpur, n. 19.
45. *Annual Report: 2006-2007*, Ministry of External Affairs, Government of India, New Delhi, 2007, pp. 25-26.
46. *Cebu Declaration on East Asian Energy Security*, Cebu, the Philippines, 15 January 2007, http://www.asean.org/23313.htm, accessed on 31 January 2007.
47. Mun-Heng Toh, "ASEAN+6 As a Step Towards an Asian Economic Community", East Asia Forum, 15 May 2009, http://www.eastasiaforum.org/2009/05/15, accessed on 20 June 2009.
48. "The ASEAN Community: Unblocking the Roadblocks", *ASEAN Studies Centre, Report No. 1,* ISEAS, Singapore, 2008, http://www.iseas.edu.sg/aseanstudiescentre/ASC1.pdf, accessed on 24 February 2010; See also P.S. Suryanarayan, "Eastern Initiatives", *Frontline*, 9 February 2007, p. 58.
49. Annual Report: 2007-08, Ministry of External Affairs, Government of India, New Delhi, 2008, p. 24.
50. *Singapore Declaration on Climate Change, Energy and the Environment*, Singapore, 21 November 2007, http://www.aseansec.org/21116.htm, accessed on 31 December 2007.
51. Statement of Lee Hsien Loong, Chairman of the 3rd EAS, Singapore, 21 November 2007, http://www.asean.org/22765.htm, accessed on 30 November 2007; See also http://www.aseansec.org/aadcp/repsf/abouteastasiasummit.html
52. For details, see Tridib Chakraborti, "India's Look East Policy: Time for Stock-Taking", *World Focus (Annual Number)*, New Delhi, November-December 2009, pp. 461-469
53. Siddharth Varadarajan, "India Looks East Amid Changing Asian Equations", *The Hindu*, 26 October 2009.
54. Statement by Prime Minister of Thailand, Abhisit Vejjajiva and Chairman, 4th East Asia Summit, Cha-am Hua Hin, Thailand, 25 October 2009, http://www.aseansec.org/23609.htm, accessed on 1 January 2010.
55. Joint Press Statement of the 4th East Asia Summit on the Revival of Nalanda University, Cha-am Hua Hin, Thailand, 25 October 2009, http://www.15thaseansummit-th.org/PDF/25-08_EAS%20Statement.pdf, accessed on 1 January 2010.
56. "Our Future With Asia: Seriously Asia", *Asia White Paper*, n. 35.
57. http://www.pmindia.nic.in/speech/content4print.asp?id=835, accessed on 24 March 2010
58. *The Hindustan Times*, 1 February 2010.
59. In 2008-09, New Zealand's export to India was worth US$ 442 million.
60. *Annual Report: 2010-2011*, Ministry of External Affairs, Government of India, New Delhi, 2011, p. 12.

61. Manmohan Singh's Address at the Annual Combined Commanders' Conference, New Delhi, 14 September 2010, http://www.pib.nic.in/release/release.asp?relid=53305, accessed on 30 September 2010.
62. Prime Minister of New Zealand, John Key's Speech at the 5th East Asia Summit, Hanoi, 30 October 2010, http://www.johnkey.co.nz/categories/4-Speech/P3.html, accessed on 2 December 2010; See also http://www.mfat.govt.nz/Media-and-publications/Features/660-East-Asia-Summit.php
63. *The Xinhua*, 30 October 2010; See also, http://www.en.rsf.org/vietnam
64. *Statement of the Prime Minister of Vietnam and Chairman, Nguyen Tan Dung,* Fifth EAS, Hanoi, 30 October 2010, http://www.aseansec.org/25490.htm, accessed on 1 December 2010.
65. *Hanoi Declaration of the Fifth Anniversary of the East Asia Summit,* Hanoi, 30 October 2010, http://www.asean2010.vn/asean_en/news/48/2DAA10/Ha-Noi-Declaration-on-the-commemoration-of-the-fifth-anniversary-of-the-EAST-ASIA-summit, accessed on 1 December 2010.
66. *Annual Report: 2010-2011*, Ministry of External Affairs, Government of India, New Delhi, 2011, p. 25.
67. http://www.inzbc.org/report-inzbc-ficci-joint-business-forum, accessed on 1 June 2011.
68. Sujay Mehudia, "India, New Zealand to Fast-track FTA", *The Hindu*, 10 May 2011.
69. *The Economic Times*, 25 March 2008.
70. For details, see http://www. meaindia.nic.in/meaxpsite/foreignrelation/new_zealand.pdf
71. Http://www.pib.nic.in, 29 June 2011, accessed on 1 July 2011.
72. "John Key Eyes Free Trade in India Visit", *New Zealand Herald*, 25 June 2011, http://www.nzherald.co.nz, accessed on 1 July 2011.
73. To facilitate the increasing tourism traffic between India and New Zealand, the two countries signed an Air Services Agreement in May 2008, which allows direct flights between Auckland and Mumbai.
74. *Minister of Disarmament of New Zealand, Phil Goff's Speech at the India-New Zealand Business Council*, 24 October 2007, http://www.gg.govt.nz/node/760, accessed on 1 November 2007.
75. For details, see http://www.iaea.org/Publications/Factsheets/English/sg_overview.html
76. *The National Business Review*, 7 September 2008; See also "India's NSG Battle to Focus on Nuclear Tech", *The Times of India*, 7 September 2008.
77. "Kashmir Nuclear Flashpoint", New Zealand Prime Minister, Helen Clarke's Interview to Saurabh Shukla, *The Hindustan Times*, 11 October 2004.
78. Annual *ASEAN Security Outlook: 2008*, ASEAN Regional Forum, http://www.aseanregionalforum.org/LinkClick.aspx?link, accessed on 16 February 2009.
79. http://www.mfat.govt.nz/Treaties-and-International-Law/02-Trade-law-and-free tradeagreements/India-Imports.php, accessed on 14 December 2009.
80. Pankaj Jha, "Reconfiguring India-New Zealand Relations: Perspectives from India", Rajaram Panda and Pankaj Jha (eds.), *India and New Zealand: Emerging Challenges,* Institute for Defence Studies and Analyses (IDSA), New Delhi, 2010, p. 160.

10

New Zealand's Re-engagement with the United States

Ruth Rhea Khan

Mutual commitment to democracy, rule of law, human rights and the market economy[1] have enabled bilateral relations between the two Pacific countries to withstand the tests of time. Occasional hiccups have not been successful in disrupting the 'longstanding friendship' between the two for very long. New Zealand Prime Minister John Key stated, "We are old friends facing new opportunities. New Zealand sees itself as a small but important partner for the US and with our shared values we believe New Zealand can work with the US on efforts to enhance global peace and security".[2]

In international politics, as the old cliche goes, there are no permanent friends or enemies, only permanent interests and the relations between the United States and New Zealand have never been brought to the brink of the latter. It has been a relationship that has experienced normal ebbs and flows with a brief tumultous interlude when ties were ruptured after the Labour Party led by Prime Minister David Lange came to power with a political commitment based on banning all atomic-powered and nuclear armed warships from New Zealand as an initial step towards making the nation a 'nuclear free zone'.[3] Consequently, in August 1986 the United States suspended its Australia-New Zealand-US, or ANZUS security obligations to New Zealand.

But much water has flown since then and the US, especially the Obama administration, is actively restoring its relationship by re-engaging New Zealand through meaningful security and economic involvement. Mentionworthy in this regard are the US Secretary of State, Hillary Clinton's November 2010 visit and the consequent signing of the Wellington Declaration and the US entry into the Trans Pacific Trade Partnership (TPP), signed in November 2011. The nuances of re-engagement are undergoing a fundamental transformation as newer concerns are mushrooming aside traditional common concerns of regional stability and security in the Southwest Pacific and archipelagic Southeast Asia, promoting free trade through World Trade Organisation (WTO) and Asia Pacific Economic Cooperation (APEC), scientific research in the Antarctic etc are making cooperation between the two absolutely imperative.

The Nuclear Factor

The decision of the Labour government of Prime Minister David Lange to implement the only practical measure of nuclear arms control available to it: the absolute exclusion of nuclear weapons from New Zealand upon entering office in July 1984 did not go well with the US.[4] The US request for a port visit by a conventionally powered warship, *USS Buchanan* was turned down because the government failed to absolutely guarantee that the *Buchanan* was not carrying nuclear weapons.[5] Lange (1985) in a *Foreign Affairs* article mentions, "the policy reflects the fact that there is simply no need for nuclear weapons to be brought into New Zealand. The strategic environment does not call for nuclear weaponry... By keeping such weapons out of New Zealand, we aim to ensure both that a nuclear dimension is not inappropriately injected into our area and that we do not, even inadvertently, become embroiled in a nuclear strategy."[6]

New Zealand's anti-nuke stance placed it in the "thick of global work on nuclear disarmament."[7] Implicit in it was the implementation of five treaties that are part of the history of international disarmament namely the South Pacific Nuclear free Zone Treaty, the Partial Test Ban Treaty, the Non Proliferation Treaty, the Seabed Arms Control Treaty and the Biological Weapons Convention. The decision to disallow *Buchanan* led to the United States unilaterally suspending New Zealand from ANZUS. Leader of the Opposition Helen Clark believed New Zealand was justified in putting nuclear disarmament measures at the forefront of its agenda, even to the point where it separated them from traditional allies and defence arrangements.[8]

Even after President George H.W. Bush's 1991 announcement that US surface ships do not normally carry nuclear weapons,[9] New Zealand has not returned to resuming its full ANZUS security obligations and partnership. Despite suspension of the US security obligations, the New Zealand Government has reaffirmed the importance it attaches to continued close political, economic, and social ties with the United States.[10]

The Obama administration has taken innovative steps to work around their past differences and is encouraging the resumption of warmer relations with its erstwhile ANZUS ally. Secretary Clinton stated that the US had created new parameters for military cooperation with New Zealand.[11] Consequently it was very significant that Prime Minister John Key was invited to the first Nuclear Security Summit hosted by President Obama in April 2010 in Washington DC. Forty-nine Leaders from every region of the world participated (46 countries, United Nations (UN), European Union (EU) and International Atomic Energy

Agency (IAEA) attended.[12] This event was historic because not since 1945 has a US President hosted a gathering of so many Heads of State and Governments.[13] New Zealand's inclusion in the inaugural summit attests its anti-nuclear credentials as being recognised by the US.[14] New Zealand has joined the Proliferation Security Initiative (PSI), the Global Initiative to Combat Nuclear Terrorism (GICNT), and the Group of Eight (G8) Global Partnership to secure nuclear materials in the former Soviet Union. In April 2010, PM Key announced a further financial contribution in support of the United States' Nuclear Smuggling Outreach Initiative.[15] PM Key mentioned to reporters that President Obama said New Zealand had "well and truly" earned its place at the table for top level discussions on nuclear security and 'could offer leadership on that issue'.[16]

It is mention worthy that the only major policy difference that remains is the ban on the visit of nuclear ships to New Zealand. However, with the United States relaxing the ban on military exercises with New Zealand[17] things are looking promising. Moreover, President Obama advocating his vision of a nuclear free world implies that New Zealand's nuclear-free legislation appears no longer to be an impediment or irritant to the United States, but rather a valued credential, making New Zealand a potentially important partner in the multilateral work required to achieve nuclear disarmament.[18] Thus, New Zealand's national policy on being nuclear free that had been an albatross in their bilateral relations is finding resonance in the US foreign policy agenda, signaling the resumption of robust and dynamic future relations.

The Wellington Declaration

At a speech to the Center for Strategic and International Studies at Washington DC in September 2010, Assistant Secretary Kurt Campbell remarked, "I think that the United States and New Zealand currently are the closest possible of friends... the United States and New Zealand see the world in such similar terms, in fact, in many respects, much closer than some countries that would be described as formal allies in the current environment."[19] The New Zealand-United States re-engagement has picked up momentum and been strengthened significantly with Minister of Foreign Affairs for New Zealand Murray McCully and Secretary of State Hillary Clinton signing the Wellington Declaration on 4 November 2010. Prior to the signing of this Declaration Prime Minister John Key stated, "The relationship between our two countries is in great shape. It's the best it's been for 25 years."[20] The Wellington Declaration is termed as a 'new strategic partnership' with the United States. The media note from the Office of the US Department of State mentions, "Our goal is a partnership for the 21st Century that is flexible, dynamic, and reflects our fundamental beliefs and aspirations."[21]

Clinton's November visit also had other agendas where both the countries have agreed to cooperate in areas where they had shared interests and common aspirations. This would include affirming their global commitment to peacekeeping, commitment to the environment, partnering on transnational issues in the Pacific etc.[22] The economic aspect of their relationship would also be a focus area as both were continuing their Trans-Pacific Partnership negotiations. Secretary Clinton mentioned, "her visit is part of a committed, concerted effort to restore America's rightful place as an engaged Pacific nation. In this, as in so many other endeavors, we have a strong partner in New Zealand. This is, for us, a very important relationship..."[23] Secretary Clinton also described NZ as a country that "punches way above its weight", after signing the agreement bringing the two countries closer than ever together.[24]

Secretary Clinton's visit to New Zealand was part of her ten day itinerary of the Asia Pacific tour that is symbolic of the US commitment to being 'back in Asia'. This statement is in keeping with the spirit of her earlier declaration, "just as Asia is critical to America's future, an engaged America is vital to Asia's future. The region is eager for our leadership and our business—perhaps more so than at any time in modern history."[25]

Having realised that New Zealand's anti nuclear stance is permanent, Washington seems to have found a new way to work around the loss of its ANZUS ally 25 years ago. Audrey Young in a New Zealand Herald article comments that the declaration is thought to have been proposed by Washington as a tangible symbol of the restoration of the relationship since its decision in 2007 to accept New Zealand's anti-nuclear stance as permanent.[26] However, Robert Ayson and David Capie argue that expecting too much out of the Wellington Declaration to expect a return to the ANZUS ties between them is highly unlikely as New Zealanders are unlikely to revert their decision of nuclear free legislation that had led to the termination of ANZUS.[27]

Viewed either way, this multifaceted re-engagement is aimed at widening the politico-security focus to engaging in economic diplomacy and also actively participating in the international system, moving beyond just promoting trade and investments to ensuring that growing linkages help firmly cement the relationship between peace and prosperity.

Coinciding New Zealand and the US interests in Asia

New Zealand has fought wars in Asia after 1945, including the Korean War in 1950 –1953, and the Vietnam War 1964 – 1972. It was part of the Southeast Asia Treaty Organisation (SEATO) in 1954, and the Five Power Defence Act (FPDA) in 1967. New Zealand was also invited to be dialogue partner and observer in the Association of Southeast Asian Nations in 1967.[28]

It was Prime Minister Jim Bolger who in 1993 at Tokyo had triggered the debate on whether New Zealand was an Asian country. He declared that he was 'proud to be an Asian leader'.[29] At that time Opposition leader Helen Clark objected strongly to Bolger's identification with Asia. Linking identity with potential economic advantages was seen as wanting to jump the bandwagon as Asian economies were taking off. However, the debate has run its course in the academia, among politicians and in business circles and New Zealand's economic ties with Asia have nonetheless strengthened over the decades.

New Zealand's active participation in Asian affairs is leading not only to closer economic integration with the region but is enabling it to be a part of the security architecture that is taking concrete shape and form in the region. It has been participating in the ASEAN Regional Forum (ARF) since 1994, a key forum for security dialogue in the region and the ASEAN Defense Ministers' Meeting-Plus (ADMM+) since 2010, the latest regional security architecture that includes the US and Russia that have sought to engage in East Asian dynamics. New Zealand is also a part of the East Asia Summit (EAS) since its formation in 2005.

The United States, by signaling its intention to join the EAS and by working to elevate its relationship with ASEAN to a more strategic level, appears to be shaping regional architectures in a way that will be more inclusive and trans-Pacific in nature.[30] In this way its bilateral relations with New Zealand is further consolidated as both meet regularly in the multilateral and regional fora such as UN and its specialised agencies, APEC, EAS, ARF and the ADMM+.

Further, New Zealand was spared from the effects of the global financial crisis of 2008 because of its amalgamation into Asian economic enterprises. Prime Minister John Key made visits to three East Asian countries in 2010 namely China, South Korea and Vietnam.[31] New Zealand was the first OECD economy to conclude a comprehensive free trade agreement with China.[32] It is said to be the biggest bilateral trade deal since the establishment of Closer Economic Relations Trade Agreement deal with Australia in 1983.[33] With the Republic of Korea, New Zealand is seeking to conclude FTA negotiations having begun them in June 2009 after President Lee Myung-bak's visit to New Zealand two months prior. New Zealand PM John Key also visited Vietnam in July 2010 to commemorate 35 years of bilateral relations.[34] Another significant milestone was the coming into force of the ASEAN, Australia and New Zealand FTA (AANZFTA) on 1 January 2010 between Australia, Brunei, Burma, Malaysia, New Zealand, Singapore, the Philippines, and Vietnam. Thailand, Laos PDR and Cambodia joined later and Indonesia is yet to join after notification of its completion of internal ratification procedures.[35] New Zealand's exports to ASEAN have increased 121 percent since 2000 to $4.6 billion in 2008. Over the same period, its imports from ASEAN countries have increased 244 percent to almost $ 7.6 billion in 2008.[36]

While NZ has involved itself in Asian economic dynamism, it has also kept the trans Pacific option open by continuing to take active interest in the Trans Pacific Partnership (TPP) negotiations. The TPP was finally signed in November

2011 after years of negotiations. The TPP has been envisioned with the goal of bringing together economies from across the Pacific into one trading community. The New Zealand Ministry of Foreign Affairs and Trade (MFAT) mentions that for New Zealand, the TPP grouping is even more important. TPP includes four of the 10 most-important trading economies to New Zealand (1st—Australia, 3rd—US, 7th—Singapore and 9th—Malaysia). Thirty-eight per cent of New Zealand's trade is with TPP countries; the highest proportion of any of the participants.[37] Further, the NZ MFAT states, "the commercial and strategic benefits that are to be expected from the Trans Pacific engagement both in the shorter term through the elimination of trade barriers, and exponentially well into the future through the increased productivity and growth will result from regional liberalisation. The Trans-Pacific Partnership promotes the APEC goal of free and open trade and investment in the Asia-Pacific region and is also one potential way to build towards the Free Trade Area of the Asia Pacific (FTAAP)."[38]

Security

The paradigm shifting events of 11 September had a profound impact on America's relations with the rest of the world. Relations with NZ too were revitalized after the 9/11 attacks on the US. Their bilateral security cooperation has benefitted from the stationing of New Zealand Special Air Service (SAS) troops in Afghanistan, as well as from New Zealand's contribution of headquarters personnel to the NATO International Security Assistance Force (ISAF) mission and to the United States Central Command (CENTCOM) Headquarters in Tampa, Florida.[39] New Zealand has sent special forces to Afghanistan with a Provincial Reconstruction Team in Bamiyan Province since 2003.[40] As part of Operation Enduring Freedom, New Zealand forces have also been deployed in the Gulf and Indian Ocean. Both have shared goals of peacekeeping, counterterrorism, non-proliferation, preventing transnational crime, stability in the Pacific etc, forging a stronger security partnership.

New Zealand has three defense policy objectives-defend New Zealand against low-level threats, contribute to regional security, and play a part in global security efforts.[41] Minister for Defence, Dr.Wayne Mapp in early 2010 described New Zealand's security in three concentric circles with itself in the first circle of strategic importance, Australia and the South Pacific comprising the second circle, and Southeast Asia and the larger Asia-Pacific making up the third.[42] The role of the US in underwriting security in the Asia-Pacific through ARF and its bilateral alliances, and its latest foray into East Asian security affairs through ADMM+ prognosticates that New Zealand and the US will be working alongside each other also in Southeast Asia, Southwest Pacific and the larger Asia Pacific.

New Zealand's Strategic Outlook to 2035 as outlined in the *Defence White Paper 2010*, the first in 13 years mentions, "the US is expected to remain the pre-eminent military power in the world over the next 25 years and a close security partner of New Zealand. Other powers may test its regional preponderance but only the US will retain a truly global military reach. It will continue to anchor NATO and a host of other bilateral and regional security arrangements."[43] The White Paper states the importance of 'longstanding and close security partnerships with Australia, the US, the United Kingdom and Canada.[44] It makes the following observation on security relations with the United States, "our security also benefits from New Zealand being an engaged, active, and stalwart partner of the US." The White Paper supports a continuing US security presence in the Asia-Pacific and notes the United States' role as a contributor to regional stability.[45]

New Zealand's role in resolving conflicts in Bougainville, Papua New Guinea, participation in peace operations in East Timor, and the Regional Assistance Mission in the Solomon Islands (RAMSI) has been in tune with its commitments with the Pacific Islands Forum (PIF). In tune with one of the two fundamental elements of the NZ-US strategic partnership is practical cooperation in the Pacific region. The focus areas are on renewable energy, disaster response management and climate change adaptation.[46] Apart from this, the US Department of State is working with New Zealand's Ministry of Foreign Affairs and Trade, Police, and Customs to disrupt and dismantle transnational criminal threats across the Pacific, particularly illicit transnational networks.[47] Since 2009, both these countries have been working in close collaboration to deal with this threat.[48] In November 2010, both the countries co-hosted the second workshop of the Trans-Pacific Symposium.[49] Thus, both have set themselves an ambitious security agenda on a plethora of issues where their interests converge necessitating a deepening of their relations to reap the full benefit of their current phase of re-engagement.

On global issues such as protecting the environment, New Zealand's foreign policy focuses on keeping the Antarctic secure and free of geopolitical rivalry. Since 50 years, both have had bases next to each other at McMurdo Sound with an aim to promote scientific knowledge and environmental conservation on the continent for the benefit of the world community.[50]

The China Angle

New Zealand-China relations have come a long way with a history of 39 years of diplomatic relations with each other. China being New Zealand's second largest trading partner and by virtue of its number two position in the world economy is very important to New Zealand as it makes its incursion into the process of East Asian integration. New Zealand was first to complete an agreement on the terms of China's accession to the WTO in August 1997, first to recognise China as a market economy in April 2004, the first developed economy to commence free trade negotiations with China announced in November 2004, and the first developed economy to complete a free trade agreement in April 2008.[51] Gary Hawke, Senior Fellow at the New Zealand Institute of Economic Research, mentions a 'fifth first' with the signing of a free trade agreement with Hong Kong, following its conclusion of an economic partnership framework agreement with the Mainland.[52]

The coming into force of the NZ-China FTA on 1 October 2008 was a momentous achievement as it was hoped that over time the FTA would result in the elimination of tariffs on 96 per cent of New Zealand exports to China, and is projected to lift New Zealand's export revenue from trade with China by between NZ$225-$350 million per year.[53] China's large market and cheap labour force are an attraction for New Zealand's thriving business community. Even though China's predatory export policies generate fear and uncertainty, both the US and NZ have taken cognisance of the fact that China's economic rise is a reality that they have to come to terms with.

In the realm of security, New Zealand has so far been successful in dexterously handling its partnership with an ascendant China that is stoking fears with its belligerent rhetoric and military modernisation. Growing concerns in the South China Sea dispute are bringing New Zealand into the scene because of its participation in the EAS. With Secretary Clinton asserting a US national interest in the freedom of navigation in the South China Sea at the ARF meeting in 2010 at Hanoi,[54] China has been at the receiving end of a firm diplomatic rebuke as this issue has become 'internationalised'. (China's preferred way of dealing with contentious issues in the past had been through bilateral means).

New Zealand's growing ties with the US should not come in the way of disrupting its relationship with China. All countries have a stake in managing a rising China—its 'peaceful rise to great power status.'[55] Intentions notwithstanding, China has to act as a 'responsible stakeholder'[56] in the international system and reassure the world of its honourable intentions by pursuing clear and coherent policies.

An unlikely case in point would be regarding the brouhaha over the US $200 million sci-fi blockbuster *Avatar* (2009). This had some parts of its filming done in Wellington.[57] After its worldwide release *Avatar* was pulled from the cinemas by the Chinese film board and replaced by the state produced biopic on *Confucius*.[58] It was another thing that the movie bombed at the box office and *Avatar* went to gross $76 million in China. In cases like these, the US-China tension might just be the diplomatic tightrope on which New Zealand will have to tread delicately.

New Zealand has demonstrated flexibility and ingenuity in its evolving relations with China. The Annual Report of the New Zealand Ministry of Trade and Foreign Affairs released in June 2011 mentions the conclusion of the China/New Zealand Film Co-Production Agreement in July 2010 (the first production under this agreement is being negotiated now), and New Zealand's first currency swap arrangement with China, agreed in 2011. Arrangements with China on fruit access, live seafood access and meat premises also were concluded.[59] Even though there has been a considerable degree of regional nervousness over China's aggressive and assertive international behavior, New Zealand has been exercising patience and realistic expectations in its expanding and maturing relations with China.

Notwithstanding the unmistakable rising geopolitical and geoeconomic footprint of China, both the US and NZ are occasionally casting a wary glance but are by and large, towards enmeshing China through a web of regional and multilateral institutions and working together towards dissipating the potential for conflicts.

Christchurch Quakes

New Zealand's second largest city, Christchurch was rocked by an earthquake of 6.3 magnitude on 22 February 2011 killing 181 people and left much of the city centre in ruins.[60] This occurred just after a meeting in Christchurch of the fourth New Zealand-US Partnership forum. All the US and New Zealand participants had to be evacuated to Auckland and Wellington by the Royal New Zealand Airforce C-130 Hercules.[61]

A Reuters report on February 2011 noted Prime Minister John Key mentioning the overall cost of the February 22 and the September 4 quakes combined would be about NZ$20 billion (9.3 billion pounds), with the second, more destructive, earthquake costing about three-quarters of the total.[62] The humanitarian fallout led the US Ambassador to New Zealand David Huebner declaring it a disaster due to the effects of the earthquake. In response, USAID/OFDA provided $100,000 through the US Embassy in Wellington to the New Zealand Red Cross (NZRC) for emergency shelter and deployed a Disaster Assistance Response Team (USAID/DART), including a 74-person USAR team from the Los Angeles County Fire Department, to support search and rescue efforts. USAID also activated a Washington, DC-based Response Management Team to support the USAID/DART and coordinate the US Government humanitarian response to the earthquake.[63]

Not only had the US government responded to the crisis in NZ with alacrity but mega corporations have generously pumped in dollars to assist in the reconstruction and rescue efforts. The US film organisations have donated generously in helping to rebuild Christchurch responding to the NZ Government's Christchurch Earthquake appeal. James Cameron's Lightstorm Entertainment and Fox Filmed Entertainment collectively contributed USD $1 million (NZD $1.26 million) and Warner Brothers has donated USD $500,000 (NZD $633,557) to support the reconstruction efforts of the government. Also mention worthy in this regard is the contribution of the American Friends of Christchurch (AFOC), an initiative that supports broad-based earthquake-relief efforts in Christchurch.[64] Furthermore rescuers from the US, the UK, Australia,

China, Taiwan, Singapore, Japan and Mexico had been offering assistance to a devastated Christchurch.[65] The wave of support that the earthquake generated for New Zealand revealed the enormous reservoir of goodwill that the country enjoys in the region.

Of Councils and Friends

The NZ-US Council in Wellington and US-NZ Council in Washington, DC, have been working in tandem to foster beneficial relations and strengthen the relationship between them. Both advocate the expansion of trade and economic links between the two countries including a comprehensive free trade agreement achieved either bilaterally or in the context of an expanded Trans Pacific Partnership Agreement.[66] Prime Minister Helen Clark while addressing the second US-NZ Partnership Forum, at Auckland in September 2007 stated, "I know that the NZ-US and US-NZ Councils play an important role in advocating for closer bonds between our two democracies and more extensive ties between our economies, and I thank them both for that."[67]

American Friends of Christchurch similarly is geared at adding a humanitarian dimension to hard security issues that have solidified Washington's 'enlightened leadership' in the world. Other institutions that are promoting the bilateral engagement are Friends of New Zealand Congressional Caucus and its New Zealand parliamentary counterpart and the more recent Partnership Forum.[68]

Conclusion

The bilateral interactions between the two countries have been evolving with time as newer dynamics are deepening and widening the contours of their relationship. Under the Obama Administration, New Zealand has welcomed and warmly responded to the re-engagement of the US in Asian affairs and both are on the threshold of crossing a new milestone in their relationship. Notwithstanding the solitary wrinkles that may remain or crop up in the future, there is also enough reason to be gung-ho as both are making serious and committed efforts to continue the strong upward trajectory in their bilateral relationship.

Since the challenges to global security and prosperity are increasing with every passing year and more and more issues that were peripheral are coming to the centre of the security discourse, both these Pacific countries realise that they have shared threats and concerns that have to be handled deftly through bilateral and multilateral initiatives. Both realise that correcting past differences are essential for the management of bilateral relations and new and innovative ways have to be devised to find solutions to the plethora of global challenges. The positive momentum of their interactions made PM John Key mention that the US-NZ relationship has 'come of age' and he is 'the lucky Prime Minister' to have been in the seat when it happened.[69]

End Notes

1. NZ-US Council http://www.nzuscouncil.com/index.php/section/the_nz_us_relationship
2. NZ-US Council http://www.nzuscouncil.com/index.php/perspectives/
3. Ted Galen Carpenter (1986), Pursuing a Strategic Divorce: The U.S. and the Anzus Alliance, Cato Institute Policy Analysis no. 67, 27 February 1986, http://www.cato.org/pubs/pas/pa067.pdf
4. Hans Kristensten (2006), The Neither Confirm nor deny Nuclear Policy: Nuclear Diplomacy at Work, A Working Paper, Federation Of American Scientists, http://www.nukestrat.com/pubs/NCND.pdf
5. Robert White (1998), Nuclear Free New Zealand-1987, From Policy to Legislation Working Paper no. 8, Centre for Peace Studies, http://www.disarmsecure.org/Nuclear%20Free%20New%20Zealand%201987%20-%20From%20Policy%20to%20Legislation.pdf
6. David Lange (1985), New Zealand's Security Policy, *Foreign Affairs*, vol. 63, no. 5 (Summer 1985), pp. 1009-1019.
7. Address by Christine Bogle (1997), Proceedings of a joint Centre for Peace Studies/Peace Foundation Seminar held at the University of Auckland, 7 June 1997, pp. 35-43, http://www.disarmsecure.org/A%20Celebration%20-%2010%20years%20of%20Nuclear%20Free%20Legislation.pdf
8. Rt Hon Helen Clark's Address to the Foundation for Peace Studies & Auckland University Centre for Peace Studies (1997), pp. 44-50, 7 June 1997, http://www.disarmsecure.org/A%20Celebration%20-%2010%20years%20of%20Nuclear%20Free%20Legislation.pdf
9. Amy Woolf (2011), Nonstrategic Nuclear Weapons, CRS Report RL32572, http://www.fas.org/sgp/crs/nuke/RL32572.pdf
10. U.S. Department of State: Background Note-New Zealand http://www.state.gov/r/pa/ei/bgn/35852.htm
11. United States Diplomatic Mission to New Zealand: Secretary Clinton on U.S. Engagement in the Asia-Pacific, http://newzealand.usembassy.gov/clinton_pacific_engagement.html
12. Sarah J. Diehl and Paula Humphrey (2010) Issue Brief: The April 2010 Nuclear Security Summit: One More Step Toward the Mountaintop, James Martin Center for Nonproliferation Studies, Monterey Institute for International Studies, 20 April 2010, http://www.nti.org/e_research/e3_nuclear_security_summit.html
13. The White House, 13 April 2010, http://www.whitehouse.gov/the-press-office/key-facts-about-nuclear-security-summit
14. Audrey Young, "Why Obama wants John Key at the Summit", *New Zealand Herald*, 13 April 2010, http://www.nzherald.co.nz/nz/news/article.cfm?c_id=1&objectid=10638030
15. Prime Minister John Key, "Speech Notes to NZ-US Council", Washington, DC, 14 April 2010, http://www.beehive.govt.nz/speech/speech-notes-usnz-council
16. Tracy Watkins, "Obama praisesNew Zealand's Nuclear Efforts", 13 April 2010, http://www.stuff.co.nz/national/politics/3576020/Obama-praises-New-Zealands-nuclear-efforts
17. Audrey Young, "Clinton ready to build on friendship", *New Zealand Herald*, 5 November 2010, http://www.nzherald.co.nz/nz/news/article.cfm?c_id=1&objectid=10685461.
18. Alyn Ware (2010), "New Zealand Nuclear Free Zone, Disarmament, and Arms Control Act, New Zealand 1997", *Berkshire Encyclopedia of Sustainability: The Law and Politics of Sustainability*, pp. 404-410.

19. Kurt Campbell (2010), Remarks on the Future of U.S.-New Zealand Relations, 9 September 2010, http://newzealand.usembassy.gov/usnz_relations.html
20. U.S. Department of State Remarks With New Zealand Prime Minister John Phillip Key and New Zealand Foreign Minister Murray Stuart McCully, http://www.state.gov/secretary/rm/2010/11/150390.htm
21. U.S. Department of State Wellington Declaration on a New Strategic Partnership Between New Zealand and the United States, 4 November 2010, http://www.state.gov/r/pa/prs/ps/2010/11/150401.htm
22. U.S. Department of State Secretary Clinton's visit to New Zealand, 3 November 2010, http://www.state.gov/r/pa/prs/ps/2010/11/150377.htm
23. U.S. Department of State Remarks With New Zealand Prime Minister John Phillip Key and New Zealand Foreign Minister Murray Stuart McCully, http://www.state.gov/secretary/rm/2010/11/150390.htm
24. Audrey Young and Derek Cheng, "Clinton: NZ punches way above its weight", *New Zealand Herald*, 4 November 2010, http://www.nzherald.co.nz/nz/news/article.cfm?c_id=1&objectid=10685337
25. Hillary Clinton (2011), "America's Pacific Century", *Foreign Policy*, 12 December 2011, http://www.foreignpolicy.com/articles/2011/10/11/americas_pacific_century
26. Audrey Young (2010) "Wellington Declaration signals US-NZ thaw complete", *New Zealand Herald*, 4 November 2010, http://www.nzherald.co.nz/politics/news/article.cfm?c_id=280&objectid=10685196
27. Robert Ayson and David Capie (2011) Evolution, not Revolution: The US-NZ Security Partnership, *Asia Pacific Bulletin*, no. 104, East West Center.
28. ASEAN Overview http://www.aseansec.org/92.htm
29. Helen Clark, "APEC at a crossroads", *New Zealand International Review*, No. 2, March/April 1999 http://www.victoria.ac.nz/nziia/publications/nzir/1999.html
30. Ian Fergusson and Bruce Vaughn (2010), The Trans Pacific Partnership Agreement, CRS Report R40502, http://www.fas.org/sgp/crs/row/R40502.pdf
31. John Key, 28 June 2010, http://www.johnkey.co.nz/archives/972-PM-to-visit-China,-Viet-Nam,-Republic-of-Korea.html
32. New Zealand Ministry of Foreign Affairs and Trade: New Zealand China FTA, http://www.mfat.govt.nz/downloads/trade-agreement/china/chinafta-booklet.pdf
33. New Zealand Ministry of Foreign Affairs and Trade: The Australia-New Zealand Closer Economic Relationship, http://www.mfat.govt.nz/downloads/trade-agreement/australia/australia-booklet.pdf
34. New Zealand Ministry of Foreign Affairs and Trade: http://www.mfat.govt.nz/Countries/Asia-South-and-Southeast/Viet-Nam.php
35. ASEAN-Australia-New Zealand FTA, http://www.asean.fta.govt.nz/what-is-the-asean-fta/
36. Key outcomes: Agreement establishing the ASEAN-Australia-New Zealand Free Trade Area, http://www.asean.fta.govt.nz/assets/Downloads/asean-key-outcomes.pdf
37. NZ Ministry of Foreign Affairs and Trade: Trans Pacific Partnership Agreement, http://mfat.govt.nz/Trade-and-Economic-Relations/2-Trade-Relationships-and-Agreements/Trans-Pacific/index.php
38. New Zealand Ministry of Foreign Affairs: The Trans Pacific Agreement, http://www.nzembassy.com/united-states-of-america/relationship-between-nz-and-the-usa/business-and-trade/the-trans-pacific-ag
39. Ernest Bower and Brian Lynch (2011), "Pacific Partners—The Future of NZ-US Relations", Report of the CSIS and NZ Institute of International Affairs, http://csis.org/publication/pacific-partners.

40. New Zealand Ministry of Foreign Affairs: New Zealand and the Middle East, http://mfat.govt.nz/Foreign-Relations/Middle-East/1-NZ-and-Middle-East.php
41. U.S. Department of State, http://www.state.gov/outofdate/bgn/newzealand/156592.htm
42. Wayne Mapp, "In Defence of Our Interests," *New Zealand International Review*, January/February 2010.
43. The New Zealand Ministry of Defence, http://www.defence.govt.nz/reports-publications/defence-white-paper-2010/chapter3-nz-strategic-outlook-to-2035.html
44. New Zealand Ministry of Defence (2010) Defence White Paper 2010, pp.18, http://www.nzdf.mil.nz/downloads/pdf/public-docs/2010/defence_white_paper_2010.pdf
45. Ministry of Defence, Defence White Paper 2010 (Wellington: Ministry of Defence, November 2010).
46. US Embassy in New Zealand, Wellington Declaration, http://newzealand.usembassy.gov/wellington_declaration.html
47. US Embassy in New Zealand, http://newzealand.usembassy.gov/factsheet_clinton2010.html
48. Department of State (2009), Chair's Report :Trans Pacific Symposium on Dismantling Transnational Illicit Networks, http://www.state.gov/documents/organization/137524.pdf
49. David Luna (2011), Combating Illicit Trade and Converging Threats: Reducing the Harm to Economic Growth, Sustainable Development and Global Security, Department of State, 27 October 2011, http://www.state.gov/p/inl/rls/rm/176279.htm
50. New Zealand Embassy in Washington Defence Relations, http://www.nzembassy.com/usa/relationship-between-new-zealand-and-usa/new-zealand-and-usa/defence-relations
51. New Zealand-China Four Firsts, http://www.chinafta.govt.nz/3-Progressing-the-FTA/1-Why-China/Four-firsts.php
52. Gary Hawke Strategy more than commerce: China-New Zealand FTA, 30 July 2010, http://www.eastasiaforum.org/2010/07/30/strategy-more-than-commerce-china-new-zealand-fta/
53. New Zealand's Ministry of Foreign Affairs and Trade http://www.nzembassy.com/china/relationship-between-new-zealand-and-china/new-zealand-and-china
54. Voice of America (2010), Clinton on South China Sea, 8 September 2011, http://www.voanews.com/policy/editorials/asia/Clinton-On-South-China-Sea—127263758.html
55. Zheng Bijian (2005), "China's 'peaceful rise to great power status", *Foreign Affairs*, vol. 84, no. 5, September/October 2005, pp. 18-24.
56. Robert B. Zoellick (2005), "Whither China: From Membership to Responsibility?", Remarks to National Committee on U.S.-China Relations, 21 September 2005, http://www.ncuscr.org/files/2005Gala_RobertZoellick_Whither_China1.pdf
57. $200m Avatar starts filming in Wellington, http://www.stuff.co.nz/entertainment/27960/200m-Avatar-starts-filming-in-Wellington
58. Avatar v/s Confucius: And the winner is... 26 January 2010, http://www.economist.com/blogs/banyan/2010/01/avatar_vs_confucius_and_winner
59. New Zealand Ministry of Foreign Affairs and Trade, Annual Report June 2011, http://www.mfat.govt.nz/Media-and-publications/Publications/Annual-report/0-outcome-contributions.php#outcome1
60. Phil Mercer (2011), New Zealand's Second City Rises Again After Earthquake Disaster, Voice of America, 29 September 2011, http://www.voanews.com/english/news/asia/New-Zealands-Second-City-Rises-Again-After-Earthquake-Disaster-130775833.html
61. NZ-US Council, http://www.usnzcouncil.org/partnerforum/2011forum
62. Rob Taylor (2011), "New Zealand to fall silent in quake memorial, toll rises", Reuters

UK, 26 February 2011, http://uk.reuters.com/article/2011/02/28/uk-newzealand-quake-idUKTRE71L04920110228?feedType=RSS&feedName=everything&virtualBrandChannel=11708
63. USAID (2011), New Zealand Earthquake: Fact Sheet http://www.usaid.gov/our_work/humanitarian_assistance/disaster_assistance/countries/new_zealand/template/fs_sr/fy2011/nz_eq_fs01_02-25-2011.pdf
64. American Friends of Christchurch, http://www.americanfriendsofchristchurch.org/
65. David Sharrock (2011), "Christchurch earthquake: British team fly in to help victims", *The Guardian*, 26 February 2011, http://www.guardian.co.uk/world/2011/feb/27/christchurch-earthquake-british-team
66. NZ-US Council http://www.nzuscouncil.com/
67. NZ-US Council Free Trade With The US: the time is now, July 2008, http://www.nzuscouncil.com/images/uploads/NZUS_Council_FTA_Marketing_Doc_FINAL.pdf
68. Bruce Vaughn (2011), New Zealand: Background and Bilateral Relations with the United States, CRS Report RL32876, 27 May 2011, http://www.fas.org/sgp/crs/row/RL32876.pdf
69. Audrey Young, "US-NZ relationship has come of age, says Key", *New Zealand Herald*, 25 July 2011, http://www.nzherald.co.nz/politics/news/article.cfm?c_id=280&objectid=10740625

11

Towards Closer Partnership: New Zealand-Southeast Asia Relations

Man Mohini Kaul and Amrita Dey

This paper attempts to examine Zealand's foreign policy towards Southeast Asia, which, in recent times has been marked by deepening of relations, reflected through a comprehensive approach towards the countries of this region. As a result of its policy of active engagement, New Zealand has emerged a key player in Southeast Asia and is no longer viewed by these nations, as a non-descript South Pacific nation, with low-level interest in Southeast Asia. According to New Zealand Statement of Intent 2011-14: "If we want to take part in the institutional changes taking place in the region, New Zealand must continue to develop positive relationships and make contributions to regional affairs that underpin our participation. It is not enough that we value highly our connections with Asia; it is important that the countries of Asia value New Zealand participation in regional dialogues and in efforts to build the ASEAN and East Asian community."[1]

Change in Perspective

Viewed as a South Pacific nation, New Zealand's foreign policy has in the 21st Century, evolved from a typical South Pacific-centric policy to one which includes Southeast Asia as an area of vital importance to its national interest. At this point in time, New Zealand's security, economic and political interests are linked with this region. Thus, from a typical 'South Pacific' power, it has evolved into an influential regional player.

For a long time, New Zealand though "physically situated in the region" and having "exercised administrative responsibility over some of the territories in the area, did not actually identify... with the region". Both New Zealand and Australia had their "affinity and orientation ... towards Europe."[2] With the independence of many of the South Pacific Island states, New Zealand accepted the fact that it is a South Pacific nation, situated a long distance away from the West, needed to link in every way with the South Pacific islands nations, who looked to New Zealand for cooperation, stability and security.[3]

However, from mid 1980's to mid-1990's, the Island states of South Pacific, witnessed internal instability, and from the point of view of regional powers, Australia and New Zealand—these incidents were a serious cause of concern to their own security. The coups in Fiji, the Bougainville crisis and unrest in Vanuatu, were some of the security challenges which were aptly called by a US official report as "Problems in Paradise."[4] Criticism by regional powers regarding erosion of democracy and bad governance in some of the island states, did lead to deterioration of relations with them, although, New Zealand did succeed, to a large extent in diffusing the critical situation through "a creative and culturally diplomatic initiative".[5] In fact, it stood solid as a bastion of democracy, in what came to be known as an "arc of instability." New Zealand increasingly played a leadership role in diffusing the situation and assumed renewed regional responsibility towards the Pacific Forum countries. To quote New Zealand academic Roderic Alley, "relations with the South Pacific encountered growing governance, resource management and equity challenges, although New Zealand contributed significantly towards a resolution of a decade of conflict on Bougainville."[6] New Zealand along with Australia assumed regional peacekeeping and stabilizing operations in the Island states.[7] According to official source, "It is in New Zealand's interests to play a leadership role in the South Pacific for the foreseeable future" a "weak or unstable South Pacific region poses demographic, economic, criminal, and reputational risks to New Zealand."[8]

South Pacific is "markedly asymmetrical in power terms, therefore, regionalism as personified by the Pacific Islands Forum (PIF) unlike ASEAN, is very "lopsided" and is reflective of "patron-client regionalism".[9] At the same time, New Zealand recognised that its 'inward-looking,' 'backyard regionalism,' positioned on the South Pacific, had to be activated by a more 'outward-looking' policy. In today's world, where interdependence is pushing nations together, the policy makers realised the importance of engaging constructively with the neighbouring region. The key factors underlying New Zealand's growing ties with Southeast Asia, can be categorized as : One, its pursuit of Free Trade Agreements (FTA's) demanding a more creative and realistic policy towards Southeast Asia.[10] Two, the shared security interests in the profound changes that have taken place in the geo-strategic environment in Southeast Asia after 9/11 and Bali bombings, justifying the need to coordinate, cooperate and strategies with the Southeast Asian countries. The New Zealand Defence White Paper 2010 stated, "Our interests are best served by a region in which all countries and especially the major powers agree on the importance of stability and prosperity, and share a common understanding of how these goals should be secured. We contribute to that stability and prosperity, including by working alongside partners and friends in structures such as the FPDA, the ASEAN Regional Forum, and the ASEAN Defence Ministers' Meeting-Plus."[11]

New Zealand and Southeast Asia towards a Closer Partnership

Although New Zealand's close engagement with Southeast Asia began in the 70's, when it became a dialogue partner of ASEAN in 1975, the Cold War perspective defined its ties with the countries of Southeast Asia. According to a well-known historian Anthony Smith, "New Zealand's commitment to SEATO reflected its ongoing allegiance to the United States, and willingness to follow American policy in relation to the Asia region. This alliance saw New Zealand contribute troops to the American campaign during the Cold War conflicts in Korea and Vietnam."[12]

With the end of the Cold War, New Zealand's engagement with ASEAN countries grew dynamically, both at the bilateral and multilateral level, showing a new maturity in New Zealand's diplomacy. Positive results followed in its inclusion in multilateral forums and the expansion of areas of cooperation from limited trade to free trade. The academic writings and policy debates replicate this view. Roderic Alley writes, "New Zealand's external orientations during the 1990s, expanded under conditions of enhanced globalisation and interdependence. Increased external activity heightened the necessity for independent assessment, strong global citizenship credentials, and active multilateralism. This served trade diversification, consolidated the anti-nuclear policy, and helped to support international law, human rights, and environmental policy objectives."[13]

From its security requirements, New Zealand has become "increasingly interdependent with other countries in the region and has a growing stake in maintaining its security."[14] In the new strategic circumstances, New Zealand signalled its interest through various White Papers. These assured of New Zealand's intentions to pull its weight "in an affordable way forward for ensuring" its "security now and in an uncertain future".[15] In the 21st Century, New Zealand's desire to build holistic links are already in shape through the Joint Declaration for ASEAN-New Zealand Comprehensive Partnership and its Plan of Action (POA) for 2010-15, across the three pillars of the Partnership, namely political-security, economic and socio-cultural cooperation. The statement at the end of the signing of this Declaration stated, "The ASEAN Ministers appreciated New Zealand's readiness to work closely with ASEAN to build an ASEAN-centered regional architecture, encompassing existing regional mechanisms, which will contribute to regional peace and stability, advance economic prosperity while enhancing socio-cultural cooperation."[16] New Zealand achieved a 'strategic partner' status in 2010, when the first ever ASEAN-New Zealand Summit between ASEAN leaders and Prime Minister John Key was held, giving great boost to New Zealand's growing ties with Southeast Asia.[17] All these proposals have helped the deepening of "cooperation in key areas such as trade, security, disaster management, education, environment, and cultural links."[18]

Security Concerns

From Southeast Asia's security perspectives there are concerns about 'China's might,' and an anxiety over declining US presence in the region, which has led to balance of power strategy by ASEAN, which in turn has led to New Zealand along with others, to play a more constructive role in the region. New Zealand's membership within the ASEAN Regional Forum (ARF) has immensely helped to narrow the gap between its disputing members. In resolving the South China Sea (SCS) problem, New Zealand has wholeheartedly supported the Declaration on the Code of Conduct of Parties on the South China Sea at the 8th ASEAN Summit in Phnom Penh, Cambodia (2002).[19] The Declaration called for the concerned parties to reaffirm their commitment to the principles laid out in the Charter of the United Nations, the 1982 UN Convention on the Law of the Sea (UNCLOS), the Treaty of Amity and Cooperation (TAC) in Southeast Asia, the Five Principles of Peaceful Coexistence and other universally recognized principles of International law. It further called for parties, to reaffirm respect for and commitment to the freedom of navigation. The concerned parties were also asked to exercise self-restraint in the conduct of activities that could complicate or escalate dispute and affect the peace and stability of the region.

For the sake of Confidence Building Measures (CBMS), the Declaration incorporated some initiatives. These were: (i) to intensify the spirit of cooperation and understanding through dialogue and exchange of views; (ii) notifying on a voluntary basis other parties concerned of any impending joint/combined military exercises and exchange of relevant information; (iii) seeking a durable settlement of the dispute through exploration and cooperative activities like search and rescue operation and combating trans-national crime—not confined to trafficking in illicit drugs, sea piracy and armed robbery at sea and illegal trafficking in arms and ammunition.[20] According to a former New Zealand diplomat and a leading strategic expert Terence O'Brian, "New Zealand analysts consider, however, that ASEAN has through the ARF, laid solid foundations for the establishment of dialogue, confidence building, and a regional *modus vivendi* with China."[21]

Mark Rolls, of the University of Waikato, New Zealand, has provided in a detailed paper, valuable insight into the importance of maritime security from a New Zealand perspective. He explains, "New Zealand is, it has rightly been contended, a maritime nation both in geographic location and from its historical experience". New Zealand's EEZ is 4,053,000 square kilometres, which is 15 times its land mass and the fourth largest in the world. Shipping trade equalled approximately NZ$20 billion and there were 2430 visits by international trading ships (excepting fishing) each year.[22]

Therefore, it is not in New Zealand's advantage to be a bystander. Consequently, it is cooperating with the regional countries in safeguarding freedom of seas, otherwise the consequences would be too grave for the economic and strategic well being of not only Southeast Asia but of New Zealand as well.[23] The safety of the sea-lanes and their choke points like Malacca straits are crucial to all. Joint military exercises with the countries of the region are a witness to the growing security cooperation.

Defence Links

New Zealand defence policy has always prioritised on the security of its 200 mile Exclusive Economic Zone (EEZ) and maintained its commitment to peace and stability in Southeast Asia. In other words, there has been a growing commitment by New Zealand to its immediate neighbours which needless to emphasise, is crucial to New Zealand's security and integrity.[24]

Commitment to peace and stability in Southeast Asia "is being approached by New Zealand, through military training, assistance arrangements, exchange programmes and exercises with the ASEAN countries".[25] Terrorism is a trans-national problem requiring active cooperation. Such cooperation is now the basic component of New Zealand's security policy goals which do take into account its limitations such as limited defence capability. Many of these cooperative efforts especially those related to intelligence sharing and enhanced military contacts will help in assuaging anxieties about security threats to all stakeholders including New Zealand and ASEAN. In order to strengthen its "military to military contacts," New Zealand through its membership of the Five Power Defence Arrangement (FPDA) continues to play an important role within the region. New Zealand through the FPDA, maintains an appropriate level of training through annual joint exercises with—Malaysia and Singapore. New Zealand was equally prompt in extending its capacity-building assistance to Southeast Asia soon after the Bali bombings in 2002 and in 2005.[26] On 29 July 2005, New Zealand along with ASEAN signed the ASEAN-New Zealand Joint Declaration for Cooperation to Combat International Terrorism. The objective of the Declaration is as following: The Participants reaffirm the importance of having a framework for cooperation to prevent, disrupt and combat international terrorism through the exchange of information, intelligence and capacity building.[27]

In the maritime arena, New Zealand Defence Force (NZDF) has continued to contribute to the freedom of New Zealand trade routes, including the Malacca Straits, by keeping regular contact and dialogue with the regional countries of Southeast Asia.[28] A NZDF liaison officer is posted at the Changi Information Fusion Centre in Singapore to assist in the collection, analysis and sharing of information to combat piracy and armed robbery against ships in the region that could disrupt trade routes. The NZDF is also a member of the Western Pacific Naval Symposium, which promoted mutual understanding, professionalism and interoperability among personnel of participating nations. In May 2011, the RNZN ANZAC frigates *Te Mana* and *Te Kaha,* and a P-3K Orion participated in the annual FPDA exercise *Bersama Lima* off the Southeast Asian waters.[29] The exercise involved the use of fast jets, submarines, warships and personnel from five nations of FPDA.[30] New Zealand troops also took part in Exercise *Suman Warrior* conducted in Singapore. The exercise was designed to develop interoperability among the participating navies, including the command and staff procedures in combined and joint operations.[31]

New Zealand's bilateral military linkages with the Southeast Asian countries has been facilitated by the Mutual Assistance Program (MAP), whereby, military officers from Thailand, Malaysia, the Philippines, Singapore and Indonesia have attended various types of training programs in New Zealand.[32] However, New Zealand's most substantial military-to-military link remains with Singapore.[33]

Membership of Regional Groupings

As stated earlier, New Zealand's efforts at intensifying relations with Southeast Asia have resulted in its emergence as an active and influential player in the Asia-Pacific region. It is a member of all important regional multilateral forums like the APEC, the ASEAN Regional Forum, the ASEAN Defence Ministers Meeting Plus and the Asia Europe Meeting. New Zealand's inclusion within the East Asian Summit (EAS) in 2005 was thus a natural corollary to its relevance to the regional countries.EAS which was formed on 26 July 2005, brought together 10 ASEAN nations, the plus three states of China, Japan and South Korea, as well as Australia, New Zealand and India; the membership criteria within EAS was determined by three main conditions: (1) Substantive relation with ASEAN; (2) Full Dialogue partner status; and (3) Accession to the Treaty of Amity and Cooperation (TAC) in Southeast Asia.

Thus by opening EAS to New Zealand, ASEAN has made EAS inclusive and not exclusive only to ASEAN plus three. Wanting US to reengage in Southeast Asia, the ASEAN has put its weight on getting US and also Russia included as members in EAS. The inclusion of New Zealand, Australia and now the US and Russia, negates the earlier version visualised by former Prime Minister Mahathir of Malaysia of "East Asia Economic Caucus minus the Caucasians." Lee Kuan Yew has explained the inclusion of non-ASEAN members in the EAS from a Southeast Asian perspective. He states, "India would be a useful balance to China," he said, "while bringing Australia and New Zealand into the Summit would erase any concern that it is a forum of 'Asians versus Whites', or an anti-American grouping. It is a neater balance".[34] The membership of EAS, has given New Zealand an opportunity to have a say in the evolving regional architecture. Similarly, ASEAN through EAS remains central to the evolving East Asia

Community and its leaders are able to give direction on political and security issues.

Economic Ties

Economic engagement with Southeast Asia has always been vital for New Zealand, and over the years it has grown in scope. According to recent figures, around 11 percent of their merchandise exports (NZ $4.7 billion) and 16 percent of imports (NZ $7.6 billion) are with this region.[35] Three of New Zealand's top 10 trading partners (Singapore, Malaysia and Indonesia are fifth, seventh and tenth respectively) and the total trade with these countries is now according to official statistics not far behind their total trade with the European Union.[36] New Zealand is a major supplier of ASEAN's dairy products, meat and wood products. New Zealand imports electronics, electrical appliances, manufactured products including motor vehicles, fruits, vegetables, petroleum products and other resource-based products from ASEAN.[37] In 2006, Japan proposed a 16-nation East Asian Free Trade Area to be coordinated by an organization similar to the Organization for Economic Cooperation and Development. The 16-nations would include the ten members of ASEAN, Japan, China, South Korea, India, Australia and New Zealand.

Economic engagement with ASEAN was further cemented by the signing of ASEAN-Australia-New Zealand FTA (AANZFTA). According to an official ASEAN source, it is described as the single most comprehensive economic agreement among its Dialogue Partners.[38] The AANZFTA entered into force on 1 January 2010, and its importance was hailed by Dr Surin Pitsuwan, Secretary-General of ASEAN as "a significant development particularly in our efforts to slowly integrate the markets in this region".[39] He further explained it thus: "What makes this particular development more meaningful is the fact that the AANZFTA is being implemented amidst such economically challenging times."[40] The Joint Statement of the ASEAN-New Zealand Commemorative Summit at Ha Noi, on 30 October 2010, reflected the positive sentiments as a result of FTA. It stated: "We affirmed that AANZFTA, as a 'living agreement' and through its implementation agenda, is a new pillar of the relationship and a strong basis on which to build deeper economic integration. Today our combined trade makes ASEAN New Zealand's third largest trading partner with trade in one week now equalling that traded in a whole year in 1975. This shows the extent to which our livelihoods have grown together. We look forward to the accelerated growth and benefits for our peoples that will flow from the AANZFTA."[41]

While New Zealand has been more liberal to ASEAN exports, ASEAN as a multilateral grouping still seems to pose some concrete investment barriers to New Zealand. According to Jose Tongzon, there are four barriers to investment that exist in ASEAN. First, there's a strong concern with political and social instability in some of its member countries. Second, ASEAN is not an integrated market like the European Union as it has inconsistent rules and regulations. Third, laws and regulations in ASEAN are highly discriminatory against foreign firms. Fourth, ASEAN lacks a coordinated set of investment policies—fiscal incentives, restrictions on entry of foreign personnel, regulations on exploitation of natural resources and other sensitive sectors.[42]

In fact initially, ASEAN's drawbacks shifted New Zealand's focus from the multilateral organisation to bilateral engagement with individual Southeast Asian countries. At the bilateral level, New Zealand has improved its trade relations, and is trying to keep pace with changing pace of economic cooperation in the region. New Zealand is a member of the Trans-Pacific Strategic Economic Partnership Agreement with Brunei, Chile and Singapore.[43] Closer Economic Partnership (CEP) agreement between New Zealand and Thailand entered into force in July 2005.[44] Also, they have negotiated arrangements on labour, environment and customs cooperation. On July 2001, New Zealand and Singapore Closer Economic Partnership came into force, and "except for Closer Economic Relations with Australia, it is the most comprehensive trading agreement that New Zealand has negotiated."[45] Over 200 Multi-National Corporations (MNCs) of New Zealand today operate within Singapore, including major firms like Fonterra, Beca, Baycorp, Fisher & Paykel, among others. Many digital media companies of New Zealand have set up their bases in Singapore. These include Lucas films, Electronic Arts, Southern Star and Digipen. Singapore is New Zealand's largest source of import from the ASEAN region, but only fifth largest destination for New Zealand exports with dairy products forming the bulk of the trade.[46] On the tourism front, New Zealand continues to be an attractive holiday destination for Singaporeans. The CDL Company of Singapore runs a chain of quality hotels in New Zealand and it has extensive land and property development interests in both New Zealand and Australia. Singapore has also served as an attractive 'education hub' for students from New Zealand. However, in areas of creative IT solutions and a number of expert service capabilities, like engineering, New Zealand companies are doing much better than their counterparts in Singapore.[47] New Zealand's trade relationship with Indonesia too is showing tremendous growth. It has gone up from $541.33 m in 2007 (both import and export) to $971.19m in 2008 (both imports and exports).[48] A Free Trade Agreement between New Zealand and Malaysia was signed in 2009. Even Vietnam has been initiating negotiations with New Zealand for greater economic cooperation.

New Linkages across Sectors

Under the auspices of the Colombo Plan of 1950,[49] international students from Asia first came to New Zealand in 1951. The six students, who came to New Zealand to study dentistry at the University of Dunedin, Otego, mainly hailed from Southeast Asia. It 'laid the foundation for some enduring relationship between New Zealand and the region' as it enabled 'Asian students returning to their home countries take back first hand experiences of New Zealand and play an important role in promoting New Zealand, as well as forming a valuable pool of potential employees for New Zealand companies. Traditional source countries of students— Malaysia and South Korea, were followed by new source countries of students-—Vietnam and Thailand. According to a 2008 report on the impact of international students on New Zealand's economy, it was found that, while in 1999, the contribution of export education to New Zealand's Gross Domestic Product (GDP) was estimated at $545 million; by 2001 this had more than doubled to $1.3 billion. In 2004 the estimated contribution from education had passed $2billion, with the industry's value-added estimated at approximately $2.2 billion. Despite a downward trend of foreign fee-paying students since 2003, in 2007/08 the export education industry generated around $2.3 billion of foreign exchange, of which $70 million came from off-shore provision.[50] In the tourism sector, a recent survey showed that there were 90,000 New Zealand visitors to ASEAN countries. The number of visitors from ASEAN to New Zealand too had grown to 252,000. Additionally, more than half of foreign students in New Zealand hail from ASEAN countries.[51] New Zealand has announced initiatives "within the framework of the Plan of Action" to assist ASEAN namely the ASEAN-New Zealand Scholarships Programme, Young Business Leaders Exchange Programme...[52] These initiatives have definitely helped in promoting people to people contact.

Conclusion

When its traditional ally Britain withdrew from the east of Suez in 1967, it brought home to New Zealand's political elite that close economic relations with booming economies of Southeast Asia were essential for its economic and trade interests. However, major policy changes only took place in New Zealand's foreign policy only after the end of the Cold War, when it started pursuing greater engagement with Southeast Asia. No longer could New Zealand afford to confine itself to its periphery of South Pacific, the new regional opportunities beckoned it, its democracy, open economy, political stability, good governance and above all its benign image attracted the Southeast nations who were looking for powers to counterbalance China's looming presence. By focusing on building ties with Southeast Asia through regional cooperation, it has become very much part of the economic integration taking place in this region. Although, in the beginning the concentration was on shared economic interests, with the profound transformation in the contemporary world after the end of the Cold War, there grew convergence on security issues as well. The process of globalisation has given a new dimension to the meaning of security, which now includes non-military threats that states and the international society face due to the complex pattern of interdependence. New Zealand's diligent pursuit of closer trade relations with the ASEAN countries and the strengthening of bilateral and multilateral ties with this contiguous region are clearly visible from its growing cooperation in all fields, from comprehensive economic cooperation to combating terrorism and ensuring maritime security in the region. New Zealand is seen by ASEAN as a likeminded country, which did not dilly dally like Australia in acceding to the Treaty of Amity and Cooperation and has supported "ASEAN's desire to remain a nuclear weapon-free zone".

Today, New Zealand has evolved into a confident multicultural nation and is quite different from the observations made in the 1990's, "New Zealand is as uncomfortable with its Asian migrants as its location on the fringe of economically affluent Asia. At the same time, it is going through an identity crisis of sorts. It appears to hanker after closer ties with the United States and Britain, but this is becoming difficult to sustain, and Australia, as a substitute provides cold comfort. On the other hand, the more realistic New Zealanders are anxious to be a part of any sort of Asian grouping."[53] Its anxieties if any in the past, are no longer relevant in the 21st Century, as pointed out in this paper, the relationship has evolved into close and thriving partnership.

End Notes

1. Statement of Intent 2011-2014, *New Zealand Ministry of Foreign Affairs and Trade*, http://www.mfat.govt.nz/Media-and-publications/Publications/Statement-of-Intent/0-foreword.php
2. The United States and the South Pacific, Conference Report, Apia, Western Samoa, November 1988, pp. 21-22.
3. Ibid.
4. Stewart Firth, "Conceptualizing Security in Oceania: New and Enduring Issues", in Eric Shibuya and Jim Rolfe ed., *Security in Oceania: In the 21st Century*, Asia-Pacific Centre for Security Studies, Honolulu, Hawaii, 2003, p. 41.
5. Ibid, p. 44.
6. Roderic Alley (2002), Asia Pacific Viewpoint, Vol. 42, Issue 1, pp. 149-155, http://onlinelibrary.wiley.com/doi/10.1111/1467-8373.00140/abstract
7. Terence O'Brien, "New Zealand foreign policy after East Timor" in Bruce Brown ed., *East Timor—The Consequences* (New Zealand Institute of International Relations, Wellington, 2000) p. 89.
8. New Zealand Ministry of Defence: Defence White Paper 2010, http://www.defence.govt.nz/reports-publications/defence-white-paper-2010/chapter2-national-security-defence.html
9. For details see Stewart Firth, "The new regionalism and its contradictions" in Greg Fry and Tarcisius Tara Kabutaulaka ed., *Intervention and state-building in the Pacific: The legitimacy of cooperative intervention* (Manchester University Press, Manchester and New York, pp. 120-21).
10. New Zealand Country Forecast 2011, *Economist Intelligence Unit201,* p. 9.
11. Ibid.
12. New Zealand-Cambodia Relations http://brothernumberone.co.nz/nzcambodianrelations

13. Abstract from Roderic Alley, *op. cit.*
14. New Zealand Ministry of Defence, *The Shape of New Zealand's Defence: A White Paper* (1991) p. 23.
15. Ibid, p. 7.
16. Press Release (2011), "ASEAN Community in a Global Community of Nations", Post Ministerial Conference+1, Session with New Zealand, 22 July 2011, http://asean2011.kemlu.go.id/index.php?option=com_content&view=article&id=416%3Apost-ministerial-conference—1-session-with-new-zealand&catid=43%3Apress-release&Itemid=57&lang=en
17. Murray McCully, The Major Economic and Foreign Policy Issues Facing New Zealand 2012-17, http://www.national.org.nz/Article.aspx?ArticleID=37344
18. Murray McCully (2010), PM to hold Summit with ASEAN leaders, 23 July 2010, http://beehive.govt.nz/release/pm-hold-summit-asean-leaders
19. Declaration on the Conduct of the Parties on the South China Sea http://www.aseansec.org/13163.htm
20. ASEAN Declaration on the South China Sea Manila, Philippines, 22 July 1992, http://www.asean.org/1196.htm
21. Terence O'Brian, No. 5, p. 90.
22. Mark Rolls (2011), Maritime Security in the Asian Region: A New Zealand Perspective http://www.asianz.org.nz/sites/asianz.org.nz/files/Mark%20Rolls_Maritime%20Security%20in%20Asia%20New%20Zealand%20Perspective_IDSA%20Presentation.pdf
23. See the Statement by PM during the State Visit of Prime Minister John Key of New Zealand, www.mea.gov.in
24. Ibid.
25. Joseph A. Camilleri, ANZUS: Australia's Predicament in the Nuclear Age (Macmillan Company, Melbourne 1987), p. 147.
26. "Clark offers assistance after bombings," TVNZ, 3 October 2005, http://tvnz.co.nz/view/news_national_story_skin/615674
27. ASEAN-New Zealand Joint Declaration for Cooperation to Combat International Terrorism, Vientiane, 29 July 2005, http://www.asean.org/17635.htm
28. New Zealand Defence Force Annual Report 2011 http://www.nzdf.mil.nz/downloads/pdf/public-docs/2011/nzdf-annual-report-2011.pdf
29. New Zealand Defence Force Annual Report 2011 http://www.nzdf.mil.nz/downloads/pdf/public-docs/2011/nzdf-annual-report-2011.pdf
30. Ibid.
31. See New Zealand Defence Force Annual Report, 2011, http:// www.nzdf.mil.nz.
32. New Zealand Army: Mutual Assistance Programme, http://www.army.mil.nz/our-army/training/map.htm
33. Anthony, L. Smith (2005), "New Zealand-Southeast Asia Relations: A Survey of the Contemporary Relationship," in *Outlook 01*, asia:nz Foundation, pp. 16-18.
34. Rodolfo, C. Severino (2006), *Southeast Asia: In Search of an ASEAN Community*, ISEAS, Singapore.
35. New Zealand Ministry of Foreign Affairs and Trade, Foreign Relations, Southeast Asia, http://mfat.govt.nz/Foreign-Relations/Asia/2-South-East-Asia.php
36. Ibid.
37. K. Kesavapany & Others (2007), *Southeast Asia- New Zealand Dialogue: Towards a Closer Partnership*, ISEAS, Singapore.
38. Agreement on Australia-New Zealand FTA Enters into Force,12 January 2010 http://www.asean.org/24194.htm

39. Ibid.
40. Ibid.
41. Joint Statement of the ASEAN-New Zealand Commemorative Summit, 30 October 2010 http://www.aseansec.org/25542.htm
42. Jose, L. Tongzan (2007), "Trade and Investment Overview: An ASEAN Perspective," in K. Kesavapany & Others, Southeast Asia- New Zealand Dialogue: Towards a Closer Partnership, ISEAS, Singapore, pp. 22-27.
43. New Zealand Ministry of Foreign Affairs and Trade, Foreign Relations, Southeast Asia, http://mfat.govt.nz/Foreign-Relations/Asia/2-South-East-Asia.php
44. Ibid.
45. Ibid.
46. Asia-NZ Online, "Niche markets creating opportunities in Southeast Asia for NZ exporters", 22 February 2012, http://www.asianz.org.nz/our-work/action-asia-business/action-asia-insights/southeast-asia
47. Tony Nowell (2007), "Learning and Growing Together: Business Opportunities for a Stronger Singapore-New Zealand Relationship," in K. Kesavapany & Others, *Southeast Asia- New Zealand Dialogue: Towards a Closer Partnership*, ISEAS, Singapore, pp. 67-68.
48. Indonesia Trade and Economic, http://www.asean.fta.govt.nz/indonesia-trade-and-economic.
49. New Zealand Ministry of Foreign Affairs and Trade, Foreign Relations, Southeast Asia, http://mfat.govt.nz/Foreign-Relations/Asia/2-South-East-Asia.php
50. Andrew Butcher (2009), "Friends, Foreign and Domestic: (Re) Converging New Zealand's Export Education and Foreign Policies," *Policy Quarterly*, Vol. 5, Issue 4, pp. 64-70.
51. Ibid.
52. ASEAN-New Zealand Relations http://www.asean.org/5826.htm
53. Michael S. Dobbs-Higginson, *Asia Pacific: A View on its Role in the New World Order* (1993), Penguin Books Ltd, New Delhi, p. 236.

12

South China Sea Dispute: Policy Options for India and New Zealand

Amit Singh

The overlapping and conflicting claims over islands and maritime zones in the South China Sea (SCS) are one of the most longstanding security issues between China, Taiwan and five Southeast Asian countries. The recent upsurge in tensions in the SCS has turned the issue into a major regional security flashpoint with global consequences.

However, the SCS disputes between the involved nations have been going on for decades, but with the United Nations Commission on the Limits of the Continental Shelf (UNCLCS) setting a deadline May 13, 2009 for submitting claims for extended continental shelves beyond 200 nautical miles, the issue has turned into a new area of global tension.[1] After Vietnam and Malaysia submitted their respective claims, China made a submission to the UN in May 2009 and claimed that it had "indisputable sovereignty over the islands in the South China Sea and the adjacent waters, and enjoys sovereign rights and jurisdiction over the relevant waters as well as the seabed and subsoil thereof."[2] Beijing is also making an effort to include the SCS as its *"core national interest"* and in the non-negotiable territorial claims category—the same phrase it uses for Taiwan, Tibet and Xinxiang province.[3]

In response, the US Secretary of State Hillary Clinton rejected China's claims to sovereignty over the 1.3 million square-mile sea at the 17th ASEAN Regional Forum (ARF) meeting in July 2010 at Hanoi. She stated that "the United States has a *national interest* in freedom of navigation, open access to Asia's maritime commons and respect for international law in the South China Sea", and reiterated the importance of "opposing the use of force or any coercion by any claimant." Further, she called for a binding "regional code of conduct" in the South China Sea—a move that would undercut China's attempts to assert its claims in a region that Beijing regards as "strategically sensitive".[4]

In the recent years, China has been growing increasingly assertive in pressing its claims over SCS matters. But the other nations in the region do not acquiesce to China's claims. In fact, during the 2010 ARF meeting, it was reported that 12 of the 27 participating countries including India had backed the United States' multilateral approach instead of China's bilateral approach for resolution of the SCS disputes.[5] However, New Zealand chose to stay silent in the company of four others from Southeast Asia, namely Myanmar, Laos, Cambodia and Thailand—although New Zealand was well aware of the critical importance of maintaining the traditional international status of the South China Sea. The silence indicated the importance New Zealand attaches to its relations with China.[6] India cannot isolate itself from the dispute especially after Beijing denounced plans by an Indian company to develop oil fields in the SCS. There are also unconfirmed reports of confrontation between the Chinese warship and INS Airavat in the South China Sea.

In this view, the paper aims to analyze the various dimensions of the overlapping and conflicting claims in the SCS. This paper highlights the strategic and economic significance of SCS vis-à-vis India and New Zealand. It also makes an assessment of the ASEAN's approach towards solving the dispute and analyzes the role of United States especially after 2010 ARF meeting. It explores the possibilities for India and New Zealand to improve their bilateral and multilateral relations with Southeast Asian countries to safeguard their interests on freedom of navigation in the SCS. Further, their approach to maritime security in the Asia-Pacific holds promise as it will help considerably in forging closer bilateral ties.

Claimants of the South China Sea

China, Taiwan, Vietnam, the Philippines, Malaysia and Brunei are claimants of the SCS. The South China Sea stretches roughly from Singapore and the Strait of Malacca in the southwest to the Taiwan Strait in the northeast. There are more than 200 tiny islands and several uninhabited rocky outcrops, atolls, sandbanks and reefs; majority of them located in the Paracel and Spratly Island chains. The Spratly and Paracel islands are two major flashpoints of overlapping territorial disputes within the South China Sea.

Beijing claims almost the entire SCS, citing 'historical' records which purportedly show Chinese control in the region over the past two millennia. Taiwan's claims are similar to those of China as the island considers itself to be the Republic of China. Indonesia is also a party to the dispute but is seeking only maritime rights without claiming any island of the region. In fact Indonesia's EEZ and continental shelf overlap China's claims, which include Indonesia's largest natural gas reserves called Natuna. Vietnam rejects China's historical explanation and asserts that Beijing had never claimed sovereignty over the islands till the 1940s. Hanoi is convinced that both Spratly and Paracels are entirely

Map: South China Sea

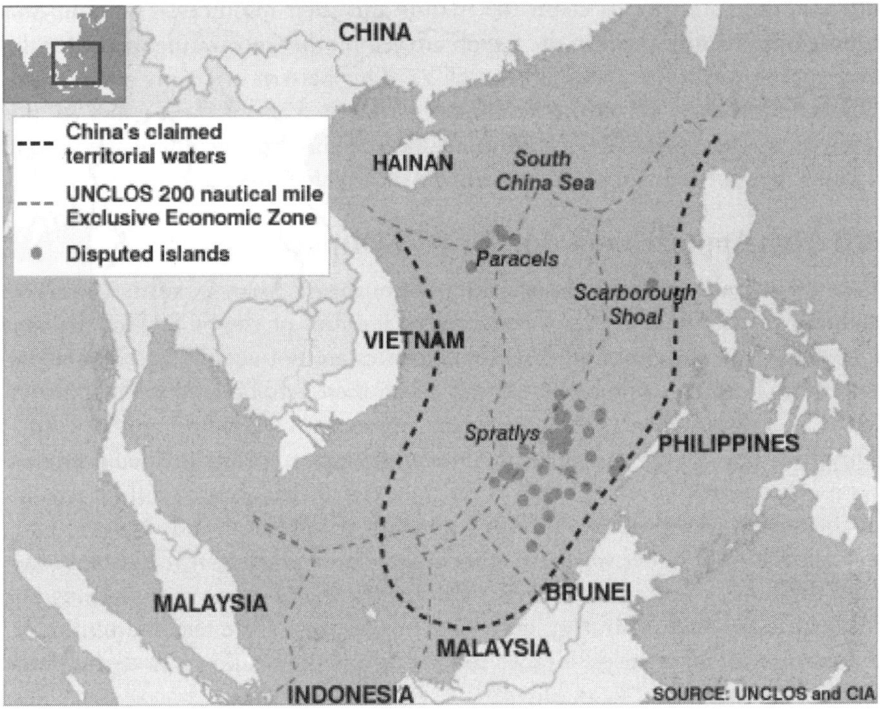

within its own territory and has the documents to prove that the islands have been ruled by Vietnam since the 17th century.[7]

Strategic and Economic Importance of South China Sea

The South China Sea region is the world's second busiest international sea lane. More than half of the world's supertanker traffic passes through the region's waters. The main reason behind the scramble for the two island chains is its richness in natural resources, especially oil and gas. On April 19, 2011 China's *Global Times* published a special report that termed the region as the "Second Persian Gulf"—a repository of 50 billion tons of crude oil and more than 20 trillion cubic meters of natural gas (about twenty five times China's proven oil reserves and eight times its gas reserves).

The SCS is not only a strategic maritime link between the Pacific and the Indian Oceans, but also a vital gateway for shipping in East Asia. 80 per cent of China's energy imports and Japan and Koreas (South and North) oil supplies pass through these waters. Almost, 55 per cent of India's trade with the Asia Pacific transits through the SCS to China, Japan, Korea and the United States. These waters are also critical to New Zealand as 98 per cent of their exports and imports are dependent on the sea lanes of communication.[8] The economic potential and geopolitical importance of the SCS are primary motivating factors for the surrounding countries to claim the islands and their resources. The bountiful fishing opportunities within the region are yet another motivating factor for the overlapping territorial claims in the SCS.[9] This pattern of claims and counter claims and military skirmishes continues in the SCS and if these issues are not resolved to the satisfaction of all maritime stakeholders including the littoral nations, heightened global tension will be inevitable.

ASEAN's Approach towards the SCS Dispute

The ten members of the Association of Southeast Asian Nations (ASEAN) maintain a deep interest in the peace and stability of the SCS. Prof. Baladas Ghoshal noted that since all ASEAN countries are not equally involved in the dispute and consequently have no equal stakes, there is not one ASEAN approach to the SCS dispute. Each member country pursues its own policy vis-à-vis China. Therefore, one can say that the ASEAN countries are in reality divided over their approach towards China, as well as on the exact mechanism to diffuse tension in the region. As a result, ASEAN's position on political and strategic issue towards China is rather weak. To compensate this weakness, ASEAN had often used diplomacy and tried involving external powers by internationalizing the regional issue. Such a strategy may have helped it to avert regional tension in the short term; nevertheless it failed to hide its inherent weakness in dealing with the regional hegemon, i.e. China.[10]

Responding to the growing assertiveness of China's territorial claims in the SCS, ASEAN Foreign Ministers adopted the ASEAN Declaration on SCS in July 1992. Pushed by the Philippines, which was chairing that year's ASEAN Ministerial Meeting, the Declaration called for the peaceful resolution of "all sovereignty and jurisdictional issues pertaining to the SCS", the exercise of "restraint", and the application of the principles contained in the Treaty of Amity and Cooperation in Southeast Asia as the basis for establishing a code of international conduct over the SCS. The former ASEAN Secretary-General, Rodolfo C. Severino pointed that the adoption of the ASEAN Declaration raised hopes for the peace and stability in the region, despite small chance of the conflicting territorial and maritime claims being resolved in a definitive manner.[11]

The joint communique of the annual ASEAN Foreign Ministers meeting in 1996 "endorsed the idea of concluding a regional code of conduct in the SCS" as something that would "lay the foundation for long term stability in the area and foster understanding among claimant countries".[12] In November 2002, ASEAN and China agreed upon a Declaration on the Conduct of Parties in the SCS. The parties unanimously consented that the Declaration has made an important contribution to the maintenance of peace and security in the region and will be instrumental in promoting regional development and cooperation. Philippine Secretary of Foreign Affairs, Blas F. Ople called the Agreement "a major leap for peace," by providing a strong framework for future talks on territorial issues among the claimants to the islands and ocean space in the SCS. Chinese deputy Foreign Minister Wang Yi said the Agreement would not solve territorial conflicts, but would allow peace to reign and help claimant countries focus on economic development.[13]

Nevertheless, efforts to turn it into a formal and binding code have got nowhere, partly because of China's anger at ASEAN's attempts to develop a common approach. China argues that ASEAN has no role in territorial issues, and insists on negotiating with other claimants bilaterally. It has been observed that ASEAN has no wish to "turn itself into a party to the dispute". Indeed, the jurisdictional issues can be resolved only by the claimants themselves through negotiations or through adjudication by a third party. However, because legal, historical and other issues are so complex and because of the deep and often conflicting interests of the claimants in their positions in the SCS, rival claims have little chance of being resolved anytime soon, particularly in the light of the fact that most points of conflict involve more than two parties.[14]

It has been also noticed that the ASEAN countries are not able to firmly oppose Beijing's overarching behavior in the SCS as almost all Southeast Asian countries are dependent on China for their developmental activities. The contact between China and Southeast Asia goes back to many centuries. That era, dominated by the mercantile links also brought Chinese culture to most of the ASEAN countries which is quite visible in today's Southeast Asian societies. There is a substantial presence of ethnic Chinese minority populations in Burma, Thailand, Malaysia, the Philippines, and Indonesia. Currently, 30-40 million ethnic Chinese reside in Southeast Asia.[15] China also receives considerable amount as remittances from the overseas Chinese communities of Southeast Asia.[16]

The year 2011 marks the 20th anniversary of the establishment of the dialogue mechanism between China and the ASEAN. In 2010, the two sides set up a Free Trade Area and signed the protocol on developing Southeast Asia into a nuclear-free region. In 1991, the bilateral trade volume was only $7.96 billion, but it soared to $292.78 billion in 2010. Currently, China is the largest trading partner of ASEAN. China has invested huge amounts in infrastructure building in ASEAN countries.[17] Since, most of the ASEAN countries depend on Beijing for their developmental activities, ASEAN's relations with China acquire critical importance. Bilateral tensions, if and when they arise, cannot be allowed to escalate as it would upset the positive momentum of their interactions.

The US Factor

It has been noted that after the end of the Cold War, the US policy on the South China Sea dispute has been consistent. At the height of the Mischief Reef Crisis in 1995, a statement issued by the US State Department articulated that Washington had a "fundamental interest in freedom of navigation" and the claimants should intensify diplomatic efforts to resolve the problem in accordance with international law and not by force.[18] As tensions have been rising, the fundamentals of this policy have remained unchanged but there has been a change in tone and emphasis.[19]

The US national interests in the South China Sea are readily apparent. The free flow of maritime trade through the Sea Lines of Communications (SLOCs) is crucial to the American economy.[20] At the strategic level, the SLOCs allow the US Navy to transit between the Indian and Pacific Oceans, greatly facilitating America's global military posture. Therefore, US policy cannot be seen to be conceding the SCS as a matter falling under the Chinese sphere of influence. Consequently, Washington has taken a series of measures to bolster its military presence in Asia, including forward deployment of a modern nuclear powered aircraft carrier i.e. USS George Washington.[21]

The US has also tightened military-to-military relations with a number of Southeast Asian countries, including capacity building support for Malaysia, Vietnam, the Philippines and Indonesia. The relationship between New Zealand and the United States was lifted to a new level when both the countries signed the Wellington Declaration during the US Secretary of State Hillary Clinton's visit to New Zealand in November 2010. The Declaration formalises New Zealand's relationship with America, after a 26-year standoff. In 1984, New Zealand banned American nuclear powered warships from entering their harbours. Consequently, they were no more considered a part of the Australia, New Zealand, United States Security (ANZUS) Treaty—the formal alliance with America. The Wellington Declaration agrees to a new US-New Zealand strategic partnership with major emphasis on working together in the Pacific region.[22]

US President Barack Obama visited Australia in November 2011, just before the Sixth East Asia Summit (EAS) in Bali, Indonesia and during his visit the US administration announced that the American military will boost its operations in the north and west of the Australian continent. The country's Northern Territory and its capital city Darwin, which is closer to Indonesia than Australia's major southern cities, will be developed into a major US staging base. From next year, 200 to 250 US marines will train for six months of the year in the Northern Territory. By 2016-17, the training will involve an entire marine air-ground task force of 2,500 troops. The increased US military presence in Australia and Asia underscore that Washington's aggressive intervention into the Asia-Pacific region is aimed at undercutting China's growing influence. The announcements in Australia are clearly intended to influence the agenda, tone and outcome of the EAS in which the US President participated for the first time. The American-Australian military cooperation will also strengthen the longstanding defence ties with the US within the framework of the 60-year-old ANZUS military alliance of which NZ was formally an ally. The deployment of American troops to northern and western Australia, along with a heightened naval and airforce presence may put the US in a better position to dominate the critical sea lanes between the Indian and Pacific Oceans, through which a large proportion of world trade passes.[23]

South China Sea and New Zealand

New Zealand is a maritime nation and has one of the world's largest Exclusive Economic Zones (EEZs), covering an area of approximately 1.3 million square nautical miles or 15 times New Zealand's landmass. Therefore, maritime security is critical for Wellington. New Zealand's Defence White Paper of 2010 highlighted that "99 per cent of New Zealand's exports of merchandise goods (by volume) travel by sea. Our economic outlook would thus be adversely affected by any physical disruption to the security of international trade, whether through civil disorder, piracy, or inter-state conflict. Therefore, New Zealand has a national interest, additional to their role as a good regional and international citizen, in supporting efforts to safeguard freedom of commerce and navigation. This is particularly the case in Southeast Asia where as much as a quarter of the world's commerce passes through the Straits of Malacca each year, but also in the Middle East and the Horn of Africa, where sea lines of communication are more vulnerable."[24]

New Zealand's Defence White Paper 2010 also underscored that the South China Sea dispute between China and half of the ASEAN countries will be the focal point in the region where a range of regional and international interests converge. Tension in SCS is likely to continue, fuelled by multiple protagonists, some of them unpredictable. Any conflict in these areas would have a serious impact on security and confidence in the wider region.[25]

New Zealand derives significant benefits from a stable and prosperous Asia. It is in Wellington's national interest to uphold and contribute to that favourable environment by supporting regional peace and security. Despite this fact, New Zealand's focus on maritime security has not always been strong and this trend continued in the 17th ARF meeting, when the US emphasized that Washington has a *national interest* in freedom of navigation, open access to Asia's maritime commons and respect for international law in the SCS, and supports multilateral approach instead of China's bilateral approach for resolving the dispute but New Zealand chose to stay silent on this crucial issue. It may be because Wellington enjoys cordial relations with Beijing and does not want to antagonize China.

On February 3, 2012, New Zealand Prime Minister John Key launched a major strategy document, "Opening Doors to China," at an official function in Auckland. It aims to strengthen economic ties by attracting more investment from Chinese state-owned companies, and more Chinese students and tourists. A new embassy will be built in Beijing to boost New Zealand's diplomatic and trade presence. The government will increase the number of business delegations to

China and set up a body similar to the US-NZ Council to develop their relations in time for the first "partnership forum" between the two nations. This is due to take place in Beijing later this year (2012) when Key makes a formal visit to China to commemorate the 40th anniversary of diplomatic relations. Since the Free Trade Agreement between the two countries commenced in 2008, New Zealand's exports to China have increased 144 per cent, supplanting the US as the country's second largest export market after Australia. Total bilateral trade stood at $12.8 billion in 2011 and is expected to reach $20 billion by 2015. China is now the biggest importer of New Zealand dairy products by value, having increased five-fold since 2008. New Zealand's education sector aims to double the value of education services to $5 billion by 2025. China is the largest source of foreign students, with about 21,000 enrolments in 2010.[26]

Efforts to establish closer ties with China have not gone unnoticed in Washington and Canberra. On the economic front, President Barack Obama announced a new trading bloc, the Trans-Pacific Partnership (TPP) in November 2011, aimed at forcing Beijing to accept US trade terms. China has expressed strong concerns over the TPP, and New Zealand is well aware of the tensions the US is generating. Therefore, the New Zealand's Trade Minister Groser recently threatened to walk away from the nine-member dialogue group if the TPP became a vehicle for the "containment" of China.[27]

On the other hand, New Zealand also enjoys strong relationship with most of the Southeast Asian countries and Wellington has been engaged with this part of the world well before the formation of ASEAN in 1967. The engagement in defence and security has included participation in the Asia-Pacific theatre of World War-II; in the Korean War under the United Nations Command; in the Malayan Emergency to help defeat the Communist Party of Malaya insurgency; in the defence of Malaysia during Indonesia's Konfrontasi; and in the Vietnam War. New Zealand, together with two Southeast Asian countries, Thailand and the Philippines, was also a member of the Southeast Asia Treaty Organisation headquartered in Bangkok. Thus, New Zealand has a long record of involvement in endeavours to maintain peace and security in ASEAN region.[28]

Since 1975, New Zealand was among the earliest dialogue partners of ASEAN and a founding member of the ARF in 1994 and a member of the EAS since its beginning in 2005, and participated in the inaugural ASEAN Defence Ministers' Meeting Plus (ADMM+8) in 2010 and also a member of the Asia-Europe Meeting (ASEM). The high-quality ASEAN-Australia-New Zealand Free Trade Agreement (AANZFTA), implemented from January 2010, binds New Zealand further to Southeast Asia. In the past, New Zealand has signed bilateral free trade agreements with Singapore (2001), Thailand (2004) and Malaysia (2009).[29] New Zealand also engaged with Malaysia and Singapore through the Five Power Defence Arrangements (FPDA) in which United Kingdom and Australia are also a party. This agreement between these five nations signed in

1971 envisages that the five states will consult each other in the event of external aggression or threat of attack. Further on November 01, 2011 Singapore hosted the 40th anniversary celebration of the FPDA.[30]

Mr. Daljit Singh, Senior Research Fellow at the Institute of Southeast Asian Studies noted that New Zealand has made itself useful and relevant to Southeast Asia and Asia in its own right. The numerous Track One and Track Two ASEAN and Asia Pacific Economic Co-operation (APEC) related meetings have exposed a whole generation of New Zealand's foreign affairs, trade and other officials, as well as scholars and businessmen, to Asian political cultures and societies, and forged invaluable networks and channels for easy communication. Today seven of New Zealand's top ten trading partners are Asian, with China, Japan, Singapore, South Korea, Malaysia, Thailand and Indonesia occupying second, fourth, fifth, seventh, eighth and tenth places respectively. Trade with Asia is growing much more quickly than trade with Europe and North America. The ASEAN region as a whole is New Zealand's third-largest trading partner, with New Zealand's merchandise trade with Southeast Asia having doubled in the past five years and the region accounting for 11 per cent of New Zealand's merchandise exports and 16 per cent of its imports. In terms of absolute value of exports, New Zealand is more important to the ASEAN region than vice versa.[31] In 2009, ASEAN countries' exports to New Zealand amounted to US$3.13 billion compared with imports from New Zealand of US$2.2 billion. The preliminary total trade between ASEAN and New Zealand in 2010 was $6.75 billion, an increase from US$ 5.3 billion in 2009. On foreign direct investment (FDI), the inflow from New Zealand to ASEAN Member States was US$ 239 million in 2009, accounting for 0.6 per cent of total FDI in the region.[32]

New Zealand is well-regarded in Southeast Asia for its governance, expertise and support of global institutions and international law but needs to be alert to the security anxieties of its friends and allies in the region. As a member of Asia Pacific, peace in the area is always important for New Zealand. Though, New Zealand is not directly involved in the territorial dispute in South China Sea, Wellington still shows strong regard for this issue.

New Zealand's Defence White Paper (2010) also recognizes that prevailing territorial disputes including those in the South China Sea will lead to "parts of maritime Asia remaining a contested space over the next 25 years and this could potentially be expressed militarily... and resource competition and narrowly defined national interest continuing to be a volatile mix".[33] It is quite certain that if the SCS dispute is going to be expressed militarily then it will easily turn into a global war as many countries have their stake in the region. And if it so happens then it would have the potential to impact on New Zealand strategically as well as economically.

Keeping the future in mind, New Zealand considers that Beijing would like to negotiate the SCS dispute with the involved nations bilaterally instead of internationalizing the issue. Therefore, China is against having this issue discussed in the ASEAN Regional Forum. However, New Zealand opposes China's view in this regard. Since many of the Asia-Pacific members are involved in this dispute, the solution should not be dialogues between nations, but "on a regional level". As a result, New Zealand strongly believes that the ARF is the best platform for members to discuss freely and reach consensus on this issue. As a country that has encountered territorial disputes, New Zealand fully understands the situation that faces each of the claimants directly involved in this dispute. New Zealand firmly believes that an open platform for members to discuss fairly and find common interest would be the best way to solve the problem peacefully.[34]

The New Zealand government also agreed during a recent meeting with the Filipino defense officials in August 2011, that the Spratly claimants—the Philippines, China, Vietnam, Brunei, Malaysia and Taiwan—should abide by the Code of Conduct they had signed in 2002 about settling territorial dispute peacefully. Both sides noted that it is necessary for claimant countries to abide by the 1982 UNCLOS and adhere to the 2002 ASEAN-China Declaration on the Conduct of Parties in the SCS, if peace and stability in the area were to be maintained.[35]

New Zealand cannot insulate itself from the South China Sea dispute as Wellington's economy is heavily dependent on SLOCs. Most scholars believe that the SCS dispute is regional in nature with global consequences especially in this globalised world. In an article, Robert D. Kaplan underscored that most of the contested areas of the globe in the last century lay on dry land but over the span of the decades the demographic and economic axis of the earth shifted measurably towards the opposite end i.e. maritime and the SCS will be the major focal point of the future conflict.[36] Therefore, this is an opportune time for Wellington to engage with the Asia-Pacific region substantially rather than symbolically.

South China Sea Dispute and India

India cannot isolate itself from the dispute especially after Beijing denounced plans by an Indian company to develop oil fields in the SCS. However, China insists on building strategic projects in Pakistan occupied Kashmir and deploying troops there but protests Indian oil exploration in SCS. There are also unconfirmed reports of confrontation between the Chinese warship and INS Airavat in the South China Sea.

The Indian Navy document "Freedom to use the Seas: India's Maritime Military Strategy", highlighted that India's area of interest "extends from the north of the Arabian Sea to the South China Sea".[37] In the 2010 ARF meeting, it was noted that 12 of the 27 participating countries including India, backed the United States' multilateral approach instead of China's bilateral approach for resolution of the SCS disputes. During the 17th ARF meeting India joined other countries to openly declare that the SCS should remain open for international navigation but unfortunately, it went unnoticed.[38] At the July 2011 ARF meeting in Bali, India noted that the parties concerned should engaged in discussions to address the SCS issue and welcomed the recently agreed guidelines on the implementation of the 2002 Declaration of the Conduct of Parties between China and ASEAN. In an address at National Maritime Foundation, New Delhi on July 28, 2011, Indian Foreign Secretary Nirupama Rao reiterated India's stand on the SCS dispute and emphasized that the SCS is an important shipping route and India supports the freedom of navigation in the SCS.[39]

India retains a strong interest in keeping sea lanes open in the SCS. Apart from helping secure energy supplies for countries like Japan and Korea, India has the unique distinction of shipping oil from Sakhalin to Mangalore through this sea route. If China controls these waters it will be difficult for India to continue its economic ventures activities through this channel. On August 31, 2011, the UK media reported that an "unidentified Chinese warship confronted an Indian Navy vessel". But India downplayed the reported confrontation between the Indian Naval ships and PLA Navy in the international waters of the disputed SCS. Actually, INS Airavat was on a "friendly visit" to Vietnam between 19-28 July, 2011. The MEA said in a statement, "There was no confrontation involving the INS Airavat." The Indian Navy, too, issued a statement stating: "There was no confrontation with any vessel." Beijing, too, maintained its silence over the incident. However, the fact of the matter is that China is closely observing Indian activities in the SCS and its growing relations with the ASEAN countries.[40]

On September 14, 2011 Beijing objected to ONGC Videsh's (OVL) venture in Vietnam and asked India to refrain from entering into deals with Vietnamese firms exploring oil and gas in the disputed SCS over which China enjoys indisputable sovereignty.[41] India has responded to Chinese objections to its companies scouting for hydrocarbons in the SCS, saying its cooperation with Vietnam is in accordance with international laws.[42] During SM Krishna's visit to Hanoi in September 2011, the External Affairs Minister of India underlined that OVL will go ahead with oil and gas exploration in the disputed region or the two offshore blocks which Vietnam claims as its own.[43] In response, China announced its plan to expand its exploration of 10,000 sq km of seabed in Southwest Indian Ocean.[44]

The question that arises here is that if India really supports freedom of navigation in the SCS then it will be necessary for India to safeguard its interest in the region as the SCS is not only a strategic maritime link between the Pacific and the Indian Oceans, but also a vital gateway for shipping in East Asia. Almost, fifty five per cent of India's trade with the Asia Pacific transits through the SCS. Therefore, it is quite visible that India derives considerable economic benefits from the SCS being an area where all actors enjoy a level playing field.

The growing influence of China in the Indian Ocean Region (IOR) and in Southeast Asia is a critical reason for both India and ASEAN to engage strategically in the region. China has strengthened its naval presence in the SCS and is endeavoring to do the same in the Indian Ocean. It has reportedly installed a listening post in the Burmese territory of Coco Islands and thus is aiming to establish its strategic presence in the Indian Ocean Region purportedly through the "String of Pearls" strategy.

After the Chinese claims over the entire SCS, Southeast Asian countries are preparing themselves against the possibility of further Chinese aggressive stances. From the ASEAN perspective, India is seen as a possible counterweight against China in the region. Therefore, India and selected ASEAN countries began holding joint maritime exercises. In February 2010, the Indian Navy concluded its Milan series of maritime exercises in the Andaman and Nicobar islands. The seventh edition of exercise Milan was held in the backdrop of India's "Look East" policy. Naval ships of Singapore (two ships), Sri Lanka, Thailand, Australia, Bangladesh, Indonesia, Malaysia and Myanmar, with representatives from navies of Brunei, Philippines, Vietnam and New Zealand participated in exercise Milan.[45] And, most of the participants of the 2010 Milan maritime exercises also participated in the recent Milan-2012 exercises hosted by the Indian Navy.[46]

China does not welcome the ASEAN move to interact with major powers. However, the Indian Navy has conducted joint exercises with the Singaporean, Vietnamese, Japanese and South Korean navies in the South and East China Seas. The Indian Navy, however, has also conducted exercises with the PLA Navy whenever Indian ships have visited the region.[47]

Witnessing overarching Chinese claims over the SCS, there is significant scope for the Indian and Southeast Asian Navy to engage constructively. India has helped Malaysia in building up its Coast Guard in the past and it has the expertise to also help the other ASEAN countries. However, maritime cooperation between India and ASEAN is still in the nascent stages.. Cooperation with regard to capacity-building and patrolling piracy-infested areas or jointly facing non-traditional threats at sea like drug-trafficking, human-trafficking and possible maritime terrorism remain inadequate. India has a strong Navy with technological credibility that can be leveraged by ASEAN. Frequent joint naval exercises similar to India-Singapore exercises and deeper cooperation in training and exchange of defence personnel could form additional and viable confidence-building measures. Collaboration on missile technology, radar systems, defence component systems and supporting hardware are again areas where ASEAN countries can work in partnership with India.[48]

India has provided training to Malaysia's Air Force pilots on MIG-29s in the past and has offered training also on the Sukhoi. It has also shown keenness to sell Brahmos missiles to friendly countries including the neighboring Southeast

Asian countries.[49] Most of the ASEAN countries have been engaged in a defence modernization programme and would like to obtain assistance in weapons up-gradation and systems integration. Like India, most of the Southeast Asian countries also rely on Russia for their defence procurements. India with its long experience in using Russian products has developed the technological capabilities for low cost servicing and hence could be a potential ally for ASEAN in this field. Assisting ASEAN will also improve India's relations with the Southeast Asian countries bilaterally and multilaterally and it will also boost India's image/standing in the region as having the potential to being capable of balancing China in the IOR.

India-New Zealand's Relations

India and New Zealand have much in common. Shared history, parliamentary democracy, Commonwealth ties, the English language, Diaspora link and of course cricket. India's importance to New Zealand is growing. New Zealand and India began talks on a bilateral free trade agreement (FTA or Closer Economic Cooperation Agreement—CECA) in April 2010. Trade between New Zealand and India is valued at over NZ$1.25 billion (up from NZ$950 million two years ago). Exports were worth NZ$917 million for the year ending March 2011, nearly double our exports two years ago. India is now New Zealand's 7th largest market. Imports from India were valued at NZ$370 million for the year ending March 2011.[50]

New Zealand has growing defence links with India. Both countries are members of the ASEAN Regional Forum (ARF) and the ASEAN Defence Ministers' Plus Meeting. A delegation from the Indian National Defence College visited New Zealand in May 2011. The former Chief of the New Zealand Defence Force (CDF), Lieutenant General Mateparae, visited India in November 2009 (the first such visit) to explore ways to expand the defence relationship. A New Zealand Defence Force Command and Staff College delegation also visited at the same time.[51]

Since 2008, the Royal Navy of New Zealand also participated in the Milan series of maritime exercises hosted by the Indian Navy. Chief of the Indian Navy, Admiral Nirmal Verma, visited New Zealand in November 2010. Naval ship visits are quite frequent: HMNZS Te Mana visited Mumbai in August 2008; HMNZS Te Mana and Endeavour visited Port Blair in the Andaman Islands in May 2007; HMNZS Te Mana visited Kochi and Mumbai ports in June 2006; and the Indian ship Tabar visited Auckland in 2006.[52]

India and New Zealand also engage multilaterally in several fora namely United Nations, Commonwealth, the World Trade Organisation, ARF, EAS, etc. The second phase of India's "Look-East" policy was directed not only towards Southeast Asia but East Asia as well as the Pacific nations. Consequently, New

Delhi became a dialogue partner of the Pacific Islands Forum in 2003. Hence, these regular meetings in these regional and multilateral fora have provided a much needed platform for regular bilateral dialogue on key issues, including climate change, piracy, human rights, counter-terrorism, maritime security, international trade and other transnational issues.

Recent Upsurge in Tension in SCS

In the past few years, aggressive maneuvers of the PLA maritime agencies in the SCS have resulted in the ASEAN countries adopting a more robust defense policy. Vietnam is in the process of acquiring six Russian Kilo-class submarines and a dozen Su-30MKK jet fighters equipped for maritime warfare. Malaysia has also paid more than $1 billion for two diesel submarines from France. Indonesia too announced that it will acquire new submarines.[53]

As China seeks to intimidate her rivals into stopping oil exploration and mining in the area, other nations, in turn, have begun to protest vehemently against Beijing's military build-up in the region. Recently, Vietnam blamed China for deliberately sabotaging two Vietnamese exploration operations which led to the huge anti-China protests in Hanoi. Consequently, Hanoi held live-fire exercises off its coast, an act described by China as a grave provocation.[54]

These skirmishes run counter to the spirit of the Declaration on the Conduct of Parties (2002) in the SCS, drawn up between the ASEAN countries and the People's Republic of China. Under the terms of the agreement, the countries had agreed to "resolve their territorial and jurisdictional disputes by peaceful means, without resorting to the threat or use of force, through friendly consultations and negotiations". But recent developments have negated the 'friendly tenor' that underpinned the agreed mechanism for conflict resolution.[55]

During the Shangri La Dialogue in June 2011, the US took a position that "the maritime security remains an issue of particular importance for the region" and followed it up by passing a resolution in the US Senate on June 27, 2011, calling for "a peaceful and multilateral resolution to maritime territorial disputes in South East Asia", deploring the use of force by naval and maritime security vessels from China in the SCS, and supporting the continuation of operations by the US armed forces to enable the freedom of navigation in international waters and air space in that Sea. The ASEAN Foreign Ministers came up with new draft guidelines on the implementation of the DOC 2002 during the Bali meeting, preparatory to the ASEAN Regional Forum (ARF) meet. In a joint communiqué issued on July 19, 2011, they stated that "they looked forward to the finalization of the same during the upcoming ASEAN-China senior officials' meeting".[56]

As Beijing seeks to neutralize the US presence in the region, the latter appears to have become more assertive and keen to play a crucial role in the SCS dispute.

In fact, the US has increased its maritime cooperation with regional countries, mainly concentrating on capacity-building with Vietnam and the Philippines. The navies of the US and the Philippines held joint exercises in the SCS from June 28 to July 8 2011. In an another move, the United States, Australia and Japan reportedly conducted a trilateral military exercise off the coast of Brunei in the SCS on July 9, 2011. These naval exercises do indicate the continuing US strategic stakes in the region. In a joint press conference with the US Joint Chiefs of Staff, Admiral Mike Mullen on July 11, 2011 at Beijing, the Chinese Chief of the General Staff, General Chen Bingde underscored that the joint military exercises held by US in the SCS with Vietnam and Philippines were "extremely inappropriate" and Washington should respect Beijing's core interests. On the contrary, Mike Mullen reiterated that the US would continue to support its allies in the region.[57]

In the August 2011, China has completed the trial run of its first aircraft carrier and has planned to deploy her in the SCS. Beijing seems to believe that deploying the aircraft carrier will act as a deterrent to keep away the other nations eyeing the region. However, Admiral Arun Prakash emphasizes that the "PLA Navy has a few years to go before it can claim to have an operational carrier at sea".[58] Beijing's showing off tactics or deploying aircraft carrier close to the SCS can only add to the tensions and fuel an arms race in the region.

Conclusion

China's recent acts in the SCS indicate that it is working on a 'revisionist agenda' in the region and trying to unilaterally change the status quo in the SCS. China's rising economic and military might could compel the ASEAN countries to rally together as well as to seek assistance from the United States' and other nations to balance China. The US posture has, in turn, raised tensions in the region as China warned its neighbours not to "play with fire". Further, Beijing believes that Washington is eyeing to control the Spratlys through Vietnam and the Philippines. If the territorial disputes relating to the SCS are not resolved soon to the satisfaction of all maritime stakeholders including the littoral nations, heightened regional and global anxiety will spiral out of control causing a bitter diplomatic fracas over this issue.

New Zealand's national interest lies in the freedom of navigation and any disruption or conflict relating to SLOCs will hurt Wellington severely and the SCS dispute has the potential to upset the status quo of the region. Therefore, it is high time for New Zealand to select their allies in the region carefully and strategically. New Zealand feels militarily threatened by no country and is itself a threat to none but keeping the volatile situation of the Asia-Pacific in mind, New Zealand should consider the much needed expansion of their defence forces especially in the maritime domain and India will be the best bet in this regard.

And, if New Zealand modernizes their Armed Forces then it will also strengthen its combined position in the FPDA.

Wellington should encourage ASEAN to control piracy and assist them in any way they can. Therefore, New Zealand should play an active role in addressing the concerns related to maritime security and promote cooperation and assistance in this regard. The enhanced maritime security of the Southeast Asian waters will also serve New Zealand's national interest of keeping the sea lanes open in the international waters of the Asia-Pacific which is crucial to Wellington's trade and shipping.

On India's part, if New Delhi is concerned about their stand on freedom of navigation in the SCS it will have to channelize its foreign policy substantially rather than symbolically. It has been also noted that the second phase of India's Look East policy is over and now the time has come for India to lay the ground work for the third phase, in which it must concentrate on the strategic aspects of the bilateral relations with all the Southeast countries. Moreover, it is an opportune time for India to interact strategically with its allies in the region. In this context, maritime cooperation and capacity building between India and the Southeast Asian countries will be of utmost importance.

New Delhi and Wellington should also support each-other's efforts constructively and work jointly in achieving the peaceful resolution of the SCS as this will also add new momentum to their bilateral relations.

End Notes

1. Tran Truong Thuy (ed.), *The South China Sea: Cooperation for Regional Security and Development,* (Hanoi: Diplomatic Academy of Vietnam, 2010), pp. 137-138.
2. Cdr. K.K. Agnihotri and Sunil Agarwal, "Legal Aspects of Marine Scientific Research in Exclusive Economic Zones: Implications of the Impeccable Incident", *Maritime Affairs,* Vol. 5, No. 2 (2009): pp. 142-3.
3. "The South China Sea: A Sea of Disputes", *The Economist,* 2011, http://www.economist.com/node/21016161 (accessed September 10, 2011).
4. "Southeast Asia Arms itself against China", *Hindustan Times,* August 10, 2010, p. 17, New Delhi.
5. Amit Singh, "South China Sea Dispute: A New Area of Global Tensions", July 20, 2011, pp. 1-5, http://maritimeindia.org/sites/all/files/pdf/South%20China%20Sea%20 Dispute,%20A%20New%20Area%20of%20Global%20Tension%20by%20Amit%20Singh.pdf (accessed on February 20, 2012)
6. Daljit Singh, "ASEAN's Perspective of New Zealand's Place in Asia" (Wellington: Asia-New Zealand Foundation, *Outlook Series,* October 2011), p. 12.
7. http://community.middlebury.edu/~scs/maps/US%20EIA,%20South%20 China%20 Sea%20Tables%20and%20Maps.htm, (accessed on February 20, 2012).
8. Summary Report, ASEAN Regional Forum Second Inter-Sessional Meeting on Maritime Security, Auckland: New Zealand, March 29-30 2010, p. 2.
9. Amit Singh, n.5, pp. 1-5.
10. Baladas Ghoshal, "ASEAN and South China Sea Dispute", *World Focus,* April 2011, pp. 207-210.

11. Rodolfo C. Severino, "ASEAN and South China Sea", *Security Challenges*, Vol. 6, No. 2 (Winter 2010), pp. 37-47. See also 'ASEAN Declaration on the South China Sea, Manila, Philippines', July 22, 1992, ASEAN, http://www.aseansec.org/3634.htm (accessed August 9, 2011).
12. 'Joint Communique of the 29th ASEAN Ministerial Meeting (AMM)', Jakarta, July 20-21, 1996, ASEAN, http://www.aseansec.org/1824.htm (accessed August 9, 2011).
13. Nguyen Hong Thao, "The 2002 Declaration on the Conduct of Parties in the South China Sea: A Note", *Ocean Development & International Law*, 34:279–285, Taylor & Francis Inc, 2003.
14. Wu Shicun (ed.), *Maritime Security in the South China Sea: Regional Implications and International Cooperation*, (Surrey: Ashgate, 2009).
15. Catharin Dalpino and David Steinberg (eds), "Southeast Asia Looks North," in *Georgetown Southeast Asia Survey, 2002-03*, (Washington: Georgetown University, 2003). See also CRS Report for Congress, China-Southeast Asia Relations: Trends, Issues, and Implications for the United States, April 2006, http://www.fas.org/sgp/crs/row/RL32688.pdf (accessed September 5, 2011), pp. 5-6.
16. Yen Ching hwang, *The Chinese in Southeast Asia and beyond: socio-economic and political dimensions,* (Singapore: World Scientific, 2008). See also Karl Malakunas, "Southeast Asia's Chinese Winning Freedoms," *Jakarta Post*, January 21, 2004. See also Eric Teo Cheow, "China's Rising Soft Power in Southeast Asia," *Pac Net* 19A, May 3, 2004.
17. Chu Hao, "Ties with ASEAN advance" *China Daily*, August 22, 2011.
18. "US warn against restriction in South China Sea, *Straits Times*, May 12, 1995.
19. "China's 'aggressive' buildup called worry", *The Washington Times*, 14 January 2010, See also "China 'more aggressive' at sea", *Straits Times*, 24 July 2010.
20. US Department of Defense, Naval Operations Concept 2010: Implementing the Maritime Strategy (Washington D.C.: US Department of Defense, 2010), p. 35.
21. James Kraska, How the United States Lost the Naval War of 2015, *Orbis*, Winter 2010.
22. Liz Puranam, "NZ, US sign Wellington Declaration", November 04, 2010 http://www.3news.co.nz/NZ-US-sign-Wellington-Declaration/tabid/419/articleID/184781/Default.aspx (accessed on February 22, 2012).
23. James Cogan, "Obama increases US military presence in Australia and Asia", November 17, 2011, http://www.wsws.org/articles/2011/nov2011/asia-n17.shtml (accessed on February 20, 2012).
24. *Defence White Paper 2010* (Wellington: Ministry of Defence, 2010), p. 20.
25. Ibid, pp. 11-30.
26. John Braddock, "New Zealand moves to broaden economic ties with China", February 18, 2012, http://www.wsws.org/articles/2012/feb2012/nzch-f18.shtml (accessed on February 20, 2012).
27. Ibid.
28. Daljit Singh, n. 6, p. 2.
29. "ASEAN-New Zealand Relations", October 2011, http://www.asean.org/5826.htm (accessed on February 20, 2012).
30. Jordan D. Green, *"New Zealand's Involvement in Maritime Security in Southeast Asia and the Pacific, from 1982 Onwards"*, (Unpublished MA thesis, University of Waikato, 2010).
31. Daljit Singh, n. 6, p. 4.
32. "ASEAN-New Zealand Relations", October 2011, http://www.asean.org/5826.htm (accessed on February 20, 2012).
33. *Defence White Paper 2010* (Wellington: Ministry of Defence, 2010), p. 32.
34. Pan Asia MUN, *ARF Position Paper, Nov. 2011*, http://www.panasiamun.com/2011/studyguides/PP_ARF.pdf (accessed on February 22, 2012).

35. D.J. Yap, "New Zealand backs Philippine position on Spratlys", *Philippine Daily Inquirer*, August 12, 2011, http://globalnation.inquirer.net/8775/new-zealand-backs-philippine-position-on-spratlys (accessed on February 23, 2012).
36. Robert D. Kaplan, *The South China Sea is the Future of Conflict* (2011), http://www.foreignpolicy.com/articles/2011/08/15/the_south_china_sea_is_the_future_of_conflict (accessed August 16, 2011).
37. "Freedom to use the Seas: India's Maritime Military Strategy" (New Delhi: Ministry of Defence, GOI, 2007) pp. 59-60.
38. Indrani Bagchi, India to discuss China with US later this month, *The Economic Times*, Sep 4, 2010.
39. http://meaindia.nic.in/mystart.php?id=530117885 (accessed July 30, 2011).
40. India, Vietnam ties irk China? *Asian Age*, September 2, 2011, p. 5.
41. Li Hongmei, "Wise to Refrain from Churning up South China Sea", http://news.xinhuanet.com/english2010/indepth/2011-09/16/c_131142806.htm (accessed September 18, 2011).
42. http://www.mea.gov.in/mystart.php?id=190018274 (accessed September 18, 2011).
43. Sachin Parashar, "Undeterred India to hunt for oil in South China Sea", *Times of India*, New Delhi, September 17, 2011, p. 18.
44. Indrani Bagchi, "India, China square off for sea fight", *Times of India*, September 19, 2011, p. 10.
45. "Indian Navy Hosts Milan 2010", http://indiannavy.nic.in/Milan12/sub-pages/history.php (accessed February 23, 2012).
46. "Indian Navy Milan-12", http://indiannavy.nic.in/Milan12/index.php (accessed February 23, 2012).
47. Faizal Yahya, "Challenges of Globalization: Malaysia and India Engagement," *Contemporary Southeast Asia*, 27, no. 3 (2005): pp. 472-98.
48. Amit Singh, India-Malaysia Strategic Relations, *Maritime Affairs*, Vol. 7, No. 1, Routledge, Summer 2011.
49. "Export Market of Brahmos Missile," Press Information Bureau, Government of India, August 9, 2010, http://pib.nic.in/newsite/erelease.aspx?relid_64459 (accessed on June 1, 2011).
50. "India's Relations with New Zealand", http://www.mfat.govt.nz/Countries/Asia-South-and-Southeast/India.php (accessed on February 23, 2012).
51. "India-New Zealand Relations" January 2012, http://www.mea.gov.in/mystart.php?id=50044506 (accessed on February 23, 2012).
52. "History of Milan: Friendship Across the Seas", Indian Navy, http://indiannavy.nic.in/Milan12/sub-pages/history.php, (accessed on February 23, 2012).
53. "Southeast Asia Arms itself against China," Hindustan Times, August 10, 2010, p.17, New Delhi.
54. http://www.bbc.co.uk/news/mobile/world-asia-pacific-13748349 (accessed July 30, 2011).
55. Leszek Buszynski, "Rising Tensions in the South China Sea: Prospects for a Resolution of the Issue", *Security Challenges*, Vol. 6, No. 2 (Winter 2010), pp. 85-104.
56. KK Agnihotri, "Concerns on South China Sea", Purple Beret *Magazine*, New Delhi: August 2011, http://purpleberet.com/details/column_detail.aspx?id=216, (accessed August 10, 2011).
57. http://www.bbc.co.uk/news/world-asia-pacific-14097503 (accessed July 20, 2011).
58. Arun Prakash, "The Implications of PLA Navy's First Aircraft Carrier", NMF Commentary, http://www.maritimeindia.org/sites/all/files/pdf/THE%20 IMPLICATIONS%20OF%20PLA%20NAVY'S%20FIRST%20AIRCRAFT%20CARRIER.pdf (accessed August 10, 2011).

Index